With love,
Maryann

Unlearning to Fly

JENNIFER BRICE

Unlearning to Fly

University of Nebraska Press Lincoln & London

Manufactured in the
United States of America

∞

Library of Congress Cataloging-
in-Publication Data
Brice, Jennifer.
Unlearning to Fly / Jennifer Brice.
p. cm.
ISBN-13: 978-0-8032-1094-3 (hardcover : alk. paper)
ISBN-10: 0-8032-1094-9 (hardcover : alk. paper)
1. Brice, Jennifer. 2. Alaska—Biography. I. Title.
CT275.B6775A3 2007
979.8'04092—dc22
[B]
2006034348

Set in New Baskerville.

For my mother Carol Heeks Brice
and my father Luther Alba Brice

Teach me, unwell swallow,
Who has unlearned to fly,
How I could with no rudder or wing
Elude this tomb in the sky.

—Osip Mandelstam,
"Lines about the Unknown Soldier"

It is not danger I love. I know what I love. It is life.

—Antoine de Saint-Exupery,
Wind, Sand and Stars

Contents

Preface

My mother kneels beside the clawfoot tub in the first-floor bathroom. It's an afternoon in April, that cruel month. Bluish light seeps through the rectangular window and pools on the worn linoleum. A baby splashes in the bathtub. She feels as safe as if she's in the womb of her world. She is me. The house on First Avenue in Fairbanks, Alaska, is my first home. My parents rent it from a widow who will, two years from now, refuse their offer of $18,000 and hold out for $19,000. Two years after *that*, a rain-swollen river will overrun the house, steeping it to the ceiling in tea-colored water. Now—more than forty years later—a parking lot splays where the house once stood.

But I'm getting ahead of myself.

In 1964, the house is white clapboard with red shutters. From the second-story window overlooking the street and, beyond it, the Chena River, you can see Saint Joseph's Hospital, where I was born. From the east window, you can see Saint Matthew's Episcopal Church, where I was christened. You cannot see the airport where my father works because it lies five miles away, on the western outskirts of town. He'll be home for dinner in an hour or two. Meanwhile, my mother sloshes a soapy washcloth over my back. I squeal with pleasure. She shifts her weight from one leg to the other and sighs, wiping a sweat-plastered curl from her forehead. She is twenty-seven and hugely pregnant with my brother Sam, who will be born in just three weeks.

What happens next is so strange that my mother struggles to make sense of it. The bathwater forms peaks and troughs, just like the ocean. The floor undulates. My mother holds onto the lip of the tub and heaves to her feet. Out the window, she sees Chitina's doghouse riding wave after wave of snow-flecked sod. She hears sirens and screams and, in the house, the heavy *thud* of furniture falling. Glass shatters. My mother yanks me from the tub, clamps me naked to her hip, and runs for the phone, which has been ringing.

"Get out of the house! Now!" my father shouts. He has guessed—rightly—that the phone will be dead within moments.

"But the baby—she's wet from her bath."

"Then wrap her in a towel and stand inside the door. If things start to fall, run into the street."

I've heard the story of the Good Friday earthquake so many times it has the force of memory, which of course it's not. At 9.2 on the Richter scale, it remains the biggest quake recorded in North America, the second biggest in the world. (The largest earthquake in recorded history struck Chile in 1960.) No one died in Fairbanks, hundreds of miles from the epicenter. Near Anchorage, a pilot saw a control tower crumble, killing the man who had, moments ago, cleared him for takeoff. The earthquake severed power lines all over the state, so the pilot's was the first eyewitness report to reach Fairbanks. In Valdez, a supply boat had dropped anchor that afternoon—a festive occasion—and a crowd gathered at the dock to watch its unloading. A young father brought his two little boys, leaving their mother and baby sister at home. Without warning, a tsunami reared up and swallowed everything: dockworkers, townspeople, father and sons, even the supply boat. All told, the earthquake and tsunamis—though mostly tsunamis—killed 106 Alaskans.

By the time I was old enough to be conscious of them, aftershocks rumbled through town like Army convoys. We'd hear them a split second before we felt them. Glass would chatter in the cupboard then beds would vibrate in the night. "It's OK," my father would call out in a sleep-deepened voice. "It's just a little one. It'll be over soon."

Usually it was.

Once, when my brother and sister and I were staying at the farm—which is what we called my grandparents' place—our milk glasses skittered away from our reaching hands. We looked up from the table, where we were eating peanut-butter-and-jelly sandwiches, to see what Grandma was thinking. In our experience, grownups seemed to have a sixth sense about whether an earthquake was going to be a big one or not. This was going to be a big one.

"Go, go!" she shouted, and we went, crunching glass under our sneakers. Grandma stayed behind, using the bulk of her body to protect Jerry. Jerry was in his twenties then, deaf and mute and probably not in full possession of his other faculties; somehow he'd strayed into Grandma's path one day, and she'd swept him up. He lived with her and Granddad off and on for years and became a fixture in our extended family. At every holiday, there were Grandma and Granddad, Mom and Dad, Aunt Nancy, Aunt Lois and Aunt Jane, Uncle Sam, Uncle Andy and Uncle Thom, a clutch of cousins, and Jerry. Whether it was the force of the earthquake or the force of terror that threw him to the floor wasn't clear. He lay there moaning in Grandma's arms. Shards of Depression glass fell around them both like colored confetti. With no grownup to hold us, Sam and Hannah and I clung together outside. The land heaved and writhed as if it were trying to buck us off its back or push us out by the roots.

My earliest memory of the land, then, is of its being unpredictable and unbenign. It didn't care whether I lived or died. Because I was a child and interior Alaska was my home, I didn't see it as beautiful—in fact, I didn't really *see* it at all—for a very long time.

I had a happy childhood. My parents loved me, and they loved each other. My two brothers and two sisters and I wore hand-me-downs or clothes manufactured on my mother's treadle Singer, but there were graham crackers in the cupboard at snack time and goulash on the stove for dinner; there was oil in the tank; and, occasionally, when my mother's godfather, John Zantginger, sent a check from New York City, enough money for us to spend a week in the tropics or on the ski slopes.

When I was very young, my mother read me fairy tales and

tucked Juicy Fruit gum in the pocket of an ugly hand-me-down shirt to convince me it was magic. My father gave me piggyback rides and, when he was away, wrote me letters in block print to say that I should help my mother with my younger brothers and sisters, and that he was very proud of me. Among my noisy extended family of aunts, uncles, and cousins, there were birthday parties, sledding parties, Easter egg hunts, my grandmother's "festas," and Liberty Falls camping trips.

Now that I think about it, my childhood was better than happy. It was close to idyllic.

Which is probably why, when I was eight or nine, I lay on my belly and slithered over the edge of a cliff that dropped 200 feet to a slavering creek that ended in Liberty Falls near Chitina, Alaska—the place for which the dog was named. I may have been acting on a dare from a cousin. No matter. I hung there by my fingernails, whimpering, until someone ran screaming for a grownup. Someone else's mother came and yanked me onto my feet then scolded me roundly. She probably swatted me on the butt. It was the early '70s, and other people's parents still felt free to do that.

What's stayed with me isn't the thrill of transgression or the humiliation of being spanked in front of my saucer-eyed siblings and cousins. It's the heart-racing feeling of hanging suspended over that frantic creek. My life could have ended. *I* could have ended my life. Sick as it might sound, I've re-created the conditions—if not the exact moment—a dozen times since: on a glacier, in a kayak, in a plane. There's a kind of fear that seeks to console itself with a bigger fear. I've seen friends do it, too. Like me, my danger-loving friends have families who love them. Why is it, I wonder, that we who feel so safe are most willing to court death?

The most salient feature of Alaska's landscape is size. Its mountains, lakes, rivers, glaciers, valleys, trees, and wildlife make their counterparts in the Lower Forty-eight look like models drawn to scale. When the Harvard literary critic Helen Vendler visited Denali National Park in the 1980s, she tartly observed that, where she came from, the word "park" meant something else entirely. In the 1990s, I flew to Vermont for a writers' conference; there, everyone kept using the phrase, "on this mountain." I kept an eye out for it then finally asked an organizer, "Just where *is* this mountain?" It was not a question that endeared me to her.

Alaska is full of North American *–ests*: highest mountain, longest river, biggest wilderness, sparsest population, coldest winter, richest oil, and kookiest politicians. (In 2002, U.S. Sen. Frank Murkowski, a Republican, won the governor's seat then promptly installed his daughter, Lisa, in his Senate seat.)

Like the rest of the circumpolar North, Alaska weeds out the weak in spirit and in body. Angst and anomie and Seasonal Affective Disorder may be rampant, but they are rarely discussed. "[One's] interior landscape responds to the character and subtlety of an exterior landscape," writes Barry Lopez, in "Landscape and Narrative," an essay set in Anaktuvuk Pass, Alaska. "[T]he shape of the individual mind is affected by land as it is by genes."

In the East, a pleasantry such as "How are you?" can net you a treatise on pollen allergies or the rising price of gas. Not so in Alaska. "The truth, my dear?" says my friend John Gimbel, a mathematician. "I've never been better!" The twenty-first-century Alaskan is the spiritual heir of the gold miner. Rex G. Fisher, author of *Dying for Alaska Gold*, told me the story of one gold miner, who, back in territorial days, was running his dog team when they broke through an epidermis of ice. The creek into which they tumbled wasn't deep or fast moving; with some effort, he dragged himself, the dogs, and the sled back on the trail. By then, the moon was shining from the bottom of its inky bowl of sky, and the temperature was minus forty or colder. The miner's cabin lay miles away. Rather than freeze to death, he tied one end of a rope around the handle of his dog sled and the other around his neck.

I'm not that tough—not nearly—but I can count on the fingers of one hand the times I've taken to my bed because of illness or injury. On two of those occasions, I was giving birth. I've still got my wisdom teeth, which came in straight and on schedule, and I've never broken a bone bigger than a baby toe. It may be that I suffer from the arrogance of the congenitally healthy. A lover once told me I'd sooner put him out on the polar ice pack than fetch a tissue for his runny nose. I handed him a Kleenex on my way out the door.

In 2000 I left Alaska to take a teaching job in Virginia. I left there in 2003 for a post in central New York. My family asks if and when I'll return to Alaska permanently. I can't answer that. For now, I try not to miss it too much, and I try to learn the names of the flowers and shrubs and birds that belong to this place. Forsythia and fireflies instead of ptarmigans and vetch.

In the East, I rarely tell people that I'm from Alaska or that I'm a pilot. If they find out on their own, they get the wrong idea. The otherwise bright and charming organizer of a local writer's conference insists on billing me as an "Alaska bush pilot." I tell him that I am to an Alaska Bush pilot as a tricyclist is to Lance Armstrong. He thinks I'm joking.

My reticence isn't born of snobbery. (At least, I hope it's not.) Some subjects seem too intimate for the slightly tipsy bonhomie that passes for friendship at faculty cocktail parties. Besides, I'm bored with the wide-eyed double take, the shocked echo, "*You're* from Alaska? *You're* a pilot? I never would have guessed!" As if I'm trying to pass for normal. As if everybody else is not.

Recently, I had a variation on this conversation with a well-heeled friend who is a radio journalist and, like me, a fool for ideas. We stood in my kitchen, she with her scotch and me with my red wine, and spoke of home. Not her home or my home, but home in general. Is it where you come from? Or where you live now? She grew up in Fresno, and she flies there often to visit her father. On the flight back to New York, she always cries. She says the tears tell her that Fresno is her true home. I say that maybe home is the place that makes you cry when you get there, not when you leave.

Two or three times a year, I fly Alaska Airlines from Newark to Seattle, from Seattle to Fairbanks. For that final three-and-a-half-hour leg, I invariably get stuck between a tourist and a local. They're equally easy to peg. Tourists wear fanny packs and mufti. Locals wear T-shirts with the Big Dipper or sled dogs emblazoned on them. The sled dog T-shirt says, "Unless you're the lead dog, the view never changes."

From the time the jet takes off from Seattle, the local is on tenterhooks. Somewhere between Mount Rainier and Mount McKinley, he cozies up to the tourist with deceptive casualness: "Where you from? This your first trip to Alaska?" Before long, he's warming to his role. In Seattle, he was just another tourist with a bad haircut. On this jet, he's Alaska Guy. The fabric of his T-shirt stretches to accommodate his expanding sense of self.

"The aurora borealis is something everyone should see before they die," he says. "Of course, you won't be able to see it in the summer. You'll have to come back in the winter, when it's cold. How cold? Oh, I've seen it fifty-five, sixty below. Spit freezes before it hits the ground."

The tourist is hooked. In a voice trembling with awe, she ventures a question.

"Traffic? Oh, I can get from my house to work in ten minutes when the traffic's light. Of course I can get there in ten minutes when the traffic is heavy, too.

"*Heh heh.*"

I travel to and from Alaska incognito—no mufti, no Big Dipper T-shirt—for the same reason I never carry snapshots of my children. What I love best I keep tucked deep inside my rib cage.

What follows is a memoir of reading and flying; of parenting and being parented; of joy and terror and grief and consolation. Above all, it's a memoir of Alaska, intimate topology of my soul.

What's set down here is as true as I can make it. No names have been changed, no composites created. Whenever practicable, I checked my memory against that of others and against the official record. Gaps remain. For instance, everyone in my family seems to have forgotten the tremors that followed the Good Friday earthquake, even though the Alaska Earthquake Information Center says they were real.

Whenever I fly back to Fairbanks, I try to get a window seat. That way, the tourist and the local don't have to talk over me. That way, I can take in the craggy coastline, the ribboning rivers, the glaciers that drape like stoles around the creamy shoulders of mountains. My eyes take them in and, as if to make more space on the inside, my tears pour out.

Acknowledgments

Several essays in this volume have appeared in different form elsewhere:

"Lullaby for Lloyd," *Permafrost* 14 (Spring 1992): 33–38. Reprinted in *Reflections from the Island's Edge: A Sitka Reader,* ed. Carolyn Servid (St. Paul MN: Graywolf, 1994).

"Three Paragraphs," *The Sonora Review,* no. 34 (Fall/Winter 1997): 143–48.

"Wild Music: Reflections on Big Oil and Innocence," *Blue Mesa Review* 15 (Spring 2003): 172–81.

"Grease Monkey," *Manoa* 6:2 (Winter 1994): 148–56.

"My Mother's Body," *American Nature Writing* 1994, ed. John Murray (San Francisco: Sierra Club, 1994). Reprinted in *The Dolphin Reader,* ed. Douglas Hunt and Carolyn Perry, 3rd ed. (Boston: Houghton Mifflin, 1996).

"The Metaphysics of Being Stuck," *The Gettysburg Review* 14:3 (Autumn 2001): 137–44. A short version appeared in *Alaska* magazine in March 1999.

"Angle of Attack," *River Teeth* 6:1 (Fall 2004): 17–40.

I am indebted to Wolfgang Langewiesche, author of *Stick and*

Rudder: An Explanation of the Art of Flying, which taught me to fly, and to William Langewiesche, author of *Inside the Sky: A Meditation on Flight*, which taught me to think about flying and writing at the same time. Invaluable assistance and advice were rendered by Peter Balakian, Gregory Beyer, Al Brice, Carol Brice, John Gregory Brown, Craig Jones, Deborah Knuth Klenck, Margaret Maurer, Rebekah Presson Mosby, Phillip Richards, Bridget Ryan, Peggy Shumaker, Sherry Simpson, Natalia Rachel Singer, Frank Soos, Alan Swensen, and Joeth Zucco. The Colgate University Faculty Research Council gave me a grant for this project. I'm grateful to my editor, Ladette Randolph—who said yes!—and to her assistant, Nina Murray—who translated Mandelstam's poem. To my friend Carrie Brown, I owe my sanity. To my daughters—Kinzea, Emeline, and Clara, I owe everything else.

Unlearning to Fly

ONE ~ At the Airport

A Romance

My father proposed to my mother in an airport. I like that sentence so much, I can hardly bear to revise it. But I must. The second time my father proposed to my mother, it was in an airport. The first time was in a car. They'd met three weeks earlier, when my father's brother, Sam, asked my mother to be my father's blind date for his own birthday party. He was twenty-seven and she was twenty-five. Back then, Al Brice was holding down three jobs: a mechanic for Pan Am, an after-hours fueler for a jet fuel-supply company, and a logger for his family's fledgling land-clearing concern. Carol Heeks was a public health nurse who'd arrived in Fairbanks in July of 1961 at the wheel of a blue Plymouth Valiant. A New Yorker by birth and temperament, she was unwilling to spend the rest of her life in a frontier outpost so unprepossessing that a person could drive the length and breadth of it—as she once had—without ever realizing she'd arrived.

Hence the need for a second proposal from my father.

And a third.

Nursing and romance don't mix. On her first day of work, my mother's supervisor, Mary Carey, made that abundantly clear. If Miss C. Heeks (known to her former patients at Columbia-Presbyterian Hospital as "Cheeks") had driven all the way from the East Coast for the purpose of finding a husband, she could repack her suitcases, slam the trunk of her powder-blue

Valiant, and head back to the East Coast. What was needed at the Fairbanks Public Health Center in July 1961 was one more dedicated public health nurse, a woman whose sensibly clad feet were meant for pounding the pavement, not dancing the night away; a woman whose calling was to care for other people's babies, not to beget any of her own. What was needed, in short, were more suppliers of medical services, not more consumers. Mary wouldn't tolerate any giddiness over boys. She herself cut a formidable figure: a woman of girth, stature, and intellect. Mary Carey had several chins to go with that Dr. Seuss name, but she wasn't jolly in the least. Had she made herself clear?

When my father showed up at the airport in his white mechanic's overalls to "press his suit," as my mother would say, she felt a welter of emotions: flustered, flattered, confused. She didn't say yes or no. Everything about Alaska seemed strange, including this man who kept saying he was in love with her. Was she in love, too? Enough to give up her job? Maybe. No, she couldn't be. Oh, she didn't know. The only thing she *did* know was that she had to board Pan Am's red-eye flight to New York. Her brother, Bill, would pick her up at Idlewild Airport. From there, they'd drive to Vermont to spend Christmas with the family. In retirement, her surgeon father had reinvented himself as a gentleman farmer. Carol thought of the spread in Vermont as a kind of refuge. There, for the first time in days, she'd be able to think clearly about Al Brice, about herself, and about where she belonged—or didn't.

On the nights when she and my father went out dancing, I thought my mother was as beautiful as the queen in "Sleeping Beauty" or "Rumpelstiltskin," fairy tales she read aloud to me nearly every night. To think of anything or anyone as beautiful, some kind of distance is probably necessary, though—the kind of distance that daily life disallows. One day when I was eight or nine, my mother found me studying the photographs taken on the day she graduated from nurse's training, in 1958. In them, she is younger and more carefree than I've ever seen her. Her hair is like a sable cap, and her skin is as luminous as the moon. In one picture, her lips are slightly parted, and her forget-me-not eyes are focused on someone or something in the middle distance. That's the formal, posed photograph. In another, candid one, she wears the same starched blue-and-white-striped nurse's uniform with its detachable collar and cuffs, white apron, and old-fashioned crescent-shaped hat. Here, she bears a wrapped box like a baby on one hip, and a breeze lifts her skirt slightly, pushing her toward whoever is holding the camera. The look on her face is joyful, as if she's just been handed the ticket to the rest of her life.

"Wow, Mom," I breathed, "you were beautiful then."

"You mean I'm not beautiful now?" Her voice was rueful.

"No, I mean, that's not what I meant," I said quickly. It was the first social lie I'd ever told. Whether or not my mother was still beautiful was beside the point. "Mother" and "beauty" seemed to me mutually exclusive categories. One was familiar, homely, accessible, vernacular, spoken in the *tu* form—something I'd learned during my Wednesday afternoon French lessons. The other was exotic, foreign, remote, formal. The mother who read "Lyle the Crocodile," who fixed me cream cheese and pineapple sandwiches, who played gin rummy tournaments with me—that woman was *tu.* The woman in the starched blue-and-white pinstriped nurse's uniform: not married, not my mother, not accessible to me in any way. I could think of her only as foreign or other, as *vous.*

Unlike my father, who is not a natural storyteller—or, more likely, whose early years didn't lend themselves to storytelling—my mother speaks often of her growing-up years. In her stories, the places figure more prominently than the people. It's almost as if she runs through the topography of her life, touching time and again the places on the map that tell her who she is. There's Lying-In Hospital in New York, where she was born; Saint Luke's, where her father worked; Columbia-Presbyterian, where she trained to become a nurse; and Babies Hospital, where she herself worked. There's Bronxville, New York, where her family lived before World War II, and North Adams, Massachusetts, where they lived after. Her grandparents owned an apartment on the Upper East Side, overlooking the East River. Her aunts lived in a house in the tiny town of Touisset, on Naragansett Bay. She attended the Emma Willard School in Troy, New York, and Colby College in Waterville, Maine. Her parents bought a farm in Stamford, Vermont. She was married out of Saint John's Episcopal Church in North Adams, and her reception was at the Williams Inn in Williamstown, Massachusetts.

This litany made me feel as if my mother had been meant for a different life—not necessarily a better one, just different. Reciting the place names of her past, she seemed to be seeking a pattern, as if applied teleology might tell her how she ended up in Alaska. It was such a surprise.

In a funny way, my mother's history, as conveyed through her stories, seemed—and seems—more real to me than my own. Certainly, the stories made her life seem richer than mine, which has always had Fairbanks as its point of origin, not its destination. Throughout my childhood, she kept telling and re-telling the stories, sanding their edges, buffing and polishing each one until it was as shining and beautiful as the platters she brought out for baby showers and Easter dinners—sterling silver that gave back a slightly distorted reflection of one's self.

Carol Ann Heeks was born in New York's Lying-In Hospital on July 10, 1936. Her father, William Garland Heeks, was a Harvard-educated surgeon. Her mother, Lucia Bell Page, came from people with enough money they didn't have to talk about it. When my mother was a child, she and her brother and sister would be dressed in their best clothes and taken, on rare Sunday afternoons, to visit Lucia's parents. After kissing the papery cheeks that were proffered, the children would array themselves on a window seat in the front hall. There, they'd pass the afternoon watching boats travel up and down the river. They did not play, nor did they partake of the conversation. If they spoke to each other at all, it was in whispers so as not to disturb the adults.

Orphaned early, my mother's father was reared by doting aunts. He put off love until after medical school, when he wooed and won Lucia Bell Page, a finishing school beauty. In her studio wedding portrait, Lucia's expression is solemn, inscrutable, her pose—pivoted at the waist, so her silk train pools at her feet—as stylized as an Alphonse Mucha painting. After the wedding, William settled into a life of daily commutes from Bronxville to the city, Lucia into a routine of shopping, gardening, dinner parties, and volunteer work. There were evenings of martinis and steak followed by one or two rubbers of bridge. Three babies in quick succession—Alexandra (Sandie), then Carol, then William Jr. (Bill)—transformed Lucia's figure from that of a willowy debutante to a prow-shaped matron. She stayed stateside with the babies when her husband, well beyond the draft age, volunteered for the army during World War II. He was sent to the South Pacific. After his return, the family bought a Tudor-style house on Cherry Street in North Adams, where they settled back into their old, pre-war routine. In June the children were packed off to summer camp; in September, they went to boarding school.

When Carol entered Lucia's alma mater, the Emma Willard School, she was an overweight, underachieving, and desperately homesick child. In yearbook pictures from 1951 and 1952, she looks lumpen in her gingham-checked uniform. Her shoulder-length hair frizzes out around her face; her legs are as straight and thick as tree trunks in bobby socks and Mary Janes. She looks sturdy and unfeminine, the kind of girl who plays goalie on the field hockey team (which she did), the kind who ends up a potted plant beside the vivacious, popular girls with smooth, butterscotch-colored hair and slender ankles. Even so, she had friends. She was popular. The girls in her circle called each other "Jacques," pronounced "Jake," as in, "Hullo, Jacques. What's up?" "Nothing much, Jacques. You?" Within a year or two, Carol had shed the baby fat. By her junior year, she was wearing her hair shorter, too, in the flattering, face-skimming style she favors today. Never more than an average student, she yearned unrealistically for a Stanford or Bryn Mawr education. A guidance counselor gently steered her toward second- and third-tier schools.

During her first year at Colby College, Carol volunteered

at the hospital in the working-class town of Waterville. During this era, nursing was still regarded as a glorified form of waitressing—a fallback for women who couldn't type. Even so, Carol convinced herself that her father would be pleased to hear, in the fall of her sophomore year, that she had decided to become a nurse. She was wrong. "No daughter of mine is going to earn a living emptying bedpans," he roared. Carol beseeched and wept, but her father wouldn't budge. Pale and despondent, she went through the motions of going to class until one day her roommate came up with a plan that was brilliantly simple. Carol called her parents for permission to spend spring break in New York City with her roommate's family, and permission was granted. While there, she visited Columbia-Presbyterian School of Nursing. On her tour, Carol saw the student nurses in their starched postulant's uniforms working on the wards. She heard in her interview that she was an exemplar of what Columbia-Presbyterian, in its drive to professionalize nursing, was looking for: young women with at least two years of college behind them, willing to split the next three years between classroom and ward. After that, they'd graduate with a bachelor's degree in nursing. Carol returned to Colby and promptly filled out the application. She said nothing to her parents, figuring it would be better to beg for forgiveness later than to ask for permission now. She spent the next few weeks on tenterhooks until the day, near the end of the term, when a slim envelope was slipped into her box. The letter's tone was apologetic but firm. While the admissions committee felt that Miss Heeks was a worthy applicant in many respects, her medical records revealed that she lacked the strength and stamina for a career in nursing. Carol's first thought was that there must be some mistake. How could she, the former field hockey standout and glowing picture of health, be holding in her hand a slip of paper that said she was too frail to do the only thing she wanted to do?

That night on the phone, her father listened in grim silence while she wept. He said, "I'm going to make some calls. I'll let you know what I find out." Within a few hours, my grandfather ascertained that the admissions committee had somehow gained access to Carol's records, which were on file at Babies Hospital, an affiliate of Columbia-Presbyterian. Twice during infancy, Carol had been rushed into surgery for strangulated hernias and intestinal blockage. After the second operation—and after my grandparents returned from an overseas trip they'd taken sans children—my mother's surgeon broke the news that she was unlikely to survive into adulthood. She survived, of course, only to become the victim of that dire prognosis. My grandfather's outrage over Carol's rejection trumped his outrage over her career choice. A couple of calls to highly placed friends and colleagues—a radiologist at Columbia-Presbyterian Hospital, for one, and a highly regarded surgeon at Babies Hospital, for another—resulted in a happier letter for Carol.

What followed were the headiest, most carefree years of her life. She shared an apartment in the city with three nursing students, including her best friend, Lois Lemmon. She and Lois spent their days off window-shopping on Fifth Avenue and standing in line for tickets to Broadway shows. By then, Carol had shed the chrysalis of adolescence. She was slender and poised, possessed of a razor-sharp wit. She has always shown affection by teasing, and there was no shortage of young men willing to be teased. I imagine those days as a 1950's version of *Sex and the City*: lots of city and very little sex.

Shortly after graduating from nursing school, she was put in charge of a ward at Babies Hospital. The most freakish and hopeless cases ended up there: hydrocephalic and hermaphrodite babies; babies born with hearts that were too small or too large; babies dying of meningitis or hepatitis or leukemia. The nurses, Miss C. Heeks among them, shushed and rocked the babies from sunrise to sunset, until their shifts ended or until the babies died.

A medical resident from San Antonio asked her to marry him, and Carol said yes. He flew her to Texas to meet his family. She has no story for what happened there. She says that Bob's mother, a Texas socialite with big hair and big jewelry, found her unacceptable. Whenever my mother says this, I picture a bejeweled dowager in a broad-brimmed, Ascot-style hat prying apart a horse's jaws to check its teeth. Did Bob's mother study my mother's work-roughened hands and see in her guileless face something of the awkward and chubby child she'd been? The engagement broken, Carol flew back to New York alone.

There, things were in flux. One roommate was getting married; the other two had accepted jobs in different cities. My mother would have to give up the apartment. She would leave New York, too, she decided, applying for two jobs: the first as a nurse on the *Good Ship Hope*, which was setting sail for Africa, and the second as a public health nurse in Alaska. She swore to herself that she'd take the first offer she got. It turned out to be Alaska; the *Good Ship Hope* came through too late. She packed her Plymouth Valiant, bid her parents good-bye, and with the neighbors' sixteen-year-old daughter, Susan Bunce, riding shotgun, she headed north.

She and Susan took the long way, crisscrossing the country. They gawked at Mount Rushmore, the California redwoods, Yosemite and Yellowstone national parks. When night fell, they pulled onto a wide spot in the highway, threw down their sleeping bags, and slept under the stars. Gradually, the road grew narrower and rougher until, somewhere in Canada, they left pavement behind. When they got to the place where their map said Fairbanks would be, it wasn't. They drove for a few more miles, then stopped at a filling station.

"How do I get to Fairbanks from here?" my mother asked the attendant.

"Lady, you just drove through it."

Susan boarded a plane for New York the next day, and my mother found herself a $240-per-month apartment in Fairview Manor, a couple of blocks from the unprepossessing brown box that was the Fairbanks Public Health Center. Her salary was $400 per month. For that, she'd be the nursing equivalent of a beat cop, swabbing throats for signs of strep, administering TB tine tests, paying visits to mothers with newborns, the elderly, and the infirm. She'd also track down the partners of patients who tested positive for venereal disease. She'd find them in such bars as The Hideaway and Tommy's Elbow Room, where my mother, acting on a tip from the bartender, would tap them on the shoulder then ruin their whole day. Anti-government and pro-privacy sentiments tend to run high in frontier towns, and not everyone would take kindly to the sight of a nurse in her light-blue uniform dress and rubber-soled shoes marching up the walk or elbowing up to the bar. My mother would get the dog bite scars to prove it.

Mary Carey was a martinet of a nursing supervisor. Years before Lyndon Johnson's Great Society, she saw herself and her nurses as fighting a trench war on disease, poverty, and ignorance. To be a good soldier in Mary's army required the elimination of potential distractions, chief among them, suitors.

Mary couldn't stop Carol from making friends, though. She found a handful of bridge partners and joined the curling club. Once in a while, she saw a guy named Sam Brice who, like her, was heartsore. His parents had forced him to break off an engagement to a young woman deemed unsuitable because of her divorce. One day in December 1961, Sam called to ask a favor of Carol. Would she attend his older brother's birthday party as his older brother's date?

I wonder what Carol Heeks thought of Al Brice. Two years older than she, he stood a few inches taller, roughly five-foot-nine to her five-foot-five. He had an overbite that stopped just shy of buckteeth, and he was going bald. On occasions such as weddings and funerals that called for a tie, serious effort was required to locate his neck. In high school, Al had had the biggest head and the smallest feet of any player on the football team. Yet he was fit from years of felling trees and hauling them through the swamps of southern Georgia and northern Florida. Among the portraits in the upstairs hall of my parents' home hangs a large-format, sepia-toned print of Al and his brothers Sam, Thom, and Andy sharing lunch on a fallen log. They're in their late teens or early twenties, and they're wearing work boots, belted khaki pants, and (except for Al and Andy) bare chests. My father is wearing a colored T-shirt, which, on him, looks even sexier than a bare chest. The boys (as their mother called them) look muscular enough to wrestle alligators in the swamp where they were stump logging. Underneath their caps, there's a sweet, aw-shucks quality to their smiles that almost—but not quite—belies the manliness of the sinewy arms, tanned chests, and work boots. My father and his brothers were the originals that James Dean and his ilk could only hope to imitate.

In short, he made hardly any impression on my mother at all.

What my father saw when he looked at Carol Heeks was a slim, stylish woman with Irish coloring: nearly black hair, pale skin, blue eyes. In her off hours, she wore oversized shirts on top of slim-fitting ankle pants and penny loafers. Then as now, she had a disarming smile and a way of looking at you as if you were the only person in the room. She was also an unrepentant tease.

Carol definitely made an impression on Al.

A few days later, they met again at a sledding party. Carol loved such parties, and even today is rarely more herself—ebullient, competitive, uninhibited, even a bit silly—than within the formal constraints of a toboggan run or Scrabble game. On the way back to town, Al engineered the seating so that Carol would ride alone with him. Then he promptly drove the car into a snow bank. Waiting for a tow, they had their first real conversation. Carol recounted how she'd driven across the country in her Plymouth Valiant, with no one but her sixteen-year-old friend for company. Al thought (but didn't say) she had grit as well as good looks.

Later, he drove her back to her apartment and walked her up the stairs.

"I was afraid he was going to try and kiss me," my mother says, in response to a question from me. She wasn't the kind of girl who kissed on the second date. Ten feet from the door, he abruptly said good night, turned, and walked away. Turning the key in the lock, Carol felt a bit hurt that he hadn't even tried.

A few days later, he took her for a drive. On a wide curve overlooking the Tanana River, Al pulled over. He asked Carol if she'd ever considered staying in Alaska beyond her two-year contract with the Public Health Service. She had not. Why would anyone want to live in this godforsaken place, where, in the winter, the temperature rarely rose above zero and a body could duck into the post office while the sun was rising only to emerge a few moments later and see it sliding down the sky?

"The reason I asked," Al said, "is you're the kind of girl I've always wanted to marry."

The guy's crazy, my mother thought. *I don't even know him, let alone love him.*

Out loud, she said she'd think about it. Given the ambiguous nature of the proposal, she wasn't entirely sure what she was promising to think about—staying in Alaska after her contract was up, marrying Al Brice, or both.

A couple of days later, she was on the ice at the curling club when her friend, Betty Waldhaus, said, "Hey Carol, who's the guy in the stands with the fish eyes looking at you?"

She looked up, and there was Al in his white mechanic's overalls. He waved. Carol glanced away. A few seconds later, he was gone.

Betty cornered Carol after the match. "Out with it," she said.

Carol burst into tears. With a wadded up handkerchief in her hand, she told Betty the whole story.

"Do you love him?" Betty asked. Tiny as a wren with a wren's piercing eyes, Betty was a decade older than my mother. A fellow public health nurse, she was possessed of the no-nonsense manner that comes with years of marching up to strangers in bars and handing them a prescription for gonorrhea.

"I don't know. I barely know him," my mother replied. Then, "Promise you won't tell Mary?"

Betty promised, but only after observing tartly that my mother couldn't lead the poor sap on indefinitely.

The poor sap showed up at the airport a few days before Christmas, while Carol was checking in for her Pan Am flight to New York. Once again, Betty saw him first. She nudged Carol and nodded in the direction of Al, who was, again, wearing his mechanic's overalls. Taking her husband, Fred, by the arm, Betty withdrew to give the two of them some privacy.

Al didn't waste a moment. He told Carol there was a diamond ring in her name waiting at Tiffany's on Fifth Avenue in New York. Picking it up wouldn't commit her to anything more than thinking about whether she could ever bring herself to wear it. Was she willing to do that much for him?

I'm in the middle of a Cinderella story, Carol thought.

Out loud, she said, "Well, I guess I could do that."

Her flight touched down at 4:00 a.m. at Idlewild Airport. Her brother, Bill, was waiting in the terminal, groggy but game for the drive to Vermont. Hesitantly, Carol explained that she had to run an errand in the city first.

"What kind of errand?" Bill asked.

Carol told him.

"Boy, are you ever going to be in trouble with Mom and Dad."

"Promise you won't say anything?"

Bill and Carol drove into Manhattan and then drowsed in the car until ten o'clock, when the security guard unlocked the front door of Tiffany's. Rumpled and red-eyed from her overnight flight, my mother sensed that everyone was watching her as she stepped into the store. She was right. All of Tiffany's was agog. The manager hovered and the salesladies fussed over the girl who'd flown all the way from Alaska to pick up her engagement ring. They were brimming with questions. How cold does it get there, really? Have you seen the northern lights? Is it dark all the time in the winter? Aren't you afraid of the bears? And what about this guy? What a romantic! How'd you find him? When's the wedding?

The next day, the florist delivered a dozen yellow roses to the Vermont farmhouse. And the day after that, more roses came. As Carol fetched a second vase, her father raised his eyebrows but said nothing. She, too, was silent. The ring was still nestled inside its blue velvet box at the bottom of her purse. On her third day in Vermont, the telephone rang. In those days, roses were cheap compared to long-distance calls from Alaska. Carol took the call on the upstairs extension. She'd barely begun speaking when her father walked into the room and plunked a three-minute egg timer on the table beside her. After she hung up, he said, "I don't know who this guy is, but if he loves you, and you love him, marry him. Tell him to save his money."

The next time my father called, my mother said yes.

"I'm on my way," he said.

They married in North Adams, Massachusetts, in February, a few days before Ash Wednesday and the beginning of Lent, which would have meant no wedding until after Easter. The dress fittings, cocktail parties, rehearsal dinner, and wedding seem now to belong to a glamorous but magical world, a kind of Brigadoon that my mother can summon from the clouds with the force of nostalgia. Whenever she trots out the story of her wedding, it has the unconscious effect of making every other wedding seem poorer, more overdone, banal, and tasteless by comparison.

For the ceremony, Carol wore a raw-silk gown with tulle underskirts and a detachable train trimmed with fabric roses. A veil of Alençon lace was bobby-pinned to her hair. The veil, along with the gown's high, unembellished neckline, gave her the look of a postulant taking vows. For the drive from the church to the reception, at the Williams Inn in Williamstown, she borrowed a white fur capelet that heightened the pallor of her skin, the red of her lipstick. Her bridesmaids wore red velvet cocktail dresses and carried white fur muffs trimmed with holly.

My parents honeymooned in northern Europe, flying there on Pan Am passes. Afterward, they settled into married life in Fairbanks. Mary Carey went apoplectic the first time my mother wore her Tiffany's diamond to work, but she got over it and grudgingly allowed my mother to keep working at the health center. By March of 1965—three years and one month after their wedding—my parents had three children: a preschooler (me), a toddler (Sam) and a newborn (Hannah). My mother had to quit working. As a joke, my uncles had nicknamed me "J. P., the Lumber Baroness." (The P stood for Page.) It was a joke because Al and his father and brothers had yet to get their land-clearing concern up and running. My parents were renting a drafty, coal-heated house on First Avenue. They'd furnished it with beds and tables and chairs purchased on a payment plan from Nerland's. The bills were piling up. I imagine that, to my mother, everything about her life must have felt fragile and provisional. Everything, that is, except for the Tiffany's diamond on the ring finger of her left hand.

In the summer of 1965, my father's company won a contract to build a runway for the village of Noorvik, which is on the Bering

 Sea, just north of the Seward Peninsula. The lease was nearly up on my parents' house, so they put their furniture in storage, and then flew to Noorvik with the three of us—Sam, Hannah, and myself. My mother had barely unpacked and settled into our quarters in the village armory before news crackled over the village radio. The warehouse in which my parents had stored not just their furniture but appliances, photo albums, wedding presents, clothes, and books had caught fire and burned to the ground. There was no insurance. My mother flew back to Fairbanks to sift through the ashes. Beneath the burned-out hull of what had been our refrigerator, she found our baby books, volumes into which she'd painstakingly pasted pictures and snippets of hair, and where she'd recorded shower gifts and first words. The books were scorched around the edges, but a few pictures from each were salvageable, protected from the worst of the fire by the bulk of the refrigerator. The only other things she found were my fourteen-carat-gold christening cross and baby bracelet, soldered together by the fire's heat. Everything else was gone.

In a photograph from our days in the Arctic, my mother kneels beside a sled bearing the three of us kids. She's wearing a pine-green corduroy parka with a white fox ruff. We, too, wear parkas with wolverine ruffs snugged up around our faces. Our feet are laced into caribou and sealskin mukluks. After Noorvik, my father had taken a second Bush job, this one in Wainwright, a tiny village perched precariously on cliffs above the Arctic Ocean. With no house or possessions waiting in Fairbanks, my mother went to Wainwright with us kids. Because there was no runway (Brice Inc. had yet to build it), my father set down his single-engine Aeronca Champ on a smooth stretch of beach. From there we rode partway in a skin boat then walked half a mile across the wind-scoured tundra. We staggered into Wainwright nearly hypothermic in skimpy windbreakers and sneakers. It was October. A few days later, three ageless Iñupiaq ladies brought gifts of fur-lined parkas and mukluks for everyone. (The nineteenth-century explorer Mary Kingsley writes of "that ever powerful factor in all human societies, the old ladies." My charming mother won them over.) My parka zipped up the front, which I loved; Hannah's went over the head, which she hated. In the photograph, it's possible to see that even Sam's parka is trimmed in the Iñupiaq way, with ricrac and colorful ribbons stitched around the pockets, zippers, and hem.

On the second day in Wainwright, my father left for the job site early. (I'd say "before dawn" except that, in October in the Far North, there is nothing that resembles dawn, just a pinkish glow that suffuses the horizon toward midday.) The rest of us hunkered down, still asleep in a house heated by a primitive coal-burning stove. When my mother awoke and tried to light the stove, it balked. Frustrated, she threw a bit of fuel on it. There was a loud *bang*. My mother says she felt nothing until she looked at us. Sam and I cowered in terror. The explosion had singed off her eyebrows, eyelashes, and much of her face. After a series of radio calls (a schoolteacher in Wainwright was able to raise someone at the newspaper office in Fairbanks, who telephoned my grandmother. She telephoned someone at the Barrow hospital, who dispatched a Medevac flight to Wainwright), my mother ended up in a hospital bed 230 miles from her family. The moment must have felt like the aphelion of a life whose perihelion was her East Coast society wedding. There she lay with her face on fire, being tended to by strangers while her children, too, were entrusted to the care of elderly Iñupiaq women in a one-room shack in a godforsaken Arctic village where her husband was working twenty-hour days and where she and her children were living by default, because they had neither furniture nor rugs nor dishes nor flatware nor blankets nor dishtowels with which to make a home. The next day, in defiance of her doctor's orders, she checked herself out of the hospital and flew back to Wainwright.

I don't remember the stove blowing up in my mother's face. I was only three. But I remember darkness so thick it seemed palpable, the wavering flame of the seal-oil lamp, the chamois-soft hands and throaty giggles of Nannie and Mae in their cotton kuspuks. They told my mother stories: an eight-year-old girl left for a neighbor's and never returned. In the spring, the melting snow gave up her body, lying between the two houses. A twelve-year-old girl fell out of a top bunk and broke her back. She languished in bed for four months before dying. A few years after Wainwright, my mother would become a founder, along with the minister from the Episcopal church, of the Resource Center for the Prevention of Child Abuse and Neglect. She would return to graduate school, earning a master's degree in education that would enable her to start a successful family counseling business. Eventually, she would serve on and even chair the Alaska Children's Trust under two Alaska governors. Her life as an activist was shaped by our stint in the Bush, but not in obvious ways. What others might have seen as unconscionable cruelty on the part of Native parents toward their children, my mother came to see as a kind of fatalism born of extreme duress—heartbreaking, yes, but not irrational or incomprehensible. Where people live under the harshest imaginable conditions, modern medicine and modern justice have little sway.

When it was time for me to enter nursery school, my mother flew back to Fairbanks with us children. She rented a street-level apartment on Fairbanks Street, near the University of Alaska campus. My father stayed in the Bush. The next summer, August 1967, the Chena River overflowed its banks. With water lapping at our stoop, my mother boxed up the only possessions she cared about, our restored baby books, and carried them upstairs to a friend's apartment. The water kept rising. She threw some clothes into bags and bundled us children into raincoats and boots. A stranger in a canoe paddled up to the door. Did she need help? One at a time, she handed us into the stranger's waiting arms. The gunnels of the overloaded canoe barely cleared the water. When my mother tried to hand the stranger our husky, Chitina, the man said no. She was firm. If the dog stayed, she stayed, too. Short of paddling off with three motherless, howling children, there was nothing the man could do. With Chitina in the bow, he paddled through the parking lot, where the antennae and roofs of cars poked through the brackish water like branches or islands. Then he paddled up the street to the base of the hill on which the university—like so many institutions of its kind—perched. There,

National Guardsmen lifted us and the other refugees out of motorboats and canoes and swung us onto the back of troop trucks. Our truck ferried us to even higher ground, a radio tower on Farmers Loop, a few miles north of Fairbanks. There, a second stranger gave us a ride in his car to my grandparents' home in the former Fairbanks orphanage, ten miles from town. We stayed nearly two weeks at the farm, as we called my grandparents' spread, even though they never kept animals there. With customary generosity, my grandmother had thrown open her doors to all comers—family, friends, and anyone else who drifted in. She and my grandfather owned a car, but it was useless without any way to buy gas. Every couple of days, my mother and a sister-in-law walked two miles to a Red Cross distribution center, where they waited in line for milk (for babies only) and emergency rations. When the floodwaters receded, my mother returned to the apartment, expecting to find that she had, for the second time in as many years, lost everything. This time she was lucky. The water had barely crested our threshold.

Eventually, my father returned from the Bush and found land-clearing work closer to Fairbanks. For a few months, he came home every evening. My mother began working more hours. One spring morning, she left for several days to assist a pediatrician studying strep among children living on Saint Lawrence Island. According to my memory (which seems suspiciously pat), my father drove us straight from the airport, where we'd put my mother on a plane, to the car dealership. There, he traded in the family's cream-colored, wood-paneled Plymouth station wagon for a four-wheel-drive Toyota Land Cruiser. It had bench seats and a rear-door latch that was accessible only after one unhitched the spare tire. We kids thought it was the coolest thing we'd ever seen. Our father even let us pick out the color: powder blue. It was to be a surprise for our mother.

Meanwhile, she and the pediatrician and a second nurse examined the children in the village of Gambell on Saint Lawrence Island. Then they left by dog team for the village of Savoonga, on the other side of the island. A member of the Alaska National Guard rode the runners of each sled, and each sled bore one passenger. On the way to Savoonga, the party ran into a blinding storm, a real tsunami of snow. The soldiers lost the trail. My mother, zipped into an ice-encrusted sleeping bag that was lashed to her sled, grew so cold that she drifted in and out of consciousness. At one point, she roused enough to realize that she was alone: her driver and her dogs were gone. The sled to which she was strapped was marooned in a sea of snow. She lost consciousness then woke to the sound of voices. Several men working together lifted her sled and then, using a primitive system of ropes and pulleys, lowered it down the sheer face of a cliff. The wind howled and swatted at the sled, but the ropes held. A short time later, two of the three sleds—the ones carrying the nurses—that had left Gambell together pulled up in front of the Savoonga school. Inside, the nurses found no furnishings, no rugs, no blankets, no pillows, and no food. When they turned on the faucets in the girls' restroom, frigid salt water poured out. The women thawed their frostbitten limbs as well as they could then fell into an exhausted, fitful sleep on the floor.

The next morning dawned clear and cold, with sunlight cutting patterns in the snow dunes. Together, the women picked their weary way to the clinic, where they found the doctor waiting for them. He was in hearty good humor after spending the night in a villager's home, where he'd been treated to a hot meal, a warm bath, a soft bed. As nearly as the nurses could tell, he hadn't spared a thought for their comfort or even their safety. What was worse, the storm had broken up the offshore ice pack, luring the village men away to hunt for seals and walrus. No one stayed behind to plow the village airstrip. Until it was plowed, no flights could take off or land. The gym floor was to be the nurses' home for the next few nights.

Back in Fairbanks, the day finally came when our father bundled us up and drove the Land Cruiser to the airport. As the plane taxied to its parking spot, we bounced up and down, irrepressible with glee. Our mother's face, snowburned and peeling, appeared in the doorway. We shouted, "Mommy! Mommy! Guess what we bought!" She couldn't guess. Even when she was standing right in front of it, she still couldn't guess. She shot our father a withering look. His boyish grin wavered. "Where's my station wagon?" she said. Her eyes swam with tears. "I want my station wagon back."

An airport is a between space. Between our leaving and arriving. Between the place we come from and the place we live now. Between childhood and responsibility. Between loss and wholeness. There, boundaries between self and other, inside and outside, home and the wider world seemed less fixed, more fluid somehow. When I was six or seven, my father's mother flew with me to Tennessee to visit her relatives. Of the trip itself, I remember next to nothing except that I nearly drowned in the deep end of someone's swimming pool while my grandmother chatted with cousins on the patio. As I thrashed and sputtered, she said, "Don't pay her any mind. She's just playing. Really, she's a very good swimmer." What I remember best is being in the airport before we left. In photographs, I'm wearing a white straw hat, a pink jacket, blue stretch pants, and red patent leather Mary Janes. I'm carrying a round vinyl suitcase, and my hair is styled in long sausage curls. My grandmother—stylish in her rhinestone-studded glasses and shrug-on coat—has a protective arm around me, as if to say to my mother, the picture-taker, "Don't worry. I'll bring her back safely." Twenty-five years after that picture was taken, I would drive to the airport to bid my grandmother good-bye on her semi-annual pilgrimage to the Mayo Clinic in Rochester, Minnesota. She would come back in an urn.

The historical and cultural convulsions of the 1960s—the Cuban Missile Crisis, John F. Kennedy's assassination, the Vietnam War, feminism, Twiggy, and the *Apollo 11* moon walk—had little bearing on our daily lives. People who kept up with the news in the Lower Forty-eight were regarded as vaguely eccentric, even suspect. A big technological leap happened right before our eyes, though. Pan Am began developing the Boeing 747-100 in 1966, and it entered the commercial market in January of 1970. While deregulation was still the dim dream of a paper pusher somewhere, the 747 slashed per-seat operating costs and made international airline travel more affordable to the average American. It also brought the outside world to Fairbanks.

With their hair in beehives or French twists under cunning blue pillbox hats, with their lipstick and manicures and impossibly high heels, Pan Am's 747 stewardesses (not yet flight attendants) embodied all that was grownup and feminine, beautiful and exotic. Then as now, they traveled through the airport in packs. After they'd passed, the scent of New York, London, Paris, Singapore, or Tokyo hung in the air, thick as perfume. They clicked past us mere mortals with a kind of energy I came to associate with going somewhere else, somewhere more alive and interesting than Alaska. In those days, "somewhere else" almost always meant the East Coast.

My mother's relatives flew in on Pan Am's New York–Tokyo flight, which stopped in Fairbanks to refuel. Her father, widowed since 1962 ("I write from the bottom of a broken heart because fifty-one is too young to die," said the telegram he sent when Lucia was diagnosed with inoperable lung cancer) stayed with us for a few weeks every summer. Her brother, Bill, now an executive in the import business, sometimes spent twenty-four hours on his way to or from what my mother always called "the Orient." Once, he brought along a pineapple, the first we kids had ever seen or tasted outside of a can. The tangy sweetness seeped into our mouths and ran down our chins as we grabbed seconds and thirds, blind to our mother's admonitory look that said, "Be on your best behavior in front of my brother. Or else."

For trips to the airport, my mother wore Shalimar—a drop on the inside of each wrist and behind her ears. Her everyday scent was Jean Naté, which she bought at the Five and Dime, later Woolworth's. She'd gone back to work part time by then. I'd come to associate public health nursing with brown penny loafers and navy-blue, double-knit pantsuits, not the starched white dresses and mortarboard crescents that real nurses like Cherry Ames wore. Like her uniforms, my mother seemed bland and careworn compared to the nurses of fiction, or even the black-habited nuns who ran Saint Joseph's Hospital, where I'd gone to have my tonsils and adenoids removed. I knew from experience that, once in flight, the stewardesses removed the bobby pins holding their pillbox hats in place and hung up their tailored jackets for frilly aprons. With a child's sense for what's real and what's not, I knew they were only playing at domesticity. Their real selves were the ones they presented in the airport or during the pre-flight briefing, when they demonstrated how to use a seat cushion as a flotation device. My mother, on the other hand, was most real, most herself, when she was wearing flat shoes and an apron, mulling over a cookbook in the kitchen.

For those trips to the airport, my mother let me wear my patent-leather Mary Janes (black before Memorial Day and white after, even if the snow hadn't yet melted) and white socks with lacy cuffs. She'd button me into a smocked cotton dress, stiff with starch and warm from the iron. She herself wore what I thought of as her airport dress, a bottle-green knit with a mock turtleneck, trimmed in contrasting blue stripes around the sleeves and hem. Under the dress, my mother wore a full slip and girdle, pantyhose and pumps. Before leaving the house, she would have spent thirty seconds in front of the mirror, which was twenty-seven seconds more than she usually spent powdering her nose and applying lipstick. Her hair was styled then as it has been for nearly sixty years: short and wavy around her face. Then, as now, she washed it once or twice a week in the kitchen sink, in the early morning, before anyone else but my father—who often left for work before 6:00 a.m.—was awake. She routinely gave it three or four quick strokes with a hairbrush in the morning then forgot about it for the rest of the day. For the airport, she might brush it once more and spray it with Aqua Net.

In the terminal, my younger brother would hang onto Mom's stocking-clad legs, hamstringing her; Hannah would perch, alert as a baby sparrow, in her arms. My mother's glance, when it fell on me, was appraising: Had my hair ribbon come untied? Had my socks fallen down? No, and no. I was a tidy child, seemingly born with a flair for ritual and pageant, keenly aware of the gap between off- and onstage persona.

In the '60s and early '70s, we were allowed to wait outside

 while the jet landed, taxied, then parked fifty yards away. There were no jet ways then, just stairs leading to the spot where we stood on the tarmac. We were almost always waiting for my mother's father, whom we called Grampy to his face and Grumpy behind his back. He'd spend the next few weeks sitting in milky-eyed judgment from the recliner in our living room, a scotch and soda sweating into the coaster beside him. When he was there, we had to be quieter and more respectful than usual. If one of us complained about what my mother was fixing for dinner, he'd say, "Go see the chaplain: end of the hall, first door on the left"—a bit of advice that was an absolute cipher to us kids. In a better mood, he'd crack one of his off-color jokes. They, too, were a cipher: "Where does hair grow the curliest? In India." Ha.

When my mother dressed up to meet her father's flight every summer, she seemed both the same and different. It was as if she—who never cared about dazzling or even impressing us—was wooing someone else, this aged foreigner to whom she constantly deferred. He told her what cut of beef to buy from the butcher, and he let her know when he thought one of us needed spanking. Even my father, who stood on ceremony with no one else, called him "Dr. Bill." Our mother, this woman who could do no wrong in our eyes, was never able to measure up in her father's. Perhaps she was a stranger to us in that airport dress because she was a stranger to herself.

Two or three times a year, my parents went dancing at Club 11. Earlier in the day, my mother would have asked a beautician friend to style her hair in waves that stood high off her forehead. After my father left to fetch the babysitter, I'd sit on her bed and watch her pull on a rustling silk blouse and long skirt, one of two she owned in Key West fabrics, a gift from her father. She'd clip on ivory forget-me-not earrings with gold nugget centers. (My mother has never pierced her ears. When she was growing up in New York, only "fast" girls pierced their ears.) She'd dab on Shalimar, apply lipstick in three quick swipes, and then, when my father returned, straighten the tie that was already making him miserable. He held her mouton coat, the one she'd worn, in one style or another, since boarding school, and she donned it with a shrug of her shoulders, a gesture that broke my heart every time. "Don't go. Don't leave me," I begged. My mother bent from the height of her black patent high heels to kiss me and to promise me a treat for being a big help to the babysitter. Behind mascaraed lashes, her eyes seemed softer and more unfocused than usual, as if she'd already left.

The sting of betrayal was worse than when my mother left for longer stretches—to give checkups and vaccines in the villages or to accompany my father on business trips. The morning after my parents had gone out, I'd pad into the kitchen and see my mother frying bacon for breakfast. Not even that familiar sight consoled me. A whole day might go by before I forgave her. Back then, I only intuited what seems clear now. My mother's nights out were practice separations, rehearsals for the bigger leave-takings—my departure for college, my getting married, my leaving Alaska, her decline and eventual death.

There was something else going on, though. The true stories of my mother's childhood had a strange and alchemical effect, mingling in my mind with the stories of fairies and frogs and princesses. I knew what a changeling was, and here was my mother—familiar, beloved—changing into a glamorous creature before my eyes. Her stories told me that marriage and motherhood had stolen her from a kingdom of wealth and beauty and fresh produce (the East) and deposited her on the farthest outpost of civilization (the North), where fruits and vegetables came in cans, where milk and juice and potatoes had to be reconstituted from powder. On my mother's Shalimar nights, I cried and clung to her until someone—the babysitter or my father—led me away and tried to distract me with the promise of hot chocolate or Chutes and Ladders. Such was the power of my mother's stories. I knew she'd come from far, far away just to be with us; when she dressed up like royalty, I thought she was going away forever.

One Thanksgiving, my mother bought tickets for the family to fly back East for Christmas. When my father found out how much the tickets had cost—nearly $2,000—he sent my mother to the airport to cash them in. He took the money and used it for a down payment on an Avalon motor home, which he and my mother drove, in shifts, from Fairbanks to Fairfield, Connecticut, in time for Christmas, then from Fairfield to Key West, Florida, where Grampy spent his winters. When it was time to drive home, they drew a line on the Rand McNally Road Atlas from the southernmost city in the United States to the northernmost one. My memories of the vacation are fragmentary, imagistic. At Niagara Falls, I vomited over the railing, sick with what my mother thought was a virus but turned out to be carbon monoxide poisoning. On the beach in Key West, I tried to pick up a cotton candy-colored jellyfish with my plastic sand shovel; I wanted it for a souvenir. After stopping somewhere in Kansas to fill up the Avalon's tanks and to buy snacks, my father pulled up to the highway, a taut ribbon stretching in both directions toward the ends of the earth. Which way were we going? Had we made a left into the filling station? Or a right? We flipped a coin.

The summer I was twelve, my parents agreed that a round-trip ticket from Fairbanks to New York was a small price to pay for a two-week reprieve from pre-teen angst and sulking. The plan was for me to spend two weeks at Aunt Sandie's house in Connecticut. Like all arrivals and departures, this was to be an event. My mother and I went shopping for a new dress: midi length, with a blue polka-dot skirt, red-striped blouse, and a wide boy's tie. I wore it with a white cardigan, white patent-leather boots and my new pageboy haircut, achieving a look that fell somewhere between Marlo Thomas and *The Mod Squad*. In that dress and that hairstyle, I felt prepared to travel back East. "Back East" was the phrase my mother uttered with roughly the same reverence and frequency as the Prayer of Humble Access at Saint Matthew's on Sunday mornings. "Back East" was the seat of civilization, tradition, and elegance. People who lived "back East" set their table with the fork on the left, spoon and knife (blade facing inward) on the right. They used cloth napkins and sterling candlesticks and Battenberg lace tablecloths. They fixed drinks beforehand, cunningly named cocktails such as vodka gimlets, whiskey sours, cosmopolitans, and greenies. Before the cocktail hour, they showered and changed from their gardening or tennis togs, and the women did their nails with manicure tools stored in monogrammed cases of red leather. Easterners set a lot of store by how you were raised, and they could tell a lot about that by the state of your cuticles. Mine tended to be red and ratty from chewing. Two weeks "back East" would do more than break me of the habit; it would transform me.

Aunt Sandie's household was a surprise. There was a lot of hollering between my aunt and my teenage cousins. When they weren't talking on the phone with boys, Peggy and Vickie were embroidering denim work shirts or polishing their toenails or slathering their skin with baby oil to sunbathe on the back deck. Compared to their work shirts, my midi dress was trying much too hard; it was, in a phrase beloved by my stylish grandmother, "too-too." My cousins shaved their legs and wore sky-blue eye shadow and left the house with girlfriends only to meet up later with boyfriends. Suspicious, my aunt sometimes sent me along to the movies or the county fair as a chaperone, a role for which I was ill suited. The last thing I wanted was to tattle on my exotic cousins—what I wanted was to *be* them. Despite my aunt's best efforts (trips to Old Sturbridge Village and Louisa May Alcott's house), I wasn't becoming more polished. If anything, I felt like more of a rube than ever.

One night, I awoke in pain. My right hand throbbed unbearably. Whimpering, I switched on the bedside lamp in order to see what was wrong. The top joint of the middle finger had swollen to the width of a thumb. Around the nail bed, the skin had turned a sickly shade of green. It looked like a finger out of the comics, just after the villain has been duped into hitting himself with a sledgehammer. In the morning, my surgeon grandfather would examine the finger and then write a prescription for penicillin. He'd shake his head and tell me I had only myself to blame for the infection, having brought it on through my nasty habit of cuticle chewing.

My mother is a paradox in a way that the nineteenth-century female explorers were paradoxes. Unlike their male counterparts, the women did their exploring under the guise of missionary work or teaching or nursing. My mother's ancestors may not have come over on the *Mayflower*, but they were from England, and they were here for the Revolutionary War. A distant cousin made a fortune in thoroughbreds and Calumet baking powder. She herself is the product of a Harvard-educated surgeon and his socialite wife, of people who summered on the Cape and the Vineyard, and who sent their daughters to Emma Willard or Miss Porter's. (The women in my mother's family never use slang. To this day, I cannot bring myself to say, out loud, "cops" for "police" or "bucks" for "dollars.") She herself may have pursued a profession, and she may have married a penniless mechanic on the Last Frontier, but she still wears that badge of belonging in East Coast society—a diamond solitaire from Tiffany's. The way she tells her story, she was leading the life she was born to lead when she was swept off her feet—and swept away from her socialite's life in the East—by my father's proposal. (I use the passive construction deliberately.) That was the romantic convention of 1950s America, pre–Betty Friedan and Gloria Steinem: Men were measured by their actions, and women were measured by how well they bore up under men's actions. In fact, my mother was anything but passive. Years before she met my father, she'd acted downright subversively when it came to applying to nursing school. And who but an adventurer would apply for work in the territory of Alaska in 1961? In many respects, she was like the British explorer Gertrude Bell, whom Jill Ker Conway describes as seeking "an alternative society where her obvious talents would be recognized, and where she could establish herself as a person of substance."

Over the course of four decades, my mother established herself as a person of substance. There's even a human services building named in her honor. While I was growing up—while I was listening to her stories—she was busy reinventing herself: public health nurse, mother, activist, graduate student, educator, parenting guru, stateswoman. I'm not sure what the lesson is. Perhaps it's that one's willingness to adapt and change depends greatly on the stability of one's personal mythology. It's odd that my mother, who's quick to latch on to new theories and fresh practices, also clings to what's old—Spode china, embossed silver, embroidered linens, monogrammed sheets, family genealogies, boarding school yearbooks, the 1942 Book of Common Prayer—with reverence bordering on awe. From her grandmother, Daisy Bell, she inherited an evening watch crusted with diamonds and sapphires. In all the time she's owned it, it has never run. The proprietor of a dusty watch-repair shop in the Polaris Building told her it never will.

My mother was in her forties before her mythology began to unravel. During a conversation with her sister, my mother mentioned some crazy antic of their mother's.

"Of course, that was because she was drunk," Sandie said.

"What do you mean, 'She was *drunk*?'"

"She was drunk all the time, Carol. Didn't you notice?"

My mother hadn't noticed. When her mother was angry, Carol assumed it was because she'd done something wrong. As a child, she did a lot of things wrong. She was never allowed in the kitchen, where she might get underfoot or break something. She was never allowed to help with the housework because she might mess up, like the time she spooled the toilet paper backward. When Carol was ten, she fell out of a tree and broke her arm. Furious, her mother yanked off the torn and dirty play clothes and stuffed Carol—her broken bone dangling—into a frilly pink dress for trip to the hospital. Her mother was angry with her then. It didn't occur to her until Sandie said so that her mother might have been drunk that day. Until then, my mother had seen her parents' drinking as genteel. She regarded her adult self as a hick or lightweight for taking only a few sips of wine, and then only on special occasions. When her doctor recommended a nightly glass of red wine to improve her circulation, she demurred. She was afraid, she always said, of liking it too much. What she never said, even to herself, was that she was afraid of becoming like her parents, who drank themselves into oblivion every night of the week.

With *The Joy of Cooking* in one hand and Dr. Spock's *Baby and Child Care* in the other, my mother taught herself how to cook a roast and how to love a child. She wasn't perfect at either one. Like every cook who came of age during the *Apollo* years, she was more smitten with TV dinners and Hamburger Helper than with Welsh rarebit or veal scallopini. As a mother, she could be remote. "I'm only one person," she used to say when we importuned her. Or, "I'm your mother, not your maid." She could also be autocratic; to our question, "Why?" she usually responded, "Because I said so." Once, memorably, she refused to stop for a policeman who wished to have a conversation with her about her speeding; she was in a hurry, she said. When speaking to salespeople or telephone company representatives, she introduces herself as "Mrs. Brice." She's grown more patient with age, but when we were children, she inscribed her anger on our bottoms. (Disclosure: as a mother myself, I, too, can be remote, autocratic, swift to anger. Worse—and unlike my mother—I am slow to forgive.)

Politically, my mother is a liberal. If she could, she would save every hurt, unloved, or undernourished child in Alaska. As it is, she's saved a lot of them, including my brother Ben, whom she and my father adopted in 1972. When I was a child, it seemed we never went anywhere—sledding at the farm, swimming at the hot springs, even camping at Denali Park—without picking up one or two extra children on the way, until every seat in the Land Cruiser was filled. Once, my mother took us to the hospital to visit a girl roughly my age who had been mauled by a pack of dogs. In part, my mother meant for us to see this red-haired stranger (whose name I've long forgotten) as Exhibit A in a cautionary tale titled "Never Pet a Strange Dog" (though why this mattered in her case, I was never sure; she'd apparently been set upon as she walked home from a friend's house. After the attack, she crawled into an unlocked car and slumped against the horn until rescuers came). We bore gifts of toys and clothes and books, charms against life with a scarred face. One way to look at my mother's impulse to care for people whom my friend Carrie calls the "woebegone and the misbegotten" is as a kind of condescension or *noblesse oblige.* Another way to look at it is as charity—in the Christian sense of loving one's neighbor—in action. Depending on my mood, I've looked at it both ways and felt, according to my point of view, either ashamed or proud of my mother.

Temperamentally, she's a conservative. She's still friends with people she met during her first couple of years in Alaska, including Betty Waldhaus, her co-worker and confidante back in the days when my father was wooing her. She still sits in the same pew (second on the left) and serves on the altar guild at Saint Matthew's Church, where her five children were baptized and confirmed, and where her daughters were married. She favors clothes from Talbots. She's never met a chintz fabric she didn't like. She considers it a cardinal sin to renege on a commitment. At age sixty-eight, she hiked the Chilkoot Trail over a strenuous pass traversed by gold rush stampeders. Whenever I visit, she wakes up earlier than anyone else (except for my father) and walks or rides her bike four miles round-trip to a bakery, where she buys scones for our breakfast. Her mantra could easily be that of Benjamin Franklin: "When you wake up, get up. When you get up, do something."

Growing up, I made a study of her virtues. The kitchen was the nerve center of our home. There, she taught me how to level off a teaspoon using the top of the baking soda box, how to separate an egg, how to make meat loaf with little more than a pound of leftover hamburger, a pinch of garlic powder, and a slice of stale bread. She showed me how to dig out a splinter using a sterilized needle and tweezers. She showed me how to read a mercury thermometer: anything higher than ninety-nine degrees meant a blessed day of rest, alternately reading and drowsing between cool cotton sheets with a frosty glass of ginger ale within reach.

By the time my high school English teacher introduced us to Conrad and Faulkner, I was an old hand at recognizing and interpreting symbols. My mother had already taught me the uses of metaphor in everyday life. When one of us was being fractious or whiny, she'd say, "Quit acting like a fried egg"—whatever that means—and we would. When she made meatloaf or piecrust or anything else that required her to knead ingredients with her bare hands, she slipped off her wedding rings and set them on the windowsill over the sink.

"Tell me about your rings, Mom," I'd beg.

"You never, ever take off your rings, even to sleep," she'd say. "Only when you're baking and you might lose them in the dough, or get them gummed up. Even then, you put them somewhere close by, somewhere safe, so you can put them back on as soon as you're through.

"The diamond is the strongest stone in the world, a sign of the strongest love in the world. You wear it on the ring finger of your left hand because it's the finger that's closest to your heart. It's a symbol to the world that you're married. You're no longer on the market."

"How come Daddy doesn't wear a ring?"

I knew it was a sore subject.

"Well, some men don't wear wedding rings just because they don't like to wear jewelry," she said. "Your father's problem is different. He keeps losing his."

It's true that my father has lost half a dozen wedding bands over the years. One time, his ring snagged on a piece of metal as he leapt off a bulldozer, nearly severing his finger. After that, he quit wearing one for a while.

Bruno Bettelheim says that every little girl wants to believe she's a princess in disguise. Such fairy tales as Cinderella and Rapunzel and the Princess and the Pea shore up this belief because, initially, the true princess is disguised as a commoner. As the daughter of a queen who'd been lured by true love into abandoning her homeland and giving up her inheritance, I felt I was a princess living in exile in the frozen North. I liked to tell other children at the playground or skating rink that the maid expected me home by 5:00 p.m. The maid was our babysitter-cum-housekeeper, a hard-as-nails widow with an Oklahoma accent. She lived in a trailer. We were supposed to call her "Grandma Fowler," but there was nothing grandmotherly about her. We called her "Fowler" instead, which seemed to fit. The school bus dropped us off at the end of our long P-shaped driveway every afternoon. Hearing us clatter up the outside stairs, Fowler would switch the channel on the TV. "Your mother don't want you watching no so-poppers," she'd say. After gobbling down graham crackers, raisins, and milk, we'd watch TV until our mother got home. I fantasized a Fowler more like Alice on the *Brady Bunch* or Sebastian on *A Family Affair.* There was nothing doing, though. Fowler wasn't even crotchety but loving like Calpurnia in *To Kill a Mockingbird.* Even though she made cinnamon rolls sometimes, we children knew what children always know: The mother who loved us had hired someone who didn't even like us very much. To be unloved by the person charged with caring for you, even for a few hours a day, is powerful stuff. To sap that power, I did with Fowler what my mother did with her own parents. Instead of vilifying her—which would, on the one hand, implicate me, and, on the other, be too easy—I turned her into a character in my own private fairy tale. She was the wicked stepmother.

By the time our beloved mother walked wearily up the steps, Fowler was already fetching her coat from the closet. She would leave, and all would be right with the world until the next afternoon. This is not to say that my mother and I never fought. The truth is, I was a good daughter—a member of the ski team, the orchestra, and honor society. I practiced the piano for three or four hours a day, studied music with a professor at the university, and performed in recitals and competitions. I didn't smoke, drink, or go to parties. My worst acting-out took the form of wrestling matches with my boyfriend in the backseat of my parents' Volvo. The rest of the time, I was, if anything, too straitlaced and driven, my self-discipline bordering on the neurotic. The battles I fought with my mother weren't over clothes or grades or independence. At the risk of sounding melodramatic, they were battles for my soul. I couldn't let go of my mother, and she couldn't—or wouldn't—let go of me. I see now what I couldn't see then. My mother was stronger because of her mythology, flawed though it was. She'd consciously constructed a self around a story that was partially true at best, but it was still a story. In her cosmology, being born and raised in Alaska meant nothing. To redeem myself, I'd have to go to college in the East. I'd have to go to Smith College in Northampton, Massachusetts. I understood that in order to win my mother forever, I'd have to leave her for four years.

 She flew out with me that first August to see me settled. Ours was the leave-taking to end all leave-takings. We postponed it as long as we could. To this day, neither my mother nor I can speak of that moment on the landing between the second and third floors of Baldwin House without weeping.

When I was little, my mother had the kind of hips that were meant to bounce a baby while her free hand stirred a pan of gravy. Then she went into the hospital for abdominal surgery and stole a peek at her own chart. According to her doctor, she was an "obese white female." After that, she took better care of herself and slimmed down considerably. Even so, I've always prided myself on being slender compared to her. A few days after my husband-to-be tucked an untraditional diamond-and-sapphire ring—one that I'd admired in the window of a local jewelry store (not Tiffany's)—under the Christmas tree, my mother retrieved her wedding dress from the box in which it had been stored in air-proof splendor for three decades. It was more beautiful than I'd imagined. I peeled off my jeans and T-shirt and stepped into it. With a bit of tugging, I was able to pull it up over my hips and slip my arms through the sleeves. By that time, my mother was bent double with laughter. There were six inches of skin showing across the back. Regretfully, I folded up the dress. In a few years, my youngest sister—taller and slimmer than I—would wear it to walk down the aisle.

My mother's fairy tale didn't fit me any better than her wedding dress. At the age of forty-three, I've only begun to ask myself what it meant to grow up in Alaska, the daughter of a Southern stump logger and an East Coast socialite. I've only begun to see the dim outline of the myths that shape and define me, and that I'll pass down to my daughters, to scoff at or embrace. Perhaps it's true, as realtors like to say, that location is everything. In his essay, "Landscape and Narrative," Barry Lopez says the place we come from and the stories we tell are inseparable. He suggests that the external, physical landscape in which we grow up, or to which we respond, has an analog in interior, metaphoric landscape. The inner and outer topology of my mother's childhood is a hyper-civilized one of rolling hills and lush lawns, businessmen taking the train into the city, window seats overlooking the East River, ice cubes clinking in cocktail glasses, smocked sundresses. The topology of my childhood is that of razor-backed mountains and blue-green glaciers, men with rubber bands in their beards, the scent of wood-burning stoves, silt rustling through glacier-fed rivers. My mother never quite lost her imperialist airs; I was born in-country. Mine are the rites and rituals of the faithful who piss off their back porch, hunt for moose in the fall, and carry tire chains in the trunk of the car. Away from Alaska, if no one stares at me, I feel as if I'm getting away with something.

Several times a year, my mother visits me in Hamilton, New York, where my children and I make our home now. In the summer, she brings plastic bags filled with wild poppies and forget-me-nots from her garden, hoping they'll "take" in mine. (They do.) She sets off walking early in the morning, before anyone else is awake. When I introduce her to my friends and neighbors, she finds a way to insert Alaska into nearly every sentence, as if it's her only source of identity: "Hi, I'm Carol. I'm from Alaska." A few months ago, the two of us spent a November weekend in the city. We ate leisurely meals, saw *Gypsy* on Broadway, and did some Christmas shopping. Being in the city made her nostalgic, and we talked about the years she spent in nurse's training and, later, as a nurse at Columbia-Presbyterian. I bought her a lacy shawl from Banana Republic that she said was too elegant for the life she leads now. As we threaded our way through the throngs on Fifth Avenue, she stopped so abruptly I nearly ran into her. She stood there staring at an impressive edifice across the way.

"I'm tempted to walk in and see if anyone there remembers the girl from Alaska who came in one day to pick up an engagement ring. They were waiting for me, you know. Everyone knew the story. Even the security guard."

I look at my mother. The gray ends of her hair, which she has never colored, peek out from under her wool hat. Her skin is the texture of parchment paper, flushed with cold and excitement. In recent years, osteoporosis has caused her to shrink an inch or two. I worry about her falling and breaking bones.

She's nearly seventy. Anyone who remembers her story would have to be at least as old, if not older. Has my mother forgotten this? Or is she wondering aloud whether her story is big enough and powerful enough to be part of the lore handed down from one generation of salespeople to the next? If the story she tells about herself is part of a bigger story that an institution tells about *itself,* then it must be true. And if it's true, then the spur-of-the-moment decision she made outside the door of Tiffany's that December morning in 1961, a decision to enter the stream of a story that had already begun to take shape in the minds of romantically inclined young women, to marry my father and spend the rest of her life in Alaska, was absolutely right.

Because I'm a coward, I said, "Let's not, Mom." She wilted a bit, then she let me loop my arm affectionately through hers and gently steer her back into the pushy river of shoppers.

TWO ~ Lullaby for Lloyd

Midwinter in Barrow and the sun won't slide over the lip of the horizon for two more months. At high noon, a kind of lavender twilight suffuses and softens this Iñupiaq village on the north coast of Alaska. Two hours later, the sky is as black and star-strewn as at midnight. Swirling snow nearly swallows the plywood-and-tarpaper houses that give onto Barrow's one-lane streets. Every village has its own background noise. Here it's the growl of the generator that supplies electricity to every house, the yelp of sled dogs, the clink of chains, the guttural pop-popping of snowmachines. The Eskimos ride them on one knee, with the studied nonchalance of cowboys keeping just one finger on the reins. It's the late 1960s, and the romance of snowmachines is new; they have yet to replace dog teams, which don't require parts to be flown in from Anchorage or Fairbanks. The sleek dogs lie curled like doughnuts, nose to tail, under a dusting of snow.

I imagine a woman on the village boardwalk. She bobs along in the side-to-side gait peculiar to people born slightly bow legged. Frances carries her baby boy in the Iñupiaq way, his sleeping body cocooned in the hood of her fur-lined parky. When Frances staggers, the baby rocks but doesn't rouse. Frances doesn't know where she's going, only what she's looking for: a place to sleep, a hot meal, her next drink.

One night this winter—not tonight, not yet—Frances will

 walk out of a bar with a white soldier. The two of them will argue, and the next morning, the villagers will pull Frances's frozen body from a snow berm. Was Lloyd there, drowsing in her hood, drawing the last bit of warmth from his mother's body? Does it matter if he was? Probably not.

That year and the next, social workers shuffled Lloyd between foster homes in Barrow and Fairbanks, four hundred miles to the south. He lived with an aunt for a while before she gave up on him. By all accounts, he was a four-year-old ball of fury. His first complete sentence may have been "Fuck you."

Lloyd Henry Ahgnatook is my brother.

My parents adopted him in June 1972. I was nine, Sam seven, Hannah six, and Rebecca, the baby, only two. Our father's construction company was going full bore by then, and he often left for weeks on what we called "Bush jobs." Barrow is in the Bush. Brice Incorporated had not yet worked in Barrow, but it had built a runway in Wainwright, seventy-five miles southeast on the coast of the Arctic Ocean. The previous fall—1971—our mother worked as a nurse at the Fairbanks Head Start, a government-funded preschool for at-risk (read *low-income* and, throughout Alaska, mostly *Native*) children. Lloyd was enrolled at Head Start, where social workers were busy casting about for a new foster family. The timing was serendipitous. Serious complications in my mother's fourth and last pregnancy had left her unable to bear more children. She and my father had been hoping for another son, a companion for Sam.

As a formality, the judge presiding over Lloyd's adoption asked me and my brother and sisters if we had anything to say about our new brother. It was like the moment in the marriage ceremony when the priest asks if anyone present can offer any reason why the two should not wed. In this case, silence felt like a freighted response. My brother and sisters looked at me, the oldest and, usually, the most outspoken. I dropped my head and swung my skinny legs below the courtroom bench. I sat on my hands and squirmed on the slippery wood that felt a lot like the pews at Saint Matthew's Episcopal Church. My prepared speech about how much we loved Lloyd, how he seemed to us to be the missing piece that made our family puzzle complete, flew out of my head. The silence stretched on, birthing more silence. Later, my mother would be angry with me—or, worse, disappointed. Then, she shot me a tight-lipped look that told me what I was in for. After the hearing, her anger dissipated quickly; nothing cast a pall over that summer day when the sun seemed to shine even more brightly on our family, with its newly minted son and brother. (In 1978, Congress passed the Indian Child Welfare Act, which requires that Native children be placed with extended family, tribal members, or other Native families.)

Adopting Lloyd, my family gained a more expansive sense of itself as a group of generous, progressive, high-minded human beings. I became a liberal, although I wouldn't have used that word (and didn't for years and years). The fact that Lloyd's adoption had driven a wedge between my mother and her father helped. Grampy's heavy pronouncement was something along the lines of, "Nothing good ever comes of mixing the races under one roof." My father's family reacted more warmly. After all, he'd grown up with three natural-born brothers and three more siblings (two boys and a girl) adopted from troubled homes. While we were in court, the rest of the Brice clan was gathering at the Travelers Inn, where they were throwing a "Welcome to the Family" party.

The judge lowered his gavel and declared that Lloyd was now a legal member of our family. From that moment, Lloyd Henry Ahgnatook became Ben Andrew Brice, the name he'd chosen for himself. For years, though, we kept calling him "Bumper," a nickname that stuck on account of the way he was always careering off the walls and furniture.

Bumper was our new favorite plaything. He was like a pet sea otter—all brown and black and chubby and shiny. His cheeks were so pink they looked as if the color had been painted on, and his thick black hair bristled like fur after one of Mom's home haircuts. He was encased in baby fat. The rest of us kids were made up of gangly white limbs, freckles, wavy hair, and (except for Hannah) blue eyes. Sam, Hannah, and I treated Ben like a life-size doll we could dress up and take to school for show-and-tell. Our baby sister toddled worshipfully after him.

 Dimly aware of unhappiness in his past, my parents put him on a regime of hugs and skating lessons, green vegetables and trips to the dentist. From the time he woke up every morning, Ben seemed happy. He ate and drank and smiled and played, even though he didn't say much. (He gave up his favorite locution after one or two mouthfuls of soap.) Yet every bedtime began with whimpering, which turned into chest-wracking sobs and kept on until his eyes swelled shut and snot soaked the placket of his flannel pajamas. There was no consoling him; his loss went deep. After thirty minutes or an hour, Ben would climb out of bed and pad over to the toy box. Then he'd pad back to bed. Clutching an armload of Matchbox cars and miniature Tonka trucks, he'd finally fall asleep.

In December, I asked Santa for a Barbie beauty kit. Sam might have wanted more snap-together orange plastic track for his racecars, Hannah a horse, and Rebecca a Baby Dear. Ben wanted to *be* a cowboy. Mom and Dad bought him a Stetson, pointy-toed boots, a bandana, and toy six-shooters. On Christmas morning, Dad photographed Ben in front of the tinsel-strewn tree: a bow-legged, brown-skinned, Eskimo John Wayne.

The first signs of trouble were like yellow lights, barely giving us pause. Unlike the rest of us, Bumper didn't seem to be interested in television. He didn't show up at the dinner table when summoned. When he finally came, he ate until Mom took his plate away. He was insatiable. After meals, we'd catch him rummaging in the pantry for snacks. Mom took him to the pediatrician for a checkup. The doctor checked his ears and mouth then shone a light in his eyes. He handed the instruments to my mother so she could see what he saw. Ben's was a case for specialists.

There was a trip to Anchorage followed by a battery of tests. Then diagnoses: Ben was legally blind, with a drifting eye too far gone to corral. Chronic infections had eroded his eardrums until he could barely hear. An early diet of candy bars, soda pop, and potato chips had rotted his teeth, too. If not fixable, these things were, to some degree, correctable. There was an operation to repair his eardrums, for example. What seemed more ominous then was Ben's inability to use words, even Iñupiaq ones, to express feelings. When he was happy, he kissed and cuddled. When he was frustrated, he lashed out with teeth and with fists. He lashed out more than he cuddled. Mostly, he lived in a haze of unseeing, unhearing, unspeaking, unknowing.

By the time he was old enough for kindergarten, my parents began to suspect that Ben's deficiencies ran deeper. A psychologist diagnosed him with Minimal Brain Dysfunction, which meant learning might be a struggle. Next, when the behavior problems started, counselors stuck him with a new and unwieldy label: Attention Deficit Hyperactivity Disorder. Finally, after ten years on Ritalin, a drug that slowed his reactions and stunted his growth, Ben was diagnosed with a disorder that often displays as MBD or DHD: Fetal Alcohol Syndrome.

Now, twenty-five years later, experts differentiate between Fetal Alcohol *Syndrome* and its milder cousin, Fetal Alcohol *Effect.* It seems, intuitively, as if heavier drinking on the part of the mother ought to produce the more severe syndrome in the child. Not so. Drinking during pregnancy is like playing Russian Roulette. Some mothers who drink give birth to babies who are, as nearly as anyone can tell, unscathed. Roughly twenty percent of heavy drinkers give birth to babies who've been pickled in the womb, who are severely deformed and retarded, and who receive the Fetal Alcohol Syndrome diagnosis. A greater percentage of mothers who drink heavily give birth to babies who suffer from MBD rather than profound retardation, ADHD rather than severe antisocial tendencies. On looks alone, these kids pass for normal. They carry all the signs of damage on the inside. In the late 1960s, drinking during pregnancy wasn't stigmatized the way it is now. Certainly, Ben's mother didn't have access to research about a link between drinking and birth defects. A few drinks more, a few drinks less: one way or the other, she could have transformed his life. Made it simpler in some ways. A cynic might say Ben was one of the lucky ones; his diagnosis was eventually modified from Fetal Alcohol Syndrome to Fetal Alcohol Effect.

FAE children tend to suffer from language deficits, poor social skills, and hyperactivity. In adolescence, their symptoms range from below-average grades to low self-esteem to weak impulse control and sudden outbursts of anger, even violence. Depression, broken relationships, alcohol and drug abuse often mar their adulthood. Like Ben, they tend to slide between minimum-wage jobs and homeless shelters, between detox units and jail. Victims of Fetal Alcohol Effect don't really live; they survive.

At twenty-nine, Ben wound up in the intensive care unit of the Fairbanks hospital after a cold developed into pneumonia, which developed into congestive heart failure—an ailment of the very old. He survived, but barely. A trip to a specialist in Anchorage yielded yet another diagnosis: a congenital heart defect critically exacerbated by binge drinking. Medication and diet could control the condition to a degree, the specialist said. But Ben's next bender—or the next one after that—would definitely be his last.

If my parents had known in 1972 what they know now, would they have adopted Ben anyway? I don't know, and I doubt they do, either. What I *do* know is that Ben's behavior led the research by four or five years. We had no context for understanding his actions outside the context of our own family. By just about any measure within our grasp, Ben was a very bad boy.

With every passing year, he acted out more and more. Like Raven or Fox, the Trickster figure from Native American literature, he stirred up trouble wherever he could. He made family car rides an ordeal; he made family car rides combined with family vacations a descent into the eleventh circle of hell. My weak spot was my looks; in the course of one year (1975, to be exact) I sprouted breasts, braces, glasses, and pimples. Ben would jump in the back seat of the station wagon beside me then gradually inch closer until his grubby brown thigh stuck to mine like Saran Wrap. He'd chant under his breath, "Jennifer is ugly. Jennifer is *ugly*." I'm ashamed to say how effective it was.

On the swing set one day, Ben casually asked the four-year-old daughter of our fundamentalist Christian neighbors for sex. Swimming in a gravel pit one summer day, he stepped on a piece of glass and nearly severed his left foot. He teased a neighbor's German shepherd until the dog turned on him, mauling his face. That time, he ended up with more than 150 stitches.

I felt sorriest for my brother Sam, though. Ben was meant to be, at best, a reward, or, at the least, a compensation for being the only boy among three girls. Instead, Ben turned himself into Sam's own special boggart, one that followed him wherever he went and left a swathe of destruction behind.

Keep an eye on your brother, make sure he doesn't get into trouble. That was my mother's mantra. There was no such thing as keeping an eye on Ben, or making sure he didn't get into trouble. One night toward the end of a disastrous family vacation, my parents left us kids alone in the hotel room. Ben's needling drove me first to distraction, then to fury. I grabbed him by the shoulders and slammed his head into the wall again and again. After that, Mom and Dad quit leaving us alone at night, even to go to a movie. For one thing, they couldn't cajole any babysitter back for a second attempt. For another, they began to fear that one of us kids might kill Ben. Not that they didn't sympathize. The mouth-washing episode came *after* my mother left nursing for a career as an activist against child abuse. The day that Ben experimented with a magnifying glass and the sun to burn holes in an expensive new sofa set, she telephoned my father at work.

"Come get him *now*," she said, through gritted teeth.

When Ben was seven or eight, we went to visit relatives in Georgia. While the adults talked, we kids wandered down to a dock along the Savannah River. One second Ben was playing by himself at the end of a dock; the next, his brown head was bobbing down the river. We screamed and ran for the grownups. My father sprinted to the end of the dock, ripped off his watch, kicked off his sneakers, and dove in. Five minutes later, Ben sat on the bumper of the car, soaked, shaking, and—for once—subdued. He looked so small and scared that I pulled him onto my lap and rocked him like a baby. For the first time in a long while, he clung to me. I remember that moment better than most. Not because I came closest to loving him then, which is true. But because, seeing him in the water, I'd thought, *Now we'll be a normal family again.* I've always been a strong swimmer. I saw him first. I could have jumped in the river to save him, but I didn't.

The phrase "*hit* adolescence" is particularly apt in Ben's case. His pilfering led to several humiliating encounters between our mother and security guards. He beat up on the less agile special ed kids at school. He was suspended several times for flying in the face of authority and for shooting spitballs loaded with sharp objects. At home, he mounted an all-out guerilla war; the skirmishes took place at the dinner table, which, as often as not, one or another of us kids left in tears. My family was falling apart. This was in the days before family therapy was invented—or, even if it had, it hadn't found its way yet to Fairbanks, Alaska.

In desperation, my mother telephoned the Alaska Department of Health and Social Services. The commissioner actually called her back. My mother said her resources were exhausted; it was time for the state to pony up some help. If it couldn't, she and my father might have to give him back. She may or may not have been bluffing. The commissioner called again a couple of days later to say that, if my parents could find an appropriate facility for Ben, the state would pay.

During spring break from Smith College, I flew to Seattle then drove up to Spokane to visit Ben. He was enrolled at Excelsior, a school that taught basic skills—getting a job, paying bills, shopping for groceries, cleaning an apartment—to problem teens. The other students were users or shoplifters or runaways. A few of the girls had gotten pregnant more than once. Tuition at Excelsior ran $30,000 a year. The State of Alaska was paying, as promised, but on the condition the commissioner had named in her call to my mother: My parents had to surrender custody, making Ben a ward of the state. My mother wept over that. Then she gave herself a talking to. When Ben entered Excelsior, he was already fifteen. Three years later, he'd be eighteen and legally an adult and on his own anyway. Meanwhile, there was no reason we couldn't keep treating him like one of our family. When I learned that, legally, Ben was no longer my brother, I

felt quick relief then guilt—the same mix of emotions I'd felt
that long-ago day beside the Savannah River.

In the Fairbanks public schools, Ben had come off as less smart and less popular than the other students. At Excelsior, among teen prostitutes and pushers, he reigned. For the first time ever, Ben was regarded as a role model: the only one in his class who'd never done time. Somewhere, I have a picture from that spring break of Ben and me, arm in arm. He was tall for an Iñupiaq. At fifteen, he stood nearly a head taller than me, and I'm five-foot-six. By then, he'd lost his baby fat and outgrown Mom's crew cut. His long glossy hair curled around the collar of his fleece jacket. Later, when I looked at the picture of the two of us, I saw him as a stranger might, and I saw that he was handsome.

Given Ben's history, my parents shouldn't have been surprised when the call came from Excelsior's headmaster. After all, Ben was a kid who'd been kicked out of the Boy Scouts, banned from the Five and Dime, and suspended several times from high school. How long could the romance with Excelsior possibly last? The headmaster was apologetic but firm. He simply couldn't keep a student who kept trying to burn down the dormitory.

So Ben came home. After a few weeks of uneasy peace, he took off again. For a while now, he'd peppered my parents with questions about his past: *How did his mother die? Why was there no father listed on his birth certificate? What about the aunt who'd cared for him for a while? Was she still alive? Did he have any other relatives?* Except for his mother's death, my parents didn't know the answers. They bought him an Alaska Airlines ticket to Barrow. The day he left, Mom carefully wrote out his full birth name, his birth date, and his mother's name on a piece of paper, which he tucked into the pocket of his jeans.

"Bye, Mom," he said. She wondered if those would be the last words he ever spoke to her.

In Barrow, Ben met a brother who'd been adopted by an aunt and uncle. The brother took him to see an ancient Iñupiaq woman who'd cared for them both as babies. The woman gave Ben a photo of three women sitting side by side on a bench, dressed in colorful cotton *qaspeqs.* The woman in the middle was Frances. The rosy-cheeked, solemn-faced baby on her lap was Ben.

Whatever Ben found in Barrow, it wasn't home. He flew back to Fairbanks full of conflicting emotions: grief for the mother he'd never known, anger at the father who'd never acknowledged him, exhilaration at finding his brother. Mostly, though, he felt confused. Did he belong in the world of white people, or in the world of the Iñupiat? On a practical level, the answer was simple. As Ben Andrew Brice, he had two parents, four siblings, a room of his own, and three meals a day. As Lloyd Henry Ahgnatook, he had only a faded photograph of three Iñupiaq women and a baby. On an emotional level, the answer was far more elusive.

Ben's next project was to get himself fired from a succession of jobs at fast-food establishments. The grounds were the usual ones: laziness, rudeness, stealing. One morning after he left for work, Mom lifted a sagging ceiling panel in his bedroom and got buried under an avalanche of *Hustler* magazines and burned-up matches. Pornography my parents could take; pyromania they couldn't. They boxed up his things and moved him into a rooming house. When he lost his job and couldn't pay the rent, they paid it for him. He went to a psychiatrist. My parents went to a psychiatrist. He wanted a snowmachine. He wanted a car. He wanted a girlfriend.

Mom's name for Delilah was "jail bait." By then, Ben was twenty-two. She was sixteen, underweight and pasty except for a neck full of angry red hickeys. Her parents spent their winters traveling the country in their worn-out Winnebago, watching cable TV, and living off welfare checks forwarded to post offices in the Lower Forty-eight. In the fall of 1989, they took Ben with them.

He called my parents collect from a truck stop. They hadn't heard from him since he'd left. It was now the week before Christmas. Delilah's parents had kicked him out of the motor home with no money, food, or clothes. There was no telling what he'd done—certainly, *he* wasn't telling—but it was probably bad. My parents asked him where he was. He had no idea.

By then, my mother had gone back to school for her master's degree in education. She'd started her own business teaching, among other things, tough love to other parents. The last thing she intended to do was to wire him money to come home. She had my father tell him to make his way north by whatever means he could, and to call collect every other day.

On Christmas Eve, Ben phoned from Seattle. He'd hitched rides with truckers all the way there from South Carolina. Mom cracked. She gripped the phone, tears running down her cheeks. "I can't bear for a child of mine to spend Christmas on the streets of a strange city," she sobbed. Dad wired Ben $100 for a hotel room and food. But Ben sensed a crack in the parental defenses. He called again an hour later. This time Dad arranged for a plane ticket home. "Spend the money on presents for your family," he told him. Early Christmas morning, Ben strutted off the jet way at Fairbanks International Airport wearing a new leather jacket and carrying a Sony Walkman. After breakfast, he called Alaska Airlines to inquire about his "lost" suitcase full of presents for the family.

Thirty-eight years old now, Frances's son has a gift for drawing and carving. He etches northern lights and dog teams into ebony-colored baleen from whale's throats. There's a market for such pieces. With more self-discipline, he might have made a career as an artist. Instead, he works an assortment of odd jobs, one of them for a quarry owned by Brice Incorporated. He lives mostly off of supplemental Social Security and royalty checks from his oil-rich Native corporation. When our youngest sister left home, there was no one left for him to torment except our parents. Ben used money to drive a wedge between them. Whenever a Native corporation check arrived, Mom would tuck it into a kitchen drawer for Ben to pick up when he was willing to accompany her to the bank, cash the check, and reimburse her on the spot for rent or groceries. Instead, Ben would call Dad at the office and ask him to drop off the check. Dad would. This went on for several years until my parents hit on the idea of turning his finances over to an outside organization that specializes in such things.

When they adopted him on that June day in 1972, they swore to raise him like one of their natural-born children. They've never given up on him, never stopped feeling responsible for his well-being, never stopped hoping that he'll be happy. My mother wrote her master's thesis on mother-infant bonding. She learned that alcohol- or drug-addicted mothers are often unable to bond with their babies. Their babies grow up with a fear of abandonment that often manifests as antisocial behavior: they sever bonds, sometimes violently, before the bonds have time to fully form. Their problems defy pharmaceutical, therapeutic or even cultural solutions. At a writer's conference, I told an elderly Yu'piq woman Ben's story. She shook her head and said, with immense sadness, "There's no hope for those kids. None at all. They're lost to us."

Hugs and kisses, fresh vegetables and whole grains, consequences, consistency, a can-do attitude: these were things my parents offered all of us, including Ben—things that fall under the headings of "stability," "nurturing," "empowerment," and "unconditional love." As nearly as any of us can tell, these things haven't made much of a difference. Or maybe they have. Ben still lives independently, no matter how tenuous the terms. His natural brother is now in prison.

When my parents adopted Ben on that June day in 1972, they taught me and my brother and sisters something about love and risk. About how much you stand to lose or gain when you promise to love someone for the rest of his life or yours, whichever ends first. Ben's adoption was a leap into the wider world: a leap of faith, a leap of generosity, a leap—some would say—of insanity. Do we regret it? The question used to interest me, but not anymore. Regret is beside the point. For better or worse, Ben showed us, and still shows us, what we're made of.

There is another question, though. The question of love. Alcohol-affected children make themselves so difficult to love that only saints can love them. I can't speak for my parents, but I'm no saint. At his birthday and Christmas, I send him cash or clothing in care of my parents. I don't even know his current phone number. When I'm in Fairbanks, my mother fixes Sunday dinner for the whole family. Before Ben arrives, I check to make sure that my purse is tucked out of sight. My mother, sisters, and sister-in-law do the same. Throughout the evening, I'm hyper-alert for signs of untoward touching between Ben and his nieces and nephews. Is he lying on the couch with a couple of boys sprawled on his legs? Is he holding one of my daughters in his lap? I wouldn't put it past him. Ben's nieces and nephews adore him. He's the only grown-up they know who plays just like a kid.

"Mommy, why doesn't Uncle Ben drive a car?" asks one of my daughters. "Isn't he old enough?"

"Yeah," says another, "and why doesn't he have a wife?"

The day after my oldest daughter was born, Ben had visited me in the hospital. He'd reeked of beer and cigarettes, and I'd sent him away in disgust. Still, I couldn't tell my daughters, *That's why he doesn't drive. That's why he doesn't have a wife.*

Later, when one of the twins climbed into my lap, I thought of Ben that day beside the Savannah River. Maybe I should have tried to save him. Maybe not. More than likely, I would have floundered, too. My father would have been forced to choose, in a split second, between saving me and saving Ben. Whatever the drawbacks, ambivalence is a lot easier to live with than Greek tragedy.

Frances's son is grown up now—old enough to marry, raise children, drive a car, serve in the military, and drink alcohol, although he does none of these things except drink, and that more rarely than he used to. The strain of living with a weakened heart has aged him. He moves slowly these days, almost as if he's under six feet of water. Ben holds a high school diploma, but he can't fill out an income tax form. He lives in a group home until he sets fire to it, holds a job until he gets demoted, works at a relationship until someone starts working back. Fine white lines crisscross the undersides of his wrists. Every few months, my parents' phone rings in the middle of the night. My father gropes for the receiver. "Hello?" he mumbles. Then, "All right. I'll be right there." My mother used to get up, too, but now she lets herself fall back asleep. In fifteen minutes, my father will pull up to the emergency room or the city jail. A few years ago, someone in my family—I won't say who—said she wished he'd go ahead and cut a little deeper, like he really meant it. Someday he probably will.

THREE Wild Music

Reflections on Big Oil and Innocence

The substitute teacher wore lipstick so red her mouth looked like a bloody gash. Her black hair was brushed off her face, as if any softness might embarrass her. Behind rhinestone-studded glasses, her eyes swept our fifth-grade classroom. She was reputed to be the meanest substitute teacher at University Park Elementary School in Fairbanks, Alaska, in 1973. We were on our best behavior around her.

The substitute teacher—I'll call her Mrs. S—wiped the blackboard clean and positioned herself beside it, facing us, with a fresh stick of chalk in her hand. *Now,* she said, *we are going to make a list of reasons why the trans-Alaska pipeline should* not *be built.* Dutifully, we parroted the arguments we'd heard at home and on the news:

It would destroy the land.
Moose and bears would die.
It could explode.
Fairbanks would be overcrowded.
Crime would get worse.
We'd have to go to school at six in the morning.
Stores would run out of food.

Next, Mrs. S instructed us to draw a picture illustrating one of the reasons on the blackboard. My best friend Lori King drew a moose sprawled beside the pipeline. It had big *X*'s over its eyes. I drew my father driving a bulldozer. He had a smile on his face. That drawing got me a big red zero for not following instructions.

Mrs. S taught me something that day that I never could have learned from a textbook. Until then, I'd felt as if I belonged to a community of like-minded people. If I'd been old enough to read the letters section of the local newspaper, I would have known better. What I did know was that the '64 earthquake and the '67 flood had brought out people's highest impulses. So had prolonged stretches of fifty below. Disaster and hardship have always done that. But politics have always torn us apart. In Alaska, the fault line is almost always over development. Those who would protect and preserve Alaska's wildlife and beauty array themselves on one side; those who would develop Alaska's resources and hunt its game array themselves on the other. That's Alaska politics in a sentence: holy fools on one side, pragmatists on the other. Of course, a book-length treatment would hardly do justice to the complexity underlying that dualism. (Even so, I highly recommend *Alaska Politics and Government* by Gerald A. McBeath and Thomas A. Morehouse.) I'm friendly with hunters who oppose development, and I know industry chiefs who've never held a gun. I've seen Alaska Natives torn between the teachings of their culture and the vicissitudes of the market. I'm tempted to say that sometimes Alaska politics go beyond the merely complicated, into the realm of the downright weird. A few years ago, two propositions won overwhelming support—well over seventy percent—at the ballot box. The first was to legalize the possession of small amounts of marijuana; the second was to ban gay marriage. In Alaska, the pro-development forces nearly always prevail. They may not outnumber environmental forces, but they're better organized, more affluent, and just plain noisier. At best, the persistence of the pro-environment movement pays off in a handful of concessions—in the softening (rhetorically, anyway) of naked exploitation into something more like "wise use."

In the early '70s, the proposal to build a trans-Alaska pipeline fractured the town of Fairbanks. There was no middle ground, nor was there any way to duck the question. You might not know whether your neighbors were Republicans or Democrats, but you knew where they stood on the pipeline. The eight hundred-mile line from Prudhoe Bay to Valdez was only a concept back then, just a squiggly line penciled in on a map. Such is the power of imaginary lines to rend communities and wreck friendships.

My parents were for the pipeline, Mrs. S against it. She was on the losing side, and she knew it. Perhaps that's why she felt angry all the time. For my part, I felt caught between two types of authority: authority at home and authority at school. I was so ashamed of my bulldozer picture that I didn't take it home that afternoon. At the time, my teacher's feelings vis-à-vis the pipeline puzzled me. One of the blissful things about being a child is the sense that everyone must think and feel as you do. If liver tastes awful, then liver *is* awful. The substitute teacher taught me a lesson in subjectivity. Also, she taught me that the forces that shape us aren't necessarily the ones we expect or welcome into our lives.

The proposal before Congress at that time was whether to let the oil companies build a conduit from Alaska's oil-rich North Slope to tidewater in the southeast. In Washington DC, environmental and industry concerns marshaled their respective lobbyists. Proponents of the pipeline predicted that bringing North Slope crude to West Coast refineries would avert a national energy crisis, reduce the country's dependency on OPEC, and improve the quality of life for every American. The cons pleaded with lawmakers to buck the oil companies, draft a national energy policy—do anything to preserve the last pristine wilderness on Earth. Both sides deployed an arsenal of rhetoric: Alaska was so big, the pipeline would be like the proverbial needle in a haystack, said the pros. (A *National Geographic* writer, Bryan Hodgson, later likened the line's zigzag pattern through the snow to "a hair on a wedding cake.") In an October 1973 letter to the editor of the Fairbanks newspaper, Patrick LeMay called the environmental forces "destructive zealots" who wanted to "hamstring" those who would use just a tiny percentage of Alaska's natural resources. The following month, in a letter headlined, "Root of all evil," Peter M. Sheff wrote that "the total destruction of the land" was a "sure thing" if the pipeline were built: "I love Alaska, I love the land, I want it to stay like God intended it to stay."

At my house, we worshiped an Episcopal God whose intentions seemed pretty much opaque to us. We tended to be of the mind that He helps those who help themselves. The success of the company my father had founded with his father and his brothers hinged on the pipeline's going forward. Brice Incorporated stood to make millions from land-clearing and revegetation contracts. Trickle-down economics at home meant more choices for my mother. She could quit working as a public health nurse and stay home with her five children, perhaps even pursue her dream of graduate school. For me, the pipeline meant whole milk instead of the blechy Carnation powdered stuff. It meant more fresh pineapple like the one my Uncle Bill had brought us from Hawaii. It meant family ski trips, dinners at the Petroleum Club, tropical vacations, more packages under the Christmas tree. It meant fewer reproaches: "I'm working my fingers to the bone," and "You kids think money grows on trees." What I wanted from the pipeline differed only in content, not form, from the grownups.

From the spring day in 1968 when Atlantic Richfield announced it had struck oil at Prudhoe Bay, the pipeline was pretty much a foregone conclusion: the real question before Congress was not whether but when—and, to some degree, how. The first hurdle was Alaska Native land claims, in limbo since statehood; the second was environmental and archeological concerns. In 1971, the Alaska Native Claims Settlement Act created thirteen native corporations, bankrolled them with a billion dollars, and set a four-year deadline for the selection of forty million acres. Meanwhile, the environmental lobby succeeded in imposing some terms on construction. An environmental impact statement contained roughly two hundred technical and environmental stipulations. Finally, in the midst of the Arab oil embargo and Watergate, in November 1973, Congress voted to proceed with the pipeline. Alyeska Pipeline Company (later

 Alyeska Pipeline Service Company), a consortium created by the oil companies, was charged with overseeing construction and maintenance.

When I think of those heady days, I think of the number eight followed by lots of zeros: at the height of the boom, Alyeska was spending $800,000 per day on construction of the eight-hundred-mile line, the total cost of which was around $8 billion. More numbers: in just four years, the population of Fairbanks grew by nearly one third, from 45,000 to 65,000. Every flight from the Lower Forty-eight disgorged dozens of wannabe pipeline workers in cowboy boots and Stetsons. By midsummer 1975, some 20,000 men and women were putting in twelve-hour shifts, seven days per week, for Alyeska and its subcontractors. A typical paycheck was $1,200 per week, which, in 1975 dollars, was more than a lot of CEOs were pulling down. The price of an apartment or a hamburger or a prostitute rose, too. My mother recalls one particular lunch with a friend at the Travelers Inn; sitting next to her were four oilmen with their boot-clad feet propped on the table. She was not amused. She was not alone. A bumper sticker proclaimed, "HAPPINESS IS . . . 10,000 Okies going south with a Texan under each arm."

I remember traffic backing up for half a mile at train crossings as dozens of yellow, four-wheel-drive Alyeska pickups whizzed by on flatbed railcars. I remember double shifting at school. Six o'clock in the morning found me and my brothers and sisters shivering in the dark at the bus stop. The older brothers and sisters of my friends quit school when they turned sixteen to work on a pipeline crew: *I can always get a GED, but I may never find another job that pays as well as this one.* Even tenured professors at the university gave up their posts because they could earn more wielding a shovel than explicating John Donne.

Alaska got rich off the pipeline. When it was over, the state got even richer off of revenues on the crude oil flowing through the line. New schools, runways, bridges, roads, and seaports sprang up in even the most remote villages. State lawmakers abolished the income tax and funneled oil profits into a permanent fund now worth nearly $32 billion. To this day, every Alaska resident receives a yearly check for as much as $1,500—a hardship bonus just for living in Alaska.

In the 1970s and early '80s, Brice Incorporated flourished; *Alaska Business Monthly* listed it among the fifty fastest-growing companies in the state. It purchased a fleet of barges and airplanes as well as heavy equipment. At home, we had whole milk and steak for dinner. We had miniature maps of Alaska sculpted from the same pipe as the pipeline. We went on family vacations to Florida and Hawaii and the Bahamas. I wore fewer hand-me-downs and, better yet, traded in my wooden skis for fiberglass racers. When I applied to college, my parents didn't bother to fill out financial aid forms. Sometime in my senior year at Smith, I received a summons to the dean's office. There, I was told that, in the college's view, I had borrowed too heavily for my education: $12,000 per year from the State of Alaska. Perhaps the dean intended to throw me out until I could pay my own way. Perhaps she was about to offer me a scholarship. In any event, I didn't give her time. Instead, I explained the terms of the loan: half would be forgiven in exchange for my return to Alaska after graduation. "Oh," said the dean. "In that case, I guess there isn't a problem."

At this point, Dear Reader, you must be thinking that my plot looks familiar. It's a moral fable, an allegory of sorts, in which Alaska—gangly newcomer to the Union, neglected stepchild, still wet behind the ears and rough around the edges—struck some kind of Faustian bargain with the oil industry. And you know where my story is headed, of course. In exchange for wealth beyond our wildest imaginings, we Alaskans sold our souls. We sacrificed Prince William Sound on the altar of our greed. As you see, biblical metaphors leap easily to mind, as do metaphors (also biblical) of rape and pillage and despoliation. Bible stories run together with the rags-to-riches allegories that resonate deeply in the American psyche (which, to some degree, is the Alaskan psyche). For many Americans, the Jay Gatsby rags-to-riches-to-hollowness story resonates even more, plucking the chord of Christian guilt: "Indeed, it is easier for a camel to go through the eye of a needle than for a rich man to enter the kingdom of God" (Luke 18:25).

When I was a baby, my mother used to push my buggy

along the sidewalk leading from our house to the Co-Op or Woolworth's or Safeway. Our husky dog, Chitina, trotted beside us. On reaching the store, Mom parked the buggy in the shade and ordered Chitina to mind me while she went in. And Chitina did. But everyone has such stories, right? Stories about doors that were never locked, strangers who stopped to change a flat in the rain, the lady at the supermarket who paid over a few cents or a dollar when you came up short. Such stories are fueled by Norman Rockwellian nostalgia for a kinder, gentler, sweeter past.

Reader, I'm not going to go there. For one thing, wrapping the past in a fuzzy glow means averting one's eyes from the present, a present in which my mother's eighty-three-year-old friend Susie spent a month in hurricane-ravaged New Orleans volunteering for the Red Cross. Or a present in which my father is, at this moment—Thanksgiving morning 2005—plowing the driveway of everyone on his street. Any misbegotten yearning for a simpler time seems to me to be yearning for time to stand still. And any yearning for time to stand still is, simply put, a yearning for the ultimate stillness which is death. At the risk of being labeled a curmudgeon, I think nostalgia is worse than simply boring (and it's always boring). Any worship of the past abdicates responsibility for the present, let alone the future. It reeks of dust and mold, of crocheted afghans and Gomer Pyle reruns, of widowers who dote on their Pekingese instead of people. If the past is always back there, irretrievable, just as the wilderness is always out there, unattainable, then how can we hope to redeem the now and here?

After the pipeline, Fairbanks kept growing like an out-of-control organism, like a cancer metastasizing from its edges outward into housing tracts and strip malls. Downtown became moribund. An entire block, consisting mostly of seedy bars but also of the building that once housed the Petroleum Club, was plowed under for a parking lot. For a while, Woolworth's and the Co-Op embraced their new identity as quaint anachronisms. Then Nordstrom left, citing the poor quality of its facility, which we Fairbanksans took to be a slur on our characters.

K-Mart shouldered its way into a market that couldn't seem to upsize and downscale fast enough. McDonald's, Burger King, and Pizza Hut thrived. So did branch banks. The virtues of drive-in businesses are the virtues of a cubic zirconium wedding ring: convenience, cheapness, and flash. Also, ease of abandonment.

"The pipeline . . . was changing the state in ways that would never be undone," wrote Joe McGinniss in *Going to Extremes.* "Not just physical changes, though they, in places, were severe; but changes in the psychological climate; deep scars cut not only across the tundra but across Alaska's very soul."

While I was at college in Massachusetts, my best friend from fifth grade, Lori King, hitched a ride with a stranger who raped then strangled her. He turned out to be a soldier from Fort Wainwright, a few miles east of Fairbanks. It would be sick to suggest any connection between the acts of a psychopathic killer and the acts of the oil industry. Even so, Lori's killing—the ease and callousness of it—seemed to me somehow inextricable from—even emblematic of—the ways the state was changing.

Years earlier, when Lori and I were in sixth or seventh grade, a husky pipeliner had said to a *National Geographic* reporter, "You can talk all you want about the last frontier. To me, it's just plain Fat City." Then he dug into his third steak.

After college, I returned to Alaska to work off my debt to the state. I took a job on the *Fairbanks Daily News-Miner.* There, if I stood on tiptoe to peer out of the newsroom's slit-like second-story windows, I could see across the river to the site, now a church parking lot, where my parents' first house once stood. From a different window in my editor's office, I could see the neon sign for the headquarters of Denali State Bank, which had gone up in place of Saint Joseph's Hospital, where I was born. It was true that Fairbanks was changing in ways that would never be undone. Was my soul in danger, too? I didn't know. For one thing, I wasn't sure then—as I'm not sure now—exactly what constitutes a soul. For another, I was seeing Alaska as if for the first time. In *An American Childhood,* Annie

Dillard writes, "Young children have no sense of wonder. They bewilder well, but few things surprise them." It's true. A sense of wonder is possible only in relation to something else, something that registers as not wonderful. To be born and raised in Alaska is to take in stride even its immense sky—tinted, at this moment, the most delicate shade of pink, like nothing so much as the inside of a conch shell.

Then, in the idiom of the oil industry, the bottom fell out of the market. In the mid-'80s, the per-barrel price of oil plummeted from thirty dollars to less than eight. The heavyweights in the Alaska economy, ARCO Alaska and British Petroleum, laid off hundreds of workers. Oil-dependent industries closed up shop. You might say the bottom fell out from beneath Alaska's middle class, too. The lucky ones who hung onto their jobs saw their retirement and benefits melt away. By the thousands, people defaulted on car loans and mortgages, declared bankruptcy, left the state. Banks collapsed. "For Sale" signs went up everywhere, but no one was buying. State government constricted. Funding for capital projects dried up. Brice Incorporated won a multimillion-dollar contract to build a boat harbor on Saint George Island in the Pribilofs, then the project was scrapped. Never what you'd call loquacious, my father turned downright taciturn. If you asked him a question, he'd start to answer then quit in mid-sentence, lost to worry. A new bumper sticker appeared: "Please God, give us another pipeline. We promise not to piss it all away this time."

By Good Friday of 1989, people's attitude toward Big Oil had grown surly. I was twenty-six. Over lunch hour that day, I walked across the bridge spanning the Chena River, from the newspaper office to Saint Matthew's Church. Inside, all of the crosses, even the heavy brass one I'd carried for years as a crucifer, were shrouded in black. Dust motes, palpable as grief, hung in the weak spring sunlight. In church, it was quiet and still. At the newspaper office, it had been neither quiet nor still. Recently, I'd been promoted to the business beat. This being Fairbanks, it might as well have been called the oil beat. Earlier that day, March 24, the AP wire had carried two big stories: Democratic governor Steve Cowper had announced he would not to stand for reelection, and an Exxon tanker, the *Valdez,* had run aground on Bligh Reef, the best-mapped hazard in Prince William Sound. Oil was gushing into the sound. By the time it stopped, 10.1 million gallons of crude oil would spill, covering an area of more than three thousand square miles.

The symbolism of that Good Friday was lost on no one. Brandishing the headline that began a public relations war—"Paradise Lost"—*Alaska* magazine's June 1989 issue hinted at a higher meaning for the events of one spring morning that turned "Alaska's emerald jewel," a thousand-mile, glacier-rimmed sound into a killing field for waterfowl, whales, seals, sea lions, sea otters, herring, and salmon. The headline alluded to Alaska's lost innocence, the degradation of a spiritual as well as physical landscape. Degradation it had suffered at the hands of the rapacious oil industry. That headline would have been unimaginable in 1980, the year that Joe McGinniss published *Going to Extremes,* with its evocation of "deep scars [that] cut not only across the tundra but across Alaska's very soul."

Below the headline, *Alaska*'s writers say,

> For the past twelve years that oil has flowed through the pipeline, the oil industry has spoon-fed the public about its ability to protect the Alaskan environment through thousands of television and print ads, and hundreds of glossy, color brochures.
>
> The message of the media blitz was this: Don't worry—we have achieved great technological feats in Alaska's harsh environment, and if anything happens, we'll have it handled before you can blink twice. Don't worry, be happy.
>
> And most Alaskans were happy. They came to believe the environmental claims of big oil. A lion's share of Alaskans had made their money from the oil industry's presence in Alaska, the state's economy was fueled by crude oil, our culture supported and largely financed by donations from the giant corporations.
>
> Yet by the second week of this man-made mess, the sense of betrayal had reached biblical proportions.

Biblical betrayal. Paradise Lost. The oil industry said be happy, and Alaskans were happy. If the metaphor stands, then who or what was betrayed? And who did the betraying? In the Garden of Eden, it was Adam and Eve, at the behest of the snake, who betrayed God's trust. But the language of the *Alaska* article—*Don't worry, be happy*—suggests it was God who betrayed Adam and Eve's trust. The unvarnished truth is that, for years, the interests of the oil industry had paralleled the interests of ordinary Alaskans. Together, we'd watched crude prices rise and fall, knowing the industry's fortunes, the state's fortunes, and our personal fortunes rose and fell, too. Together, we'd invested the bulk of our capital in what financial planners describe as a volatile commodity. By 1989, there may have been one or two holdouts—a handful of Alaskans who turned down the Permanent Fund check, who rode their bicycles to work year-round, who heated their homes with gas or even wood (itself a questionable environmental practice). Intentionally or not, every Alaskan had benefited in substantial, measurable ways from the oil industry's presence in the state. (Even my former substitute teacher, Mrs. S, had, with her family, embarked on a successful retail venture. For a while, she and my mother shared the same cleaning lady. The cleaning lady told my mother that Mrs. S's house was so big, with so many rooms and labyrinthine hallways, that she sometimes got lost while trying to clean it. I may be wrong, but I don't think Mrs. S's pro-environment convictions paid for that house.)

In the end, the biblical metaphor is too imprecise for me. Instead, I return time and again to the image of petulant children. As oil prices fell, our anger and indignation mounted. The *Exxon Valdez* simply gave it an occasion to overflow. Afterward, we raged and ranted like children who've just been told by their parents that they must grow up, must take responsibility for their own actions, must understand that there's no such thing as a free lunch—no one gets to have their cake and eat it, too. Above all, they must see the ways in which they, too, were culpable in a tragedy that irreparably harmed a place ("the emerald jewel") whose purity and beauty they themselves had ranked behind their own comfort and prosperity. I say "they" only because it's still too painful to say "we."

Here's a guy as unlike Mrs. S as he can be. Inasmuch as there is such a thing as a typical Alaskan, he's one. His name is Tom

Brennan, and he was working in public relations for Alyeska when I met him two months after the spill, in May 1989. The occasion was a journalists' junket that began in Valdez and ended in Prudhoe Bay. It was a canny undertaking in the sense that, at the time, images from the spill were still dominating the nightly news. Johnny Carson cracked wise on late-night TV about guys on cleanup crews using cocktail napkins. By reversing the order of events that led to the *Exxon Valdez,* Alyeska might shift the public's gaze from the spectacle of an alcoholic tanker captain toward its relatively safe extraction and pumping operation.

Back when Joe McGinniss arrived in Alaska to research *Going to Extremes,* he stayed with Tom and Marnie Brennan. Tom was an old colleague of McGinniss's from the Worcester, Massachusetts, newspaper. With tact and gentle humor, McGinniss described his pal's career change: "You just never know. You come to Alaska in search of freedom and adventure and whatever the future might bring. Sometimes the future brings oil."

In May 1989, Tom was angry—as angry as Mrs. S, but for a different reason. He was angry at how quickly Alaskans had turned on the industry in their self-righteous frenzy. He had a point. The outpouring of rhetoric that followed the oil spill smacked of romanticizing a past that never really existed, of mourning a present that was never even possible. At last, Alaskans had found a handy target to blame for the fact that they had had to grow up. The human face of that handy target was Tom.

I met him in the Anchorage airport, where he and I and the rest of our group caught a flight to Valdez shortly after noon on the first day of the tour. Since the spill, tents had blossomed like crocuses in every campground. Pedestrians in knee-high rubber boots dodged mud puddles. We ordered hamburgers from the driver's-side window of a Winnebago-turned-Burger King near the docks.

Afterward, we rode in an Alyeska Suburban to where the Alyeska helicopters were hangared. An Alyeska employee logged each of us in then made us step on an enormous cargo scale—a bit of revenge, perhaps, for what Alyeska regarded as our liberal bias. Our helicopter took off. As it neared Bligh Reef, the water below turned from emerald green to greasy black. I counted several floating objects that may or may not have been the bloated corpses of seals, sea lions, or even small whales. The *Exxon Valdez* was still snagged on its underwater reef, listing slightly, like a half-bored adult listening to a whiny child.

We landed on Block Island. The rotors were still cooling down when the pilot turned to us. "I'd appreciate it if y'all would please wipe the oil off your feet before you get back in the chopper," he said. I stepped outside. Clots of tar-like oil clung like runny cow pies to the rocks. With my every step, black goo oozed up the sides of my knee-high rubber boots. On the beach, some fifty people wearing Helly Hansen rain gear stood silent and motionless, shoulder-to-shoulder, washing the rocks with high-powered hoses. They turned an apathetic gaze on us. Returning it, I had the surreal sense that they were extras in a movie being made about the oil spill, and we were tourists from Kansas who'd been bussed onto the set.

The next morning, five of us journalists and Tom crowded into another Alyeska Suburban to begin the long drive north. The Richardson Highway parallels the pipeline for roughly three hundred fifty northwesterly miles, from Valdez to Fairbanks. After that, the Dalton Highway—also known as the Haul Road—takes it the rest of the way to Prudhoe Bay. Throughout, road and pipeline travel together like old companions, slipping together occasionally for an intimate conversation, then drifting apart so one or the other can follow the contours of an intriguing rock formation or valley.

Tom's mood lightened as we put more and more miles between us and Valdez. He was brimful of anecdotes. Crossing the Yukon River bridge, he recounted how Miss Texas, along on a junket similar to ours, once heeded nature's call in nearby bushes, unaware of the high-powered video cameras that Alyeska had set up to detect saboteurs.

The old Chandalar Lake construction camp sits at the entrance to Atigun Pass in the Brooks Range, well above tree line. An ocean of snow stretches out to either side of the road. Beyond the camp lie mountains with peaks as sharp as spindles. We pulled into the deserted parking lot, and Tom turned off the engine. No one said anything. The enormous sky was gun-metal gray; the wind made wild music with the truck's antenna.

A while later, as we crested Atigun Pass at 4,739 feet, the boiling sun slipped below the horizon. The North Slope rolled out before us like a red-tinted ceremonial carpet. We arrived at Pump Station Three, roughly fifty miles from our destination, shortly before 11:00 p.m. Mist flirted with the surface of a nearby pond; ducks slept with their beaks burrowed into their wings. I found the guest bedroom to which I'd been assigned. There, two foil-wrapped mints lay on my pillow.

As we drove the next day, the season changed so subtly that I couldn't say just when we drove from spring into winter. Rain turned to snow and clogged the windshield. A chill crept into my toes, and Tom switched on the floor heat. This was May at the northernmost tip of North America.

Caribou grazed alongside the highway. In the distance, we saw herds of musk oxen and, once in a while, a solitary grizzly. Kamikaze ptarmigan dive-bombed our Suburban. Suddenly, the headlights gripped a peregrine falcon, talons outstretched, swooping for a ptarmigan. The terrified prey nearly roasted itself on our grille.

"Damn pedestrians," Tom muttered.

Then we saw the "skyscrapers" of Prudhoe Bay: black metal drilling rigs probing the sky. Named in 1928 after Great Britain's Baron Prudhoe (Algernon Percy), the bay's original pronunciation rhymed with "spud-HOE." Now it's pronounced "PRUDE-oh." Over the past three-quarters of a century, far more has changed than the pronunciation of the name: Prudhoe Bay has gone from an unpopulated tract of tundra to a wasteland of steam and steel. Outlined against the dirty spring snow, it is unremittingly, irredeemably ugly. Also, it is rarely seen by anyone outside the oil industry (although it's gaining popularity with trophy-hunting tourists who want to brag that they've set foot on the top of the continent). Prudhoe Bay—and, by extension, the *Exxon Valdez*—is the juggernaut we Alaskans created when we invited comfort and prosperity into our lives.

By jet, Fairbanks lies three-quarters of an hour south of the North Slope. I stepped off the Arco jet and back into spring. In the few days that I'd been gone, the buds on birch trees had burst, and the temperature had climbed into the sixties. In the taxi, I peeled off my wool socks. Back at the office, a week's worth of phone messages and press releases jammed my in box. Unwritten stories, fragmentary notes, and transcribed interviews clamored for my undivided attention. What they (and my editors) wanted from me was order, resolution, completion. Was the oil industry doing everything in its power to clean up a mess that was made by one bad employee? Or was it doing everything in its power, as *Alaska* magazine said, to throw up a PR "smokescreen" that disguised deeper "corporate paralysis"? Was the *Exxon Valdez* a fluke, a tragedy on the order of being struck by lightning, or was it an avoidable accident brought on by corporate arrogance and neglect? I suspected it was some of each—both tragic and accidental, both a fluke and avoidable. But I couldn't say that, not when the journalist's mantra is to "Simplify, simplify, simplify."

A couple of years later, *Outside* magazine trumpeted a study saying that seven out of ten Americans regarded themselves as environmentalists. My first thought was, That's nice. My second was, What are the prerequisites for being a self-described environmentalist? I don't mean to be flip. Truthfully, I'd like to think of myself as an environmentalist in the same way I'd like to think of myself as a good person. Am I worthy of the title? I don't know.

On the one hand, I've worn Birkenstocks through several fashion waves.

Not the kind with fake leather.

Alas.

For years, I owned a fleecy vest made out of recycled plastic bottles that were made originally from crude oil. Talk about wearing your politics on your sleeve.

Or not.

In the years when I was a journalist, I lived in a cabin heated with wood. It had no running water or electricity. Living there was an aesthetic and, admittedly, an economic choice. It was also an act of rebellion against my parents. That phase ended by the time my first daughter was born, in 1992.

I recycle plastic, tin, glass, and paper, including propaganda from Greenpeace and the Nature Conservancy.

If I didn't recycle, the neighbors would talk.

Two or three houses ago, before I left Alaska, I had a routine of driving my first-born daughter and her twin sisters to school before going to my job at the university. The odometer on my trusty Toyota Corolla read 90,000 miles. Eventually, I moved up to a Sienna minivan—a gift from my parents—now with 120,000 miles. On forty-below mornings, I'd inevitably pass people on bicycles. I felt a twinge of—what? Envy? Regret? Moments later, I'd tuck my station wagon into a parking spot in front of the Montessori school. The girls and I ran a gauntlet of gargantuan SUVs: Expeditions and Explorers and Navigators and Yukons and Tundras. I felt another twinge, this one unmistakable: envy.

My youngest daughters are now in fourth grade, a year younger than I was during the pipeline brouhaha. The proposal before Congress now, in 2005, is to permit oil exploration in a coastal strip of the Arctic National Wildlife Refuge. I've been to ANWR. It's beautiful, forbidding, and foggy—the Arctic equivalent of England's moors. Democrats and moderate Republicans in Congress oppose the measure, calling instead for a national energy policy that weans America off oil while gradually increasing its reliance on alternative power sources. President George W. Bush has made drilling in ANWR one of the top priorities of his presidency, saying through a spokesman that he supports "environmentally responsible exploration." The opening of ANWR, he says, is vital to reduce America's dependence on foreign oil and make energy affordable. There's not much question of what the majority of Alaskans think. They vote a pro-Bush, pro-Republican, pro-development ticket. These days, a popular bumper sticker proclaims, "EARTH FIRST: We'll mine the other planets later."

If the way we live is a gesture, who or what is it a gesture toward? And which is better: paddling a kayak in the wilderness or driving an Expedition in the city? Is it OK to answer yes to A *and* B?

In a diner just off Virginia's Route 29, a world-famous butterfly researcher once asked if I, too, was a passionate environmentalist. I took too long to answer, and his face fell. Then I said, slowly, "I guess I'm tree-hugger with a sense of complexity. Does that count?"

FOUR ~ Three Paragraphs

Within hours of graduating college, I stuffed my diploma in my trunk, changed out of my white eyelet dress and into jeans, and boarded a Eastern Air Lines jet at the Hartford-Springfield airport. Nearly eighteen hours later, I stepped off an Alaska Airlines jet in Fairbanks. I moved back into my old bedroom with its honey-colored carpet, rose-patterned wallpaper, and gold-framed portrait of Jenny Lind. It was only temporary; in the fall, I was to begin law school at the University of Washington. To pass the time and to earn a little money, I took a job on my hometown newspaper. My title was newsroom receptionist—meaning, I supposed, that I was to answer the phone, direct visitors, smile a lot. On my second day, I learned that the receptionist at the *Fairbanks Daily News-Miner* performs the functions carried out on larger dailies by interns or cub reporters. The best part of the job was writing obituaries. My beat (as I thought of it) was bereavement, my job the packaging of death like airline meals into bland but palatable news-bites for community consumption. Because Fairbanks averages only two or three deaths per day, I also typed up the weather forecast, births, marriages, divorces, United Way meetings, petty thefts, bankruptcies, Chamber of Commerce luncheons, and drunken driving convictions. In all, death took up only half an hour between eight and nine every morning.

One or more of the local morticians called or stopped by

 then. Early in our relationship, they of the slicked-back hair and moist palms misremembered my name, calling me "Dear" or "Sweetie." Perhaps their line of work invited false intimacy. "My name is Jennifer," I'd say.

"Yes, dear," they'd reply.

Occasionally, bypassing official channels, a friend of the bereaved family brought in a brief biography. Usually a woman in late middle age, she looked as though she could be one of my mother's friends. (Fairbanks being Fairbanks, there was a one-in-three chance that she *was* one of my mother's friends.) The obit-bearing friend was the kind of woman who owns white gloves and folding chairs, who volunteers at the hospital and at church rummage sales, who plays duplicate bridge on Thursdays, and who, in the crisis occasioned by a birth, hysterectomy, nervous breakdown, car accident, or cancer can be counted upon to materialize at the back door with a covered casserole. Her male counterpart is often described as a pillar of the community, but she is its spinal cord. If this were Ireland and someone died, she would keen at the wake. If this were Israel, she would sit shiva. But this is America, so she handles the publicity.

I'd grown up watching *Mary Tyler Moore*, so I knew my role. In the brand-new suit (khaki, Banana Republic) I'd bought for law school interviews, I was cool and professional toward the overly friendly morticians in their wide ties and shiny suits. I was sweet and deferential toward the over-competent family friends who wanted to get every detail just right. But I was utterly undone in the presence of the father who twisted a corduroy bill-cap in his hands, the sister with ravaged make-up, the numb spouse or hollow-eyed mother. Where was my script? On those occasions, my bulky IBM was the only thing between me and pain beyond my ken. I murmured questions and typed in answers, avoiding eye contact lest I be the one to break into tears. I was twenty-two years old, and no one I loved had ever died; I saw my future in those faces, and I was afraid.

The bereaved came to me for a written tribute to the richness, beauty, and ambiguity of a particular life. They wanted to convey in a phrase—say, "born in Peoria"—a son's restlessness

and yearning to trade Midwest corn fields for Alaska's ice fields.
To them, "homemaker" meant more than a plate of warm Toll House cookies after school: It conjured a mother who decorated the house every Thanksgiving with turkeys the kids had made in kindergarten, from construction paper tracings of their hands; a mom who scrimped by wearing penny loafers in the seventies when every other kid's mother wore lace-ups; a mom who broke down in tears at the airport every time a kid left home for a week at camp or a semester at college. They wanted me to stitch a queen-sized quilt out of scraps. They wanted me to make a man or a woman out of words. I couldn't help but disappoint them.

In *Playing Dead*, a slim volume of essays on the Arctic, Rudy Wiebe writes of the "overwhelming doubleness to death: it brings sorrow and at the same time it makes possible the story which is our memory of the dead." In modern society, the obituary functions as the first and most official version of that story. Its purpose was lost on me then, though. Newspaper work is all about deadlines, and empathy is invidious to speed. After only one or two weeks on the job, I prided myself on nailing down an obit faster than the city editor could shout across the newsroom, "Hey Jennifer, how many morts ya got this morning?"

The woman who'd held my position before me had been promoted to the features section, where she now wrote a weekly religion column. She passed along the paper's obit formula. Really, it was as simple as an algebraic equation: my only task was to plug in the variables. Name, age, hometown, date, and cause of death went in the first paragraph; career and hobbies went in the second; family names and funeral arrangements went in the third. Flyfishing went in; Budweiser swilling went out. Among the survivors, we listed second cousins thrice removed but not longtime companions. A couple of unwritten corollaries: the older the deceased, the older the photograph; the older the deceased, the longer the obituary. Infants were tricky. No one, least of all the grieving parents, wanted to make a newborn's life seem slight and insubstantial. In such cases, the editors let in one or two flowery euphemisms that stretched a solitary inch of typeface into a more fulsome three or four, thereby lulling the average reader into perhaps thinking that little Johnny had not, in fact, died but been carried off by a troupe of angels singing the *Hallelujah Chorus.*

The obituary formula was relatively new when I arrived at the paper. Before then, the editors had reprinted verbatim (and gratis) whatever the family or morticians turned in. That policy had had troublesome loopholes. Every year or two, a practical joker or a malicious ex-spouse submitted an obituary for a person who was not, in fact, dead. These fake obits resulted in some red-faced retractions. One particular obituary put a permanent end to the paper's lax policy, however. It was for a guy named Jack "Junior" Cunningham, age sixty-three. It read, in part: "He was a world-class rodeo bronco rider and calf roper and also an interior paper hanger, specializing in silver leaf and fabric, a talent he learned in Japan at the end of World War II." The obit went on to describe the deceased as a founder of a Washington resort and an "acclaimed" irrigation specialist at a Montana lodge. To the editor's chagrin, the "resort" and "lodge" turned out to be federal prisons where Cunningham had served time for counterfeiting, the origami-like talent he'd learned in Japan at the end of World War II.

Occasionally, the newspaper departed from its own three-paragraph rule. The demise of politicians or pillars of the community warranted front-page coverage. Other reporters wrote such articles, not I. What landed on my desk were the everyday, garden variety, next-door-neighbor kind of deaths.

It wasn't easy shoehorning these lives into three paragraphs, even for a born tidy-upper like me. I remember a childless woman of my age, struck down by an asthma attack at a crowded hockey game less than a block from the hospital. A flight instructor whose plane crashed on take-off with his six-year-old nephew on board. Teenage twins killed near Denali National Park by a drunken driver while their parents were taking a dream vacation to Australia. The sewer-mouthed scourge of the Pioneers Home, a turbaned madam who'd once reigned over a row of tiny houses whose goings-on were an open secret. A newborn who smothered in his mother's sleeping bag during a family camping trip. The taciturn typesetter for the newspaper who asphyxiated himself while masturbating—the victim, according to his obituary, of a "tragic accident." Fifteen-year-old boys—too many of them—who turned their fathers' hunting rifles on themselves.

In an essay for the *New York Times,* Joyce Carol Oates once wrote of the irreconcilable conflict between the human desire for stasis and the truth that will not be comforted. Obituaries, with their pre-fab structure that reduces human life to its lowest common denominator—X was born, X lived, and X died—reflect the human desire for stasis. The truth that will not be comforted flits fractal-like in the spaces between paragraphs, sentences, words, letters. All of our rituals for dealing with death—obituaries, wakes, visitations, funerals, the wearing of black—imply there is a time to grieve and a time, somewhere in the foreseeable future, not to grieve.

When I was in my early twenties, typing up obituaries as efficiently as possible, I rarely thought of grief. When I did, perhaps I imagined it as water gushing from a faucet, eventually slowing to a trickle, finally shutting off. Ten years later, a close friend gave birth to a baby boy who lived for only a few minutes. She showed me that grief is not a faucet but a tide that flows and ebbs forever.

I think obituaries fail not because of arrogant writers or insensitive editors but because the form itself is flawed. Neither tribute nor eulogy, neither biography nor allegory, an obituary is all of these and much less. A newspaper is the document of record for a community, an obituary merely a single entry in that ledger: a debit balanced by the columns of marriages and births that frequently appear on the same page. The obituary is the mechanism by which the private experience of a life—and death—becomes a public moment. Something crucial always gets lost in translation.

Difficult as it is fully to know people in life, it is impossible to set down their fullness, flaws, cares, and complexity in the pages of a newspaper, or even a book—not with all the space and time in the world. The obituary writer is thus confined to a kind of purgatory, the gap between a life well or poorly lived and the words available to describe it, the future perfect and the imperfect past, reverberant possibility and hard closure.

Nine months into my job, the editor promoted me to the news desk. By then, I'd moved out of my parents' house and into a cabin of my own. I had a circle of friends who were all reporters or photographers. I was pretty sure I was in love with one of them. In the spring of 1986, I let the University of Washington know I wouldn't be attending law school after all.

Being a real reporter was great. For one thing, I got out more—to cover school board meetings, ribbon-cutting ceremonies, and the Tanana Valley State Fair. On Election Day, I stood in the snow outside of polling places to ask people how they'd just voted. I interviewed a fourteen-year-old cancer victim who chain-smoked the whole time, and a trio of Argentines who'd hitchhiked all the way to Fairbanks from Tierra del Fuego. I made a kind of specialty of two-fers: the sheet-metal salesman who was also a square dancer, the union pipe-fitter who was also a concert pianist. The newspaper paid my way to concerts and plays, and in return, I wrote upbeat reviews. (The newspaper's policy was never to run a negative review.) Things were going along pretty well. Even so, I missed my old job. I missed writing about the virtuous dead who never complained, unlike the red-faced conductor who barged into the newsroom like an enraged walrus and bellowed at me for confusing the Fairbanks *Concert* Association with the Fairbanks *Symphony* Association.

One day, I was sitting at my new desk, twenty feet deeper into the newsroom than my old one. I was on the telephone with the president of the chamber of commerce, who was nattering on about an upcoming rubber ducky race or some such thing. I was bored. When I'm bored, I tend to think subversive thoughts. If I'm in a roomful of people, for instance, I try to imagine which of them I'd *least* like to have sex with. Stuff like that. So I tried to compose an obituary for the president of the chamber of commerce while dutifully taking down rubber ducky statistics. I didn't get far. Unbidden, an image came to me. It was an unpleasant image, that of aluminum siding being slapped over the worn-out boards of a beloved house. At that moment, I saw that I missed my old beat not because it was easier or less stressful but because I'd moved on without mastering it. Why hadn't I paid attention? Tried harder? Why hadn't I peeked into people's closets, checked their magazine subscriptions and voter registrations, read their letters and college essays, listened to the voices of those who'd loved them? I might not have stumbled on beauty or nobility—not every time, anyway—but I might have found a way to elevate human life above the level of mathematical equation. I might have borne witness to what Don DeLillo calls the "luminousness of the everyday." I said nothing to my editor. He would have laughed. Who did I think I was, anyway? The obituaries editor of the *New York Times*?

A couple of years out of college, I left the daily newspaper for a moribund weekly that had just been bought by a group of investors, liberals and intellectuals all. They were energetic and optimistic, determined to perk up the *All-Alaska Weekly* with in-depth coverage and sparkling commentary. I was too young to see the ways in which their venture was bound to fail. My first week on the job, the editor asked me for standing feature suggestions. We should run one in-depth obit every week, I said. Its focus should be an ordinary person, someone who would not otherwise merit a front-page story. He agreed.

Around Valentine's Day, I read a brief obituary in my old newspaper. It began this way:

> Lonnie Moore Jr. was born in California on Aug. 26, 1953, and died Tuesday in Fairbanks of injuries sustained when his automobile was struck by another vehicle on Jan. 28.

Names, dates, places: pin dots on the topo map of a human life. The second paragraph described Moore as an ordained deacon in his church, president of the youth group Young People Willing Workers, a volunteer carpenter. As if the achievements made the man, not vice versa. Names of his wife, children, parents, brothers, sisters—the family tree from which a single leaf had fallen out of season—filled up the third paragraph. It was this last paragraph, this stark list of the living that touched me. I reached for the phone book and dialed Lonnie Moore's widow.

That was twenty years ago. I still remember Linda Moore as a statuesque beauty with golden skin and upswept hair. She lived with her two school-age children in a newly built subdivision of three-bedroom houses painted varying shades of neutral. She was an interior decorator, and the walls in her entryway were painted robin's egg blue, hung with straw wreaths and hand-painted "God Is Love" plaques. It was immaculate, as was the rest of the house, and I caught myself wondering what a woman thinks when she pushes a vacuum past the side of the bed where no one sleeps anymore.

This is what Linda Moore told me: one Saturday morning in January, Lonnie, a maintenance worker for the city of Fairbanks, roused her and the kids at five o'clock and drove them to Fred Meyer, a vast K-Mart clone, where the family helped with inventory to raise money for their church, Lily of the Valley Church of God in Christ. Afterward, the Moores attended choir practice, and then picked up friends at the airport. By the time the family pulled into their own driveway, it was nearly 9:00 p.m. The grownups were exhausted, the kids cranky. Linda urged Lonnie to put away the car and call it a night, but he said no. He was bent on doing what he did every Saturday night, which was to drive fifteen miles to his parents' home just to knot his father's tie for church the next morning. His father's arthritis had gotten so bad that he could no longer do it himself, and Lonnie's mother was helpless at such things.

So Lonnie helped his wife and his children into the house, and then climbed back in his car, negotiating the snowy streets of his subdivision before pulling onto the southbound expressway. He was nearly halfway to North Pole when the front wheel of a Trans Am in front of him slipped off the pavement. The sixteen-year-old driver overcorrected, and the car spun around on the ice, striking Lonnie's Mazda head on. One passenger in the Trans Am, a teenage boy, died at the scene, and two girls suffered crippling injuries. Lonnie Moore lingered in the intensive care unit of the Fairbanks hospital for two weeks. On a February afternoon with darkness closing in, he squeezed Linda's hand and kissed her good-bye.

In the summer of 2003, one of my closest friends, Reetika Vazirani, killed herself and her two-year-old son, Jehan. Afterward, there was a flurry of news stories in the *Washington Post,* the obvious comparisons to Sylvia Plath and Assia Weevil, and a moving tribute in Edward Hirsch's poetry column. A few months went by, and then I got an e-mail from a *Post* writer working on a Sunday magazine story about Reetika. Would I be willing speak with her? Regretfully, I would not. Now I'm trying to explain why, even to myself. After all, I'd been in the *Post* writer's shoes myself, calling up grieving friends and family to ask for comments. The writer said she meant well, and I believed her. Yet my reaction to her request was visceral, even ugly. *Don't do it, don't write about her,* I wanted to say. *Leave Reetika be. If you try to put her story "in context," you'll only muck it up more.*

If a reporter were to come nosing around my death, what would my friends and family tell her? I've been to Paris and Prague but not the Galapagos Islands or the Grand Canyon. I'm a sucker for Jane Austen novels and for Cy Twombly paintings. I love anything by Anne Carson. Coconut ice cream. Pinot noir. Ginger dipped in dark chocolate. Mud between my bare toes. Conch shells. Pedicures. White T-shirts. Cashmere sweaters. Clogs. Flounces. Mussorgsky and Mahler. The Buena Vista Social Club. My daughters' freshly washed hair. The *New York Times* crossword puzzle. The color chartreuse. The word "synecdoche."

I was born too late for drive-in movies, too soon for Title Nine. When it comes to following directions, I don't have the sense God gave a gnat. I believe that when the cows are lying down, it's going to rain; it'll clear up when there's enough blue sky to make a Dutchman's pants. I don't believe in the interpretation of dreams—mine or anybody else's. I bite my fingernails and pick my scabs. I wash my hands fifty times a day. I floss my teeth twice a year, just before my semi-annual dentist appointments. When someone breaks my heart, I buy shoes I can't afford that don't match anything else in my closet. Sometimes when I sneeze or laugh, I have to cross my legs to keep from peeing my pants.

Who will write my obituary? Is it possible for me to speak with her now? To do a little advance work? If so, I'd like to say, Ignore the diplomas and the fellowships and the books. Pay attention to the Mussorgsky and the Cy Twombly, the coconut ice cream and the lying-down cows. They matter.

One day a year or so ago, a brusque X-ray technician handed me a form letter. "Dear Ms. _____," it began. "Your mammogram showed something which is probably normal. Some additional pictures are required to confirm this, however . . . "

"What does this mean?" I was dressing as quickly as possible. The exam room was as cold as a meat locker. The technician kept her eyes on her clipboard as I tucked my breasts into my bra and covered them with a T-shirt. Poor things. I'd always taken them for granted.

"The X-rays showed some calcification."

"What's calcification?"

"Just what it sounds like," she said. "Some lumps. Probably nothing. But I'm really not allowed to talk to you anymore."

Near the end of my grandfather's life, a flock of Jehovah's Witnesses pestered him nearly every day. A Southern gentleman, he was too polite to shut the door in their faces, so he let them proselytize away in his living room while he sipped on his whiskey. He was the only man to call my father "Bubba" and get away with it. In a Bahamas casino over Christmas one year, he matched my ten-dollar stake and, when I hit the jackpot on a silver-dollar slot machine, claimed half of my $500. His favorite drink was Old Granddad on the rocks, his favorite smoke unfiltered Camel cigarettes.

I spent two or three spring breaks from college jouncing around his ranch in the back of his open Jeep. Every spring, he told me that his stand of oak trees, draped with melancholy strands of Spanish moss, was the largest in northern Florida. And every year, I acted as though this was news to me. Once—I think it was in my junior year—he showed me a calf born without eyes. Its mother had rejected it. Granddad fed it milk from a bottle every day until it was old enough to be weaned. Not a sentimental man, Granddad never named the calf. But he never sold it, either.

Granddad's brother, Uncle Earl, rode shotgun in the Jeep. Cancer was piecemealing him to death: first an eye, then a leg. At lunchtime, the three of us would drive up the street to my great-grandmother's house in a suburb of Gainesville. There, she'd fix us ham sandwiches, fuss at Granddad for not protecting his bald pate from the sun, and double-check that my shorts were long enough for modesty, or that I was wearing a slip under my skirt.

Two or three times, Granddad and I ate dinner at Mildred's house. Mildred had hair the color of fireweed and a buxom voice that never stopped bossing Granddad. She and my grandmother—from whom he was never divorced—had that much in common. When Granddad died, Mildred sent a red rose bush to my grandmother in Alaska. Grandma planted the bush in her garden, where it blooms still, more than a decade after *her* death. To say more about whatever understanding was between the three of them would be the most bald-faced presumption on my part. The embroidering of private lives into public documents that can withstand strangers' scrutiny is the work of an obituary writer, not a granddaughter.

The Camels got Granddad before the whiskey did. A year or so before he died, he gave up the ranch and moved to back to Alaska to be near his wife and children and grandchildren. That was just after I graduated from Smith. He planted barley in the field behind the farm. On good days, he was up and about, tending his crop. On bad days, he stayed in his room, which my grandmother had furnished with couches and chairs, a television and a bar. The intervals between trips to the hospital, where nurses tied his hands to bedrails to prevent him from ripping out his ventilator tube, grew shorter. The last time my grandmother called an ambulance to fetch him, he sent it away, saying he felt fine. My mother called the newspaper office where I was working late. She told me not to worry, which made me worry. In the middle of the night, I awoke to knocking. I think I knew before I opened the door and saw my parents standing there, white faced and grim. Granddad's funeral was on Good Friday, a day of ritualistic grieving, a day devoid not only of joy but of hope.

After the service, I hung around my grandmother's kitchen with my cousins and my friends. We were sad, but we weren't scary sad like some of the grownups, who seemed to have lost whatever ballast had propelled them through the world. Danny Nordale was the mayor's son and a friend of my brother's. He and his brother, Jim, sometimes did off jobs for the family business. He told this story:

> One day I was working on some cabinets in this room when Granddad shuffled in. He said, "Helen, what have we got to eat around here?" Your grandmother said, "Daddy, you know it's Monday, and Monday is the cook's day off." He looked at her for a while, then he muttered, "And Tuesday and Wednesday and Thursday . . ."

A day or two earlier, my grandmother's secretary had telephoned to say that I was to write the obituary. That was all. Just write it. I interviewed my father and my uncles, pored over scrapbooks and photo albums, double-checked documents and dates, then wrote and rewrote all night long. I thought it was as close to a masterpiece as an obituary could be: a paean in three paragraphs. I thought my grandmother would probably hate it. Always a complicated woman, she grew more unpredictable with age, whizzing in and out of her family's lives like a natural force—usually a force for entropy. Her highly honed sense of drama had sustained her through Granddad's service. Now that his ashes had been spread on the farm and all of the relatives had gone home, there was no telling what she'd be like. Formidable, I imagined. Even so, I printed out the obituary and drove out to the farm. Once there, I hugged her then handed over the envelope, hoping to beat a hasty retreat.

No such luck.

"Read it out loud," she said.

So I did.

"No, that's not right. Not right at all." She put out her hand. I handed over the piece of paper and a pen. She crossed out everything about his illness, his birthplace, his World War II service, his role in founding Brice Incorporated, and his beloved Gainesville ranch. All that was left was this:

> Luther Liston Brice, 78, died Monday at Fairbanks Memorial Hospital.
>
> He leaves his wife, helenka [she spelled her name with a lowercase *h*]; a daughter, Lorena; sons Bob, Nick, Tom, Andy, Sam and Alba; son-in-law Sam, and daughters-in-law Bonnie, Leta, Jane, Lois, Nancy, Joan and Carol.
>
> Grandchildren Samantha, John and Stevie; Andrea, Steven and Tommy; Jennifer, Sam, Theresa, Hannah, Rebecca and Ben; Alba, Matthew, Sarah and Katherine; Helen, Luther, Vernon and Deloris; Mark, Wendy, Skipper and Kyle; Victor, Cindy, Gayle and Ernie.

And I saw that it was enough. Like my grandparents' marriage, the obituary stubbornly refused to yield up any public meaning. To a stranger, it would be as smooth and opaque as a marble tombstone. To those of us who loved my grandfather, it told not one story but many. The stories were among us; they were in us; they *were* us.

FIVE ~ Grease Monkey

Ten minutes before we were due to land in Dutch Harbor, unseen currents unsettled the sky. The jet lurched like a steel coffin hefted by rummy pallbearers. As it punched through low-lying clouds, snow battered my window. I looked down: Bering Sea whitecaps lunged at the belly. I looked out: granite loomed off the left wing tip. *I believe in one God, Father Almighty, Maker of Heaven and Earth, and in His Son, Jesus Christ* . . . The jet struck the runway with its brakes fully engaged, what's known as a short-field landing. The skin on my face crawled toward my ears. Earlier, friends had described this rocky, storm-swept Aleutian island as unforgiving, but I hadn't believed them until now. Even Unalaska's runway is carved out of stone.

"Rough ride?" my father asked, after I found him pacing in the terminal. We hugged awkwardly. I'd worked for Brice Incorporated during breaks from college—buying parts, stake hopping, occasionally spelling a sick truck driver. Messing around on jobs, I'd learned to drive everything from a dump truck to a D-6, but I wasn't cut out for the construction business, and Dad knew it. Even so, a few weeks earlier, over Scrabble with my parents, I'd started crying and couldn't stop. My mother jostled the board as she rose for Kleenex. My father focused on lighting his pipe. Naked displays of emotion, especially from women, unnerved him. *I'm so unhappy,* I said, or something like that. *I need to change my life.* My father said he was looking for a truck driver at Dutch Harbor. The pay was good, and I'd be home in three months. At the time, it seemed simple to say yes. A few weeks later, as my father and I gobbled hamburgers and fries at the Unalaska airport restaurant, I thought it might have been simpler to say no.

Minutes later, we were jouncing over potholes in the company's ancient Land Cruiser. I was wishing for the thousandth time I were someone I'm not: a girl who grew up tough, maybe in a trailer court, with a key on a soiled shoelace around her neck. Straight brown hair, runny nose, Keds scuffed from playing tag on the asphalt with the wild boys. Wiry, tough, confident, street-smart. Nobody's baby. The kind of girl whose life had never been proscribed by *can't.*

I grew up in a comfortable, chaotic, six-bedroom house. There were two kinds of power in the house, masculine and feminine. My brothers took out the garbage and chopped kindling. My sisters and I emptied the dishwasher and dusted. On school nights, my mother did up my hair in pink foam rollers and Dippity-Do. French lessons, ballet lessons, sewing lessons, violin lessons, and piano lessons turned me into the prissiest thing you ever saw. I didn't even *own* a pair of blue jeans until I was in high school. At Dutch Harbor, behind the wheel of a truck, I'd be a fraud; worse, everyone would know it.

That Halloween morning, I saw my worry reflected in my father's face, in the way he kept repeating that I *had* to be on the job by seven in the morning. This was no princess-to-pauper switch. I was trading an $11-an-hour job as a newspaper reporter for an $18-an-hour one as a truck driver. With overtime, I'd bankroll enough to travel in Central America for six months.

The third island in the Aleutian Chain off the southwest coast of Alaska, Unalaska is bordered on the west by the Bering Sea, on the east by the Pacific Ocean. There are no roads or bridges from the mainland; the only way to get there is to grope your way by air or by sea.

In the late 1980s, Japanese investors poured millions of dollars into Unalaska's bottom-fish industry, and Dutch Harbor expanded into the second-largest U.S. exporter of fish products (read "surimi" or "krab"). When waterfront property for processing plants and warehouses grew scarce, investors threw money at the problem. Dad's company won a contract to dynamite a mountain and dump the rock into the ocean, thereby creating multimillion-dollar real estate out of the rubble.

It's a nice metaphor for what I was up to on the island: making a new self from the rubble of the old. Following my father from Fairbanks to Unalaska meant trading rolling hills for roiling sea, distant mountain ranges for the silhouettes of bonsai spruce. A woman who has always been most at ease in the company of other women, I'd be surrounded on Unalaska by men—truck drivers, fishermen, pile drivers, welders, carpenters, surveyors, my brother Sam, my father, an uncle or two, and the men who'd worked for Brice Incorporated since I was a girl. Their evening telephone calls used to interrupt family Parcheesi games with problems that furrowed Dad's brow and tensed his jaw. The men were the ones my father was with for the weeks and months when he wasn't with us, his family. The practical reasons for my being in Dutch Harbor were easy to articulate, the emotional ones harder, but I sensed they had something to do with the one-sided phone calls during which my father listened a lot and said little, with the mystery of where he went whenever he went away. I was curious about the unknown and, heretofore, unknowable language that men speak among themselves.

At 6:45 the next morning, I left the trailer I was sharing with my father, my brother, and two other men. I carried a thermos of coffee, an apple, and a copy of John Nichols's *Milagro Beanfield War.* I knew from experience that truck driving involved long stretches of waiting—to load or unload—punctuated by short spurts of driving and dumping. That first morning, darkness disguised the terrain, making it tough to tell what was underfoot, frozen mud or a membrane of ice over two feet of water—enough to top my steel-toed Extra Tuffs. Together, the four of us picked our way down Dutch Harbor's pockmarked main street, past a dun-colored two-story hotel, a liquor store, a hydraulics shop, the Peking Restaurant (a neon sign promised Chinese, Japanese, and Korean), a diesel-engine and machine shop, and Luciano's Pizzeria.

By seven, I was scaling the five-and-a-half-foot-high tires and hoisting myself into the cab of a DJB. Named for its British inventor, David John Browne, a DJB is basically an articulated, oscillating, self-leveling, off-road dump truck. It's tennis-ball yellow, and it weighs fifty tons fully loaded. The emergency brake hisses when released. I shoved the truck into first gear and maneuvered it under the loader's shovel. I was out of practice. After watching me wriggle this way and that, trying to mate the truck's bed to the loader's tires, Paul, the loader operator, smiled thinly under his black mustache and raised one hand. *Stop, just stop.* Then he twirled the loader—a ten-ton, lime-green Fred Astaire—swinging it around and dumping rocks into the bed of the DJB. My molars felt the sound of boulders striking steel.

I pulled away, shifting from first to second. The truck carved a wake in mud the texture of chocolate mousse. After negotiating Dutch Harbor's lone stop sign, I shifted into third. At thirty miles an hour, top speed for a DJB, the truck has the momentum of a freight train. Its steering system operates on hydraulics, which means you must press down on the gas pedal in order to steer. Swerving and braking simultaneously in order to avoid running over a small object in the road—a car or, God forbid, a child—is outside the DJB's operating parameters.

I chugged along on that first pitch-dark morning, and on every pitch-dark morning that followed, from wherever we were loading to wherever we were dumping. There, I backed the truck down a steep ramp to the water's edge. When wavelets lapped at the rear wheels, I stood on the squealing brakes, lifted the dump lever, and threw the transmission into first, playing gas and brake pedals like a church organist. With the fully loaded DJB's weight concentrated in the rear and its bed raised, the brakes alone can't keep it from rolling into the North Pacific: the trick is to apply just enough gas to keep the truck from rolling backward or forward. Within a yard or two of shore, the ocean shelf drops a couple of hundred feet. A few days earlier, a pile driver had slipped off his post. The ocean gulped.

Some dumps were trickier than others. Tricky ones are known as "technical" dumps. For those, Dad often materialized out of the fog to guide me. In my side mirror, I saw him, hatless and gloveless in his green Filson coat. Other men hunched their shoulders into the wind; Dad seemed impervious to it. Every morning, he left the trailer with a pair of yellow work gloves. Within fifteen minutes, they were usually gone, dropped on the ground when he stopped to light his pipe, or left behind in an engineer's trailer. He was forever working bare-handed in the twenty-below wind chill. One morning, the gloves went missing even before we left the trailer. On the way out, I opened the fridge to grab a Coke and saw them on the top shelf, next to the milk.

"Always drive with the window open, no matter how cold it is," my father had told me on the first day. "That way you can get out if you have to." *If you have to* meant *if the truck rolls in the water.*

He continued: "If anything happens, the most important thing is to save yourself." Then he grinned. "If you were to hit the 'kill' switch on your way out, I'd appreciate it."

A week or so into the job, Dad guided me onto a pile of dirt so high that the right side of the DJB reared up at an alarming angle. He made a fist, indicating I should stop there. Then he pointed up. *Here? I'm supposed to dump* here? With some trepidation, I yanked the dump lever. There was an ominous creak, like the groan of an old house confronting the wrecking ball. Now Dad was pointing down, emphatically. I hesitated, yesterday's instructions running through my head: "*Never, ever* lower a loaded bed." I lifted my shoulders, an unspoken query. In that split second, gravity took over. The creaking crescendoed. Dad stumbled backward. A moment later, the fifty-ton bed flopped over with an earth-shaking, windshield-shattering crash.

When he opened the door and saw my face, Dad laughed. Rivulets of spilled coffee made streaks through the dirt.

"Are you hurt, Pumpkin?"

I shook my head. Something else was making rivulets through the dirt now.

"Hey, it's OK. There's no harm done. These things happen on a job."

Right, I thought. *I bet they don't happen to my brother.*

All of my life, my feelings toward my father have been tangled up in my desire for his affection. Temper tantrums, straight As, broken curfews, and piano recitals elicited a range of responses from awkward shoulder pats to benign tolerance. Leafing through an album once, I came across the note my father wrote to my mother in the hospital after Sam was born. I was barely old enough to walk then. It says, "Thank you for giving me the only thing our perfect marriage lacked." A son. Maybe the real reason I was in Dutch Harbor was to try to extend the range, to hit a new and unfamilial note. On the job and off, my father treated Sam like a colleague, me like a pumpkin.

We worked six ten-hour days plus one morning every week. Hiking Mount Pyramid one Sunday afternoon with my brother Sam and with Craig, the man I would marry the following summer—although I didn't know it then—the first thing I felt was silence. Gone were the clanging pile drivers, shouting foremen, beeping bulldozers. Climbing, we heard only the sound of our own heavy breathing and our boots scrabbling on the loose shale. At the top, we inhaled deeply of sun-soaked rocks and dry-as-flint moss. From the peak of Unalaska's highest mountain, we could just make out the smoky outline of the distant island of Akutan.

Like everything else on Unalaska, Mount Pyramid is not the untouched wilderness it appears to be. The local newspaper had run an article recently detailing how two teenage boys found a box of unexploded grenades near the foot the mountain. Bunkers, cannon mounts, lookouts, underground tunnels, and tumbledown buildings are everywhere on Unalaska, once you know where—or how—to look for them. What I first mistook for rocks and seaweed strewn along Unalaska's beaches turned out, on closer inspection, to be rusted strips of rebar encased in cement blocks. For fifteen months from 1942 to 1943, Japan and the United States waged a brutal campaign for control of the thousand-mile territory from Unalaska to the island of Attu, at the tip of the Aleutian chain. Some 10,000 soldiers, many of them native Aleuts, died in what has been described as "the forgotten war." Stan Cohen even wrote a book by that title.

Nearly fifty years later, in 1989, another war was ending. Every morning, in the chill of early dawn, we buttoned a second layer of woolen shirts and gulped gullet-warming coffee while we watched CNN footage of East Germans and West Germans chipping away at the Berlin Wall. Within months, they would all be simply Germans. We felt the thaw in foreign relations even on that tiny island. Every day, shifts of thirty or forty Soviet (not yet Russian) fisherman were disgorged from the pod-like orange lifeboats that shuttled them between their gargantuan fishing vessels and shore. Clad in fur hats and olive drab parkas, the fishermen marched into Dutch Harbor in groups of twos and threes, looking for the world like a ragtag navy on shore leave.

They stopped first at the Alaska Commercial Company store, a two-story brown clapboard structure descended directly from the nineteenth-century dry-goods dealers of the American Plains. Inside, the fishermen gazed on the goods with starving eyes. The ones with money in their pockets—perhaps from selling a fur hat on the way into town—bought up batteries, nail polish, electric mixers, bananas. I was too shy to approach them, even though they waved and whistled when I passed them in my DJB. One of the construction guys bought a beaver hat from a fisherman who told him they believed the ACC store was stocked specially for their visits—that, ordinarily, its shelves sat as empty as theirs in Vladivostok.

I swept, mopped, and scrubbed our living quarters once a week. Even so, it smelled like the inside of a dirty sock. The four of us went through laundry detergent at the rate of a thirty-pound box every two weeks. On morning TV, the CNN anchors with their crisp suits and lacquered hair began to look more foreign than the Soviet fishermen in their mink or beaver hats. I bathed every evening, but stubborn half-moons of dirt still crusted under my fingernails. At night my bed sheets rattled with grit. I was earning close to $4,000 a month and living in something like squalor.

We ate lunch and dinner every day in a shipboard cafeteria. After lunch one day, I was stacking my dishes when a woman about my age strode up to me. I'd seen her around. She was stocky in her navy-blue snowmachine suit, ruddy-cheeked like women who train horses or raise sheep for a living.

"So, do you get harassed a lot?"

I thought about this. The Unalaska volleyball league required every team to carry at least one woman on its roster. Unless repeated requests to play volleyball counted as harassment, the answer was no.

"Not really. I'm bigger than most of the guys around here." It was a weak joke. I meant that, in my truck, I was bigger.

"So am I." She wasn't joking.

At the end of every workday, I gassed, greased, and oiled the DJB, pampering it like a beautician fluttering over a prized client. Weary and stiff from ten or even twelve hours of driving, I unrolled ice-stiffened hoses one at time from the service truck, dragged them over to the DJB, climbed onto the narrow steel lip alongside the engine, then filled the gas and antifreeze tanks. To reach the anti-freeze valve, I had to curl my toes over the top of a slippery headlamp. The first time I tried this, I opened the valve too quickly and a sickly sweet green geyser erupted in my face.

On a middling day—muddy, rainy, a miserly few degrees above freezing—greasing the DJB's joints was about as unappetizing job as can be imagined. There are twenty-four joints total, some directly beneath the truck, others tucked deep within its bowels. I slithered under the truck on my belly then rolled over onto my back in the mud, squirting the grease gun straight up. At first I approached greasing the way I do cooking: if a pinch is good, then a cupful must be better. I learned this: moderation in all things, and always grease with your mouth shut.

Paul, the loader operator, had fought with the Green Berets in Vietnam, and he was no shirker when it came to bellying up to a grease pan. Yet his tan overalls were as spotless at seven every evening as they had been at seven in the morning. I, on the other hand, dragged myself into the trailer every evening looking and smelling like a junior-high science project gone awry.

Once a week, I checked the truck's oil. This is not a technically demanding task, but I wasn't strong enough to hold up the cowling while simultaneously sliding the support pole into its slot. So I jerry-rigged it. One evening, the pole slipped, and the ninety-pound cowling crashed down on my head. Lunch washed into my throat. I came to a couple of seconds later, feeling as though someone had soldered a steel band around my head. Back at the trailer later, when I guided Dad's hand to the goose egg, he chuckled and treated me like an eight-year-old who'd just fallen off her bicycle. But then, what did I expect? A kiss to take away the hurt?

Once I got the hang of it, truck driving was mainly a matter of putting up with boredom: long hours of tedium punctuated by occasional moments of terror. We drivers regarded the weather as a potential complication—inconvenient or uncomfortable, especially when snow blew horizontally through the cab, or when wind threatened to yank the door out of our hands, and us with it—but essentially harmless. By mid-afternoon on a typical day, the sky was clad like a court jester: to the west, a whitewashed sky and ducks scudding along the glassy surface of the water; to the east, sky and sea merged into something monolithic and awful, the color of factory smoke. A month rarely passes without a word of a sinking somewhere off the Aleutians or Kodiak Island. Sudden gales blow up, catching ships off guard that are bulging with king-crab pots. Rime ice coats the mesh pots, doubling or tripling their weight. Too quickly for an SOS, the top-heavy vessels groan and roll over on their sides.

Typically, ships anchored off Dutch Harbor for two or three days to unload their catch and resupply before going back to sea for several weeks, even months. Crewmembers spent their leave anesthetizing themselves against the hard work, danger, and boredom of fishing in the North Pacific. The Elbow Room was a nondescript plywood building roughly the size of a doublewide trailer that hunched in the shadow of Unalaska's onion-domed Russian Orthodox Church. Inside, it had the bare essentials: a stage, a dance floor, and a few booths. The floor was linoleum. Serious customers drank at the bar, standing up. According to a quote in the *Seattle Post-Intelligencer*, the bar pulled in about $1 million a night during its heyday, an era when the likes of Jimmy Buffett performed there. *Playboy* magazine once named it the second-most dangerous bar on the planet. I was dying to go.

We'd been there for only a few minutes on a Friday night when a husky fisherman, dazed-drunk, stepped onto the dance floor. As he swayed to the canned rock'n'roll, a dreamy expression washed over his face. He unzipped his pants and started dancing *with* himself. (Two facts ruled Dutch Harbor's nightlife: (1) alcohol was in abundant supply; (2) women were not. One night, one of the men on our crew returned to his trailer after a night of drinking. There, he positioned himself over his roommate's bed as if he were standing over the toilet. The sound of the zipper woke up the roommate, who rolled out of the way just in time.) The bouncer, a wiry woman in her thirties wearing more blue eye shadow than I'd seen anyone wear since 1975, wrapped an arm around the guy's shoulder and eased him into a booth.

"Hey, bitch, keep your hands off my friend!"

The bouncer shot the guy a look. A few minutes later, the same guy pitched a glass of beer at a waitress. That time, the bouncer grabbed him by his waistband, hauled him out of the booth, and began dragging him backward toward the door.

"Out! Out! You're out of here!"

He twisted like a salmon on the line and grabbed a hank of the waitress's hair.

"Fucking bitch! Don't tell me what to do!"

"Out! Out!"

The bartender flipped the light switch and strangled the music. He didn't help the bouncer, but he didn't serve any more drinks either. The men at the bar motioned threateningly toward the drunk. He experienced a moment of clarity, rose sheepishly to his feet, and slipped out.

The woman sighed dramatically, leaning her 140 pounds or so against the door. It hiccupped once, then twice. The drunk was back. He pried open the door just enough to inject an arm and swing at her. That was it. Roaring like a herd of angry sea lions, thirty fishermen charged the door.

When it was over, the bouncer plopped down on a stool and muttered to the only female customer in the joint, "I love my job. I love my job. I love my job."

The storms blew themselves out quickly. Afterward, the weather turned as benign as a trio of seal pups playing hide-and-seek in the wavelets along shore. From their perches atop light posts, bald eagles spread their wings to dry as they appraised the salmon in the stream below.

My father flew home a couple of days after Thanksgiving to work on bids. His younger brother, my uncle Andy, replaced him. Andy's goal was to wrap up the job by Christmas. As November turned to December, though, the weather worsened. Every morning, the roads shone like mirrors. "Hogs on wheels," the boys called the Kenworth tractor-trailers. A heavy-equipment dealer in Fairbanks shipped out tire chains, but they were the wrong size. It would be days before new ones arrived.

One of our usual routes was a three-mile stretch between a rock pit at one end of the island and the community of Captain's Bay. In places, the one-lane road slunk around the contoured faces of cliffs, climbing as high as two hundred feet above the ocean. I was making my second run of the day. At the turnoff to Captain's Bay, I pulled over to let a car pass, a courtesy that costs me momentum at the foot of a short but steep hill. Standing on the gas, I stormed it. A third of the way up, I downshifted from third into second. I gained fifty feet then shifted into first. Twenty feet shy of the top, the truck faltered. There wasn't enough juice in the brakes to hold it. The next thing I knew, I was sliding backward, *fast.* The transmission was screaming, the steering was shot. The possibilities of my life funneled down to three, four at most. I might plummet into the ocean, a hundred feet below on the right. (That would have been the quickest.) I might crash through the trailer park on my left. (Survivable, but expensive.) I might get lucky and slide straight to the bottom of the hill. In that case, anyone traveling behind me would be very unlucky. My right hand clawed at the door handle. "That's pointless," I thought. Then, "This is not how I thought it would end."

The DJB slid straight back to the bottom of the hill, crushing no one. When it stopped, I shoved the now-whimpering transmission into reverse, backed into the nearest driveway, and dismounted. On legs gone rubbery as hoses, I struck out for Dutch Harbor. The guys would tease me at lunch, but I didn't care. I heard a door slam somewhere. Yapping. A marshmallow-colored poodle was pistoning down the driveway toward the DJB. The poodle was so small it would have fit between my tire treads. But what is luck to a poodle? It sniffed a tire, lifted its leg, and peed. Then, head held high, without a backward glance for the slain monster, it marched home.

Minutes later, the Land Cruiser pulled alongside me, Andy at the wheel. The truck had been in my family for nearly as long as I had. It had belonged to my uncle Sam and his wife, Nancy, when their kids were little; now the kids were in college, and Nancy and Sam were divorced. The Land Cruiser's brakes worked every third day, and its horn honked whenever the wheels turned left. At this moment, though, its battered green-and-white exterior seemed so absurdly comforting that I nearly cried.

"You can put me on the next plane to Fairbanks if you like," I told Andy, "but I'm not getting back in that truck until the road is graveled."

"OK." Andy sighed. "Let's go find out what schedule the city's on. If they're not going to gravel the roads this morning, I'll drive for you."

As I get older, I get better at reading between the lines. I don't always like what's written there. What Andy meant—what anyone in his position would have meant—is, "If you were a better driver, this wouldn't have happened. If you were a man, you'd have the nerve to get back in the truck. If you were your brother . . ."

An insulating silence falls over the island on wintry mornings. Andy and I were in a huff with each other and therefore not speaking, so the rhythmic *swish-swish* of the windshield wipers and the wheezing of the Land Cruiser were the only sounds. We crossed the bridge that separates the villages of Dutch

Harbor and Unalaska. Suddenly, sirens startled the silence. A police jeep and ambulance rode up on our tail. Andy pulled over. They careered past us, topped the hill then skidded into a left turn toward Captain's Bay. Wordlessly, Andy turned the Land Cruiser around and followed them. My heart thudded louder than the windshield wipers.

Just fourteen months apart, Sam and I have always been unusually close, like Irish twins. When I was nine or ten, I told my mother about a recurring dream in which he died. "People tend to dream about things they dread—or want—the most," she replied.

As children, Sam and I played together in the sandbox with Tonka trucks and brown plastic construction men. The men's yellow hard hats unscrewed. Before becoming playthings, they'd held the iron supplements that Sammy, who was anemic, took every day. Even though I was physically stronger, at least until high school, I did not grow up in a society or a family that had the same expectations for girls as for boys. I was probably preparing for a ballet or piano recital on the evening when a trooper pulled Sam over for a broken taillight, checked his license, and fined him for driving a Kenworth tractor-trailer underage. He was fourteen. After graduating from Oregon State University with a degree in construction management, he slipped seamlessly into a job at Brice Incorporated.

Before Dutch Harbor, Sam spent his days collecting quotes from subcontractors or crunching numbers on the computer. Then, in the mid-eighties, Alaska's fuel-driven economy collapsed. Oil prices plummeted by two-thirds, and state-funded capital projects—roads, runways, and boat harbors—dried up. Dad watched his competitors put their equipment on the block and move to California. Week after week, he worried about meeting the office payroll. He smoked a pack of pipe tobacco a day, paced a path in his office rug, nursed an ulcer. Sam, who'd married his college sweetheart, quietly inquired about jobs in the Pacific Northwest.

The company had hardly anything left to lose when it won the Dutch Harbor job. The contract was huge: 350,000 cubic yards of rock—roughly 15,000 truckloads—to be moved within six months. My brother cleaned out his desk and put a dust cover over his computer. Then he flew to the Aleutians to do the kind of work he hadn't done since college. He drove a truck, every day. No complaints.

As Andy sped toward Captain's Bay, passing the driveway where I'd parked the DJB, I rocked back and forth in the passenger seat, keening to myself. It is what I do when I am very, very scared. At least a hundred men worked at Captain's Bay: pile drivers, operators, surveyors, engineers, fishermen. In weather like this, something could have happened to any one of them. Then we rounded a bend and saw the Kenworth in the bay. Boulders were scattered down the fifty-foot embankment. The tractor lay at an unnatural angle to the trailer, like a dislocated bone, and the crushed fiberglass cab was partially submerged. The exhaust pipe belched steam and bubbles.

Andy swerved to the side of the road and stopped. Before either of us could get out, a policeman strode over. He stuck his head through my open window.

"Was it you?" he asked, concern written on his face. I had this reputation.

I shook my head, no. Then where was the driver? Before he could ask anything else, a pickup pulled alongside. Gray-faced under his freckles, Sam unfolded himself from the passenger seat. It turned out that, after the wreck, he'd scrambled up the hill and hitched a ride into Captain's Bay to telephone Andy. Andy, of course, wasn't in the office. A passerby had seen the truck and called 911. The policeman gently took Sam's arm and led him away from the growing crowd. First he wanted to know if Sam was OK (he was), then he wanted to know what happened. Apparently, the rear wheels had locked up on an icy patch then skidded off the embankment, dragging the rest of the Kenworth along. From the looks of it, the truck rolled over two or three times before sliding into the water. Sam didn't remember. He must have been unconscious for a few seconds, even a full minute. He didn't remember turning off the engine, but he did.

On the drive back to Dutch Harbor, it was just me and Sam in the Land Cruiser. I drove. We'd left Andy talking to a knot of policemen, medics, and gawkers. He'd wonder eventually where his wheels had gone, but I didn't care. Sam said very little. I said a lot. *Dad would never have let us drive on a morning like this. Andy is in such a goddamned hurry to finish this job and get home in time for Christmas, he doesn't care if he kills us.* I was being totally unfair—Andy was, if anything, more cautious than my father—and I knew it, but my coiled-up fear was opening out into rage, and rage always needs an object.

Sam wasn't angry at anyone but himself. When we got to the office, he gently asked me to go. He wanted to call his wife. Then he wanted to call Dad. I knew what Dad would say: *As long as you're not hurt, nothing else matters. The truck can be fixed.* It was exactly what he'd said to me after my accident. In their conversation, neither he nor my brother would second-guess Andy's decision to send out the trucks that morning. They'd never break the unwritten code that even I, a mere girl, knew by heart: never complain, never cast blame. I drove back to the site as slowly as possible. If I'd hoped the crowd would be gone, I was disappointed. If anything, it was bigger. Andy stood at the center, as animated as I'd seen him. The men were following a script as ancient as Greek drama. Everyone had a camera and an opinion. The hero of the moment was the guy who'd given Sam a ride into Captain's Bay.

"Yeah, he's fine. A little bruised is all. Sonofabitch dumped a load in his pants, though."

It's a truism in travel literature that people change while places stay the same. Don't believe it. The landscape of my life constricted during the months I spent on Unalaska, months when the island's mass grew like a tumor, proliferating in ways that nature never intended. In a sense, I felt as foreign there as the Soviet fisherman climbing aboard their orange lifeboats in brand-new Levis and Reeboks. When I left my job as a reporter in the city to work as a truck driver in the Aleutians, I thought changing my lifestyle would change my life. Instead, the ill-fitting job only clarified for me—in the negative, if nothing else—who I am and where I belong. Looking back from the vantage point of nearly two decades, I see that my relationship with my father remains essentially the same. Perhaps a bit closer as we've aged, but essentially the same. I see something else—how my craving for his affection, even his admiration, is a necessary and valuable tension in my life. Perhaps the truer thing is this: we humans must travel to exotic ports in order to recognize home, and our real selves, when we return.

SIX ~ My Mother's Body

Winter solstice. Festive and frail as a Chinese lantern, the sun hung on the horizon where it seemed to refract rather than radiate heat. Outside my parents' guest bedroom, where I was dressing for my sister's wedding, ice fog wisped around the frost-filigreed branches of birch trees. Glittering snow carapaced the ground. The window was a mirror into which I leaned, struggling with the old-fashioned clasp on my pearl necklace. In the lamplight, I saw my reflection—a slender, dark-haired woman in green velvet—and next to me that of my sister-in-law, pink-cheeked from exertion. Impatiently, she tugged the lace bertha of the bridesmaid's dress up over her shoulders and stepped back, cradling her belly in both hands. "I was crazy to say I'd be in this wedding," she said. "I look obscene." Her first child, Julia, would be born in just a few weeks. I told her she was beautiful and meant it, but she shrugged disbelievingly. Then I turned sideways to the window and slid my hands over my collarbones, breasts, stomach, hips. Then up. At the center of my body, I probed for something smaller than the mole above my right breast, something more mysterious than the black spots on the sun. I've never been good at secrets. "Can you see my baby yet?"

Hannah was married by candlelight at Saint Matthew's Church, where my husband and I had made our vows eighteen months earlier. It had been June then, summer solstice, the church doors flung open to the watery sunlight. My family goes in for pageantry, so there was plenty of it then as now: Baskets of roses and peonies spilling down the stairs to the nave. Bridesmaids in pastel organza with dyed-to-match pumps. Purcell's trumpet voluntary. The Episcopal bishop of Hawaii, a family friend, flown in to perform the ceremony.

On the night of Hannah's wedding, though, the earth was pitching away from the sun. Afterward, guests shrugged into furs and parkas against the thirty-five-below night. While the church emptied, a photographer shaped my family into a V headed by helenka, the matriarch, in her sequined evening gown and fluffy bedroom slippers. The slippers caught me unawares. They reminded me that everything living is dying: this was likely to be Grandma's last wedding.

When my grandfather died in 1987, he left her in possession of eighty acres and a farm as well as a substantial share of the family construction business. Grandma hired a landscaper to fill in the swimming pool—a failed experiment—with soil, and she planted a rose garden there with as many bushes as grandchildren. Hardly anyone grows roses in Fairbanks, 150 miles south of the Arctic Circle, but Grandma fertilized her rose bushes with backbone. They bloomed only for her. Whenever one of her children or grandchildren fell ill, she sent a sterling silver or crystal bowl of fragrant roses instead of chicken soup. In the winter when her bushes slept, their colors tumbled off her tongue, incantatory as the descendants of Abraham: Sunflare, Summer Fashion, Summer Sunshine, Allspice, American Pride, Touch of Class, Tropicana, Mr. Lincoln, Legend, Prince Charles, Fountain Square, White Lightning, Double Delight, Sheer Bliss, and Peace. "Jennifer's color is American Beauty," she declared once. Deeper than pink but softer than red, I saw that color in the northern lights that stained the sky on my sister's wedding night.

At the reception in a faux gold rush saloon, surrounded by her children and grandchildren, helenka perched like a plump chickadee. I whispered the news in her ear. She had a knack for planting familiar words in unfamiliar gardens, so I wasn't surprised when she said, serenely, "I loved making my babies."

 The way she used *make* emphasized the *-creation* in *procreation*, as though a baby were a bowl crafted from clay on a pottery wheel and glazed for strength and beauty, or a seed pressed into the womb of the earth and nourished with food and water until it was strong enough to bend in the wind. I've never been good with my hands, never thrown a pot, never painted a still life with fruit, never even grown a Mother's Day geranium from a seed thumbed into a Styrofoam cup. But my body was making a baby.

Vernal equinox. The myth of Demeter and Persephone lay at the heart of the Eleusinian Mysteries, the secret rites that Grecian women celebrated for more than two thousand years. The myth describes the seasonal cycle—death and renewal, rending and healing, loss and joy—that flows from rifts and reparations in mother-daughter relations. In *Our Mothers/Our Selves*, Nancy Friday writes that every household reverberates with the voices of three women: mother, daughter, and grandmother. My mother's voice was reverent when she unveiled the mysteries of cycles, Kotex, and garter belts for me, her firstborn. Everything was in place, waiting in a bathroom drawer for the special moment when I would shed the chrysalis of childhood. I was hundreds of miles from home, in an airport restroom, when I saw blood in the toilet. I was traveling with my grandmother. We were running late for our next flight. "Do you need anything?" she asked when I told her. *Yes, everything.* She marched into a gift shop and bought a box of OB tampons the size and shape of bullets.

The year of my first pregnancy, spring came late. Torn between mother and lover, Persephone tarried in the Underworld. Jealous Demeter stirred up blizzards in May. My grandmother flew to the Mayo Clinic for gallbladder surgery. While she was away, no one else could coax her roses, dull green sticks brandishing thorns, into bloom. No one wanted to. The surgery went badly. Melting snow and mud puddles painted everything in drab grays and dingy browns on the morning of the funeral. I wore pearls for the first time since my sister's wedding. Also my first maternity dress. The week before, in the electromagnetic imaging lab at the hospital, I'd watched my healthy baby girl somersault in her swimming pool of amniotic fluid. Now the family gathered, seventy strong, to spread Grandma's ashes over the farm and to recite the Prayers for the Dead: *In the midst of life we are in death.*

Afterward, my mother and her sisters-in-law passed around coffee and croissants. The rest of us milled about on the lawn, avoiding each other's eyes, saying as little as possible. What is the purpose of any ritual, whether social or religious, if not restraint? I wanted to writhe on the wet grass and gouge the soil. I want to howl like an animal. Instead, I sipped decaf coffee from a Limoges cup and repeated for one of my aunts the deathless joke that, yes, my baby was due on Labor Day. On that day, my daughter's cells multiplied by the million; my grandmother's ashes fertilized her rose bushes. In *The Lives of a Cell,* Lewis Thomas writes: "Everything that comes alive seems to be in trade for something that dies, cell for cell. There might be some comfort in . . . synchrony." It may be that there's some comfort in synchrony, but it wasn't much. Not then, anyway.

Evenings when I was growing up, I'd nudge open the bathroom door then roost on the edge of my mother's tub, soaking my feet in the steaming, scented water. "Tell me all about your day," Mom would say. As we talked, I studied surreptitiously the landscape of her body. Blue-black varicose veins, like tangled rivers and their tributaries, roped their way up to the sparse triangle between her legs. Scarlet moles punctuated a stomach puckered and seamed by surgeries, including the hysterectomy that had proscribed her motherhood. One side of her belly was firm as a ripe pomegranate; the other, collapsed in folds of flab and scar tissue. Illness and childbirth had damaged her body in ways that I, with the vanity of youth, had sworn they'd never touch me.

Pregnant, I found myself back on the edge of my mother's bathtub where I studied a landscape of possibility while we designed flower gardens in our heads. "You know the gravel pit off Peger Road?" she asked. "I saw wild iris growing there last week." I thought such garden talk was code: "Plant perennials instead of annuals so you won't have to work so hard next summer, with the baby." The only roses in my mother's garden are portulaca, moss roses, whose silver-dollar-size blooms poke through the sandy soil of her wildflower garden. From Memorial Day until Labor Day, Mom lets spiders spin webs in her basement and dust bunnies confer under the beds. Wearing a one-piece, navy blue terry-cloth sun suit, she kneels outside in the dirt from eight in the morning until seven at night, or even later, digging troughs in the topsoil, planting seeds one at a time, sprinkling mounds with fertilized rainwater. She weeds a little every day then coaxes more blooms by snipping off deadheads. By mid-July, the plants are often so profuse that my mother disappears inside them, a living *I Spy* conundrum: find the mom in the field of mums. Fiddlehead ferns, delphinium, tiger lilies, snapdragons, geraniums, daisies, begonias, pansies, lobelia, Johnny-jump-ups, creeping Jenny, forget-me-nots, lettuce, tomatoes, peas, carrots, radishes, squash, and pumpkins: my mother's garden is a hymn to the regenerative power of earth, a drunken orgy under the midnight sun.

Summer solstice. The summer after I was married, 1991, my mother flew to Anchorage for what was expected to be routine gallbladder surgery. Afterward, she nearly died from complications. Her garden withered while she lay in a hospital bed on life-support machines. Watching my mother weaken and realizing she might die kindled a deep fear in me. I was working in Fairbanks from Monday through Friday and flying to Anchorage on the weekends; for the first time in my life, I thought I might die in a plane crash. Strangely, I felt safe on takeoff and landing; what I dreaded were elements beyond human control—turbulence, wind shear, electrical storms—that might tear the jet apart in midair. On landing, I left the pressurized cabin of the jet for the silent, gray, temperature-controlled corridors of Humana Hospital. The tinted windows in my mother's room watered down harsh sunlight and drained the landscape of color until it looked like an old-fashioned sepia-toned print. Every day, Mom shrunk farther into a chaos of plastic cords. I knew it was the natural order of things for my mother to die before me. But not in her fifties. Not before she'd taught me how to be a mother, too. Not until I'd come to terms with my own mortality. My mother's near-death taught me that my strongest sense of myself comes not from my friends or lovers or sisters or grandmother but from my mother. She is my road map. Without her, I'd be completely lost.

By the following summer, Mom was nearly her old self. Working in her garden, squeezing dirt between her fingers, she grew stronger daily. I lacked the patience to let things grow. I over-fertilized in a fit of solicitousness, or I forgot to weed in a loam of laziness. Even so, that summer of my pregnancy, I craved the physicality of gardening. Sometimes in the morning, Mom and I went to visit local greenhouses. She discouraged me from temperamental species; I yearned toward hothouse roses. Every afternoon I lugged baskets onto my own back porch, filled them with dirt, dug shallow holes with a trowel or my fingers, popped the seedlings out of their six-packs, and set them in their new nests. Mosquitoes buzzed around my head. Hugely pregnant under a shapeless denim jumper, I trekked back and forth to the kitchen sink carrying jugs of water mixed with pink fish fertilizer. My front yard then was a typical Alaskan lawn, which is to say no lawn at all—just a few spindly spruce trees, willow bushes, a delphinium here and there, and a ground covering of ferns, wild roses and cranberry bushes. If I could not have long-stemmed roses, I wanted wildness. I strewed wildflower seeds everywhere. By midsummer, daisies overflowed a rusting wheelbarrow, impatiens sprung from the hollows of rotting stumps, and nasturtiums cascaded off the doghouse roof. Before, I had chafed at gardening because of the waste: all that money and energy spent on something that was going to die anyway. One afternoon, two friends—married to each other then but not anymore—stopped by on their bicycles and stayed to help me plant a lilac bush. A lilac bush: *that* was optimistic. Afterward, we rode together to an ice cream shop. There, on the deck, my friend Liz—a writer, whitewater rafting guide, and environmental activist—said to me, "How can you justify bringing a child into a world that's already so over-populated, where people are killing each other by the thousands, and there's famine and acid rain and holes in the ozone layer?"

I felt as if I'd just been punched in the stomach. A moment before, we'd been friends eating ice cream outdoors on a cloudless day. Then my friend—my childless friend—had turned on me. How dare she connect my pregnancy to the apocalyptic events in Third World countries?

"I guess," I answered slowly, "because I hope." It was a naïve and unsatisfactory answer, but I couldn't think of a better one. Not then, not now.

Lewis Thomas finds comfort, not despair, in the fact that everything living is also dying. Cultivating a garden that will surely die in September can be seen as an act of senseless futility or one of consummate hope. So can having a baby. It's also true that everything dying is also living.

On the Fourth of July, friends invited Craig and me to float the Chena with them. The river is a shallow, slow-moving artery that winds through town, binding enormous chateau-style houses to rectangular ranches with Rottweilers lunging against chain-link fences. Some guy on the radio said it was seventy-five degrees that day. A cooling breeze riffled birch leaves. We paddled the stretch of river downstream from the city's power plant, a stretch that never freezes, even at fifty below. Nearing the takeout, we rested paddles on our knees and floated, trading banter between canoes. The first bucket of river water that sloshed down my back caught me by surprise. I saw the second one coming and leaned heavily to the right. Quicker than regret, the canoe spilled me and Julie into the river. I made a panicky lunge for the gunnels, but my lifejacket rode up over my belly, hampering my arms. Paralyzed by cold and fear, I let myself go under. Then my friend Charles grabbed my lifejacket while Craig paddled the second canoe to shore.

Then we were back on the river, and the late-afternoon sun was drying my hair and my clothes. Julie and I were both laughing at me. "I must've looked like a harpooned whale," I said. "You were pretty funny. 'The baby, oh, the baby,'" she mugged. In that moment, I saw something of how motherhood was going to be. How it was going to carve me away from these friends and their harmless, childish pranks. Already, my unborn baby filled up space inside of me that once was wilderness untouched by anyone, least of all me. In the deepest possible sense, she was civilizing me. Hugh Brody, the anthropologist and author, has spoken of finding the center at the edge, in the most remote hut in the most remote village in the most remote region of the country farthest from home. I have found certain truths at the edge but, for me, the center is always at the center: in my family, in my flower boxes, in my womb. For the rest of that Fourth of July afternoon I let someone else paddle while I rode in the middle of the canoe with hands cupped protectively over the mound of my belly, as if to comfort the baby within.

When my due date was still six weeks off, I felt like the Venus of Willendorf whose squat, comically exaggerated form—all breasts, belly, and hips—had flashed on the screen of the darkened art history auditorium at Smith. Instead of walking or riding my bike, I drove the half-mile to my mother's house. She'd lay down her trowel and fix us sandwiches of turkey breast, garden lettuce, and tomatoes. Afterward, we'd work on Sunday's *New York Times* crossword puzzle. Deeply afraid of giving birth, I yearned for the only solace my mother could not—or would not—give. Casually, while she looked up a four-letter word for an African gazelle, I asked what labor had been like for her. She told me of water breaking in the middle of the night, evenly spaced contractions, the urge to push, a swaddled baby drowsing in her arms. She never used the word "pain." During one of our Lamaze classes, Craig and I had watched three films of women having babies: an "easy" labor, an "average" labor, and a "difficult" labor. My friend Katherine, who'd just given birth to Timothy, said it wasn't any worse than bad menstrual cramps. When I asked my friend Lucy, the one who cut my hair, she set down her scissors, spun my chair around, placed one hand on either side of my face, and said, in her Colombian accent, "Don't let anyone tell you having a baby doesn't hurt. There is no worse pain in the world." What does that feel like? My mother wouldn't answer the one question I was too scared to ask.

My mother knows. My garden grows. There is mystery as well as synchrony. Some comfort.

The first contraction tore through me just after midnight

on the last day of August. A bad menstrual cramp it was not. I'd made a pact with my doctor to try to get through it without drugs, but I instantly wanted something—a shot, a pill, a talisman—against the pain. A few hours later, my mother walked into my hospital room. She looked pale but crisp in a madras plaid jumpsuit, carrying a pile of books and newspapers against her chest. Armor against my wildness, her helplessness. For a while, she and I and Craig played rummy between contractions. Then she and Craig took turns walking the corridors with me, pushing the IV tree with its bag of sap-like fluid. Only water and electrolytes at this point, but the doctor was predicting a long labor; she wanted to be able to administer drugs quickly, if necessary. We stopped in front of the nursery windows. I gazed at the newborns sleeping in their pink and blue cocoons. Soon, soon. The nurse swabbed the inside of my cervix and studied the cells under a microscope. Had the amniotic sac broken, she would have seen ferns. "No ferns," she said.

My contractions were prolonged but irregular. After seven or eight hours, the doctor used a crochet hook–like instrument to puncture the bag of waters. It was the strangest sensation, like a warm flood inside the body. After that, the contractions came faster. Daylight waned outside the window. The nurse added pitocin to the IV line. Within minutes, my body traveled to a place inhabited by insatiable pain, a place where language will never go, a place where I was no longer someone's daughter and not yet someone's mother. The nurse grabbed hold of my hands. She was the mother of one of my childhood friends. "Mrs. Cooney" then, "Jacquie" now.

"Jennifer, listen to me. *Listen* to me. Open your eyes. Don't go inside the pain. You'll only make it worse."

What was she saying? This pain had no inside or outside. The plate tectonics of childbirth remolded the peaks and valleys of my body. My mother held my hand. Her bones felt as frail as a fledgling's skeleton. Breakable. I wanted to break something.

"I'm going to die," I whispered to my mother.

"No you're not," she said, matter-of-factly. "It just feels that way now."

For a baby, the violent, bruising passage through the birth

canal must feel like expulsion from paradise. Before, amniotic bliss; after, cold and hunger and hands. As the mother's pain ends, the daughter's begins.

Autumnal equinox. In Alaska, spring and fall are sometimes figments of the calendar's imagination. The birch trees had barely begun to shed their chattering leaves when the first snow fell in big, wet clumps. In a defiant blaze of color, the blossoms in my garden faced death, their stems and leaves collapsing around them like tattered seaweed. Turbulent postpartum depression runs in my family; still, it blindsided me. During the day, I studied for my graduate school exams. At night, grief for my grandmother, who would never name a rose for my daughter, was a subterranean place into which I burrowed. Among the Iñupiat of northern Alaska, babies traditionally receive the same name and the same respect due to a recently deceased elder. Kinzea slept in a basket at my feet as I read.

"Grandmother," I said quietly. Then, louder, "helenka." She stirred a bit and made a sucking sound.

I had left the hospital the day after she was born without seeing her naked. I was so tired, the nurses so smoothly efficient. A few days later, as she wriggled and cooed in the bathtub, I studied her body for the first time: the parallel lines beneath her lips, the pearls of dirt underneath her chin, the nearly invisible nipples, bracelets of fat at her wrists and ankles, a tulip-shaped birthmark on her left buttock, the arch of a tiny foot. Her fifth toes are shriveled like mine, with nails the size of carrot seeds.

Earlier that evening, I'd called my mother. "How do you bathe a baby?" She'd driven over to help me take off the tiny garments, heat the water to the perfect temperature. I decided to get in the tub, too. There was nowhere for my mother to sit except on the closed lid of the toilet. When I was naked, she handed Kinzea to me, and I cradled her between thighs gone flaccid from lack of exercise. My belly slid back and forth like Jell-O melting in the sun at a church picnic. Violet stretch marks formed a complex system spreading upward from the fork of my legs, where the baby's head rested. My breasts were blue-veined, heavy with milk. Looking down, I saw my mother's body, my grandmother's body, my great-grandmother's body. Flawed, but familiar. Living and dying at the same time. There is some comfort—even grace—in synchrony, in being the daughter of a mother and the mother of a daughter. I read somewhere that a child needs the care of someone for whom she is a miracle. Mother love, I think, is born of wonder at that miracle.

SEVEN ~ The Metaphysics of Being Stuck

That morning in March held out the promise of spring. The sky was cobalt, the bottomless blue of Mediterranean tile. Overnight, a wind had come up, sweeping away the clouds, even the wispy lenticulars that usually flutter from the summit of Mount McKinley. East of it, the Alaska Range peaks of Deborah, Hess, and Hayes zigzagged across the horizon. In the idiom of the North, the mountains were "out."

It was a false promise. I once tried reading a book on chaos theory—mostly because I liked the *idea* of my reading a book on chaos theory. I found myself reading the same sentences over and over again, trying to absorb their meaning by something like osmosis. In the end, the only thing I gleaned from the book can be summed up in one sentence: There is chaos in the universe, and weather is a good example of it.

I dialed my father's office. It was Sunday, but I knew he would be there. Weekend mornings, he likes to pace the empty corridors, smoking his pipe and muttering to the walls. When the dialogue in his head heats up, he bangs his pipe against the rim of a wastebasket, spilling red-hot ashes onto crumpled papers. It's not much of a stretch to say that you can pull into the Brice Incorporated parking lot just about any day of the week and see a charred wastebasket sitting in the snow.

The liveliness of my father's internal dialogue is not always reflected in his external discourse. Chitchat is anathema to him. If you ask him how his arthritis medication is working, or if you observe that the weather is balmy for spring, he's apt to ignore you. He doesn't mean to be rude. It's just that if you can't say anything worthwhile, you can't get a word in on the conversation he's already having with himself.

On the third ring, he picked up the phone and growled into the receiver, "Brice."

"Want to go flying?" I asked.

The Arctic Tern is a high-winged two-seater whose namesake migrates twenty-five thousand miles a year, from the Arctic to Antarctica. Built in Alaska, the airplane possesses the old-fashioned virtues of sturdiness and slowness. Which is not to say it's easy to fly. Instead of the standard tricycle-style gear, it's equipped with two wheels up front and a tail wheel, which makes it prone to a peculiar dance-like maneuver called a "ground loop."

Years ago, I went for a weather briefing in a dingy office on the small-plane ramp of the Fairbanks airport. The FAA guy on duty asked the usual questions: destination, number of passengers, fuel on board, tail number, make. The idea being that if your plane goes down, it can be verified whether you did or did not bother to check the weather before you left. The guy kept his eyes tethered to his computer screen. He didn't even glance up until I said, "Arctic Tern." Then he shot me a look that may or may not have been admiring. "So, you're learning to fly a *real* plane, are you?" he asked. In fact, I'd learned to fly the Arctic Tern more than a decade earlier. But I didn't say so: I can take a compliment in the spirit it's intended. Besides, in a way, the guy was right: I *was* still learning to fly and always would be—in the same sense I'm still learning to live.

That morning in March, the Tern was on skis instead of wheels. I shoehorned myself into the rear passenger seat while Dad took the controls. Our plan was to find a field or pond, then switch seats so I could practice stop-and-go's safely away from other planes, or what the FAA aptly calls "targets." Sundry domestic dramas had grounded me since summer, and I wasn't feeling as confident as usual. I could have hired an instructor for an hour or two, but my father is the best pilot I know.

The Inuit of northern Canada have different words for the same object when it is moving and when it is still. In Inuktitut, a sailing ship scudding across the Atlantic toward unmapped territory and undiscovered riches is one thing; that same ship frozen fast in the polar ice pack is another. This distinction between water and ice, between linear movement and aereal stillness, eluded the earliest European explorers. By the time they caught on, it was, for many of them, too late.

In *Playing Dead,* the Canadian writer Rudy Wiebe contemplates the fate of the Franklin expedition during Queen Victoria's reign. The ships and their crews disappeared, destroyed by stillness. Writes Wiebe:

> Perhaps in one or another of those endless, gigantic ice pressure ridges, shifting, sinking, reshaping themselves forever in the ice streams that flow between the islands of the Canadian archipelago, *Erebus* and *Terror* are still carried, hidden and secret. Their tall masts are long since destroyed and their decks gouged, splintered, walled in by impenetrable floes, the ice a shroud scraping over these great oaken sailing ships of empire, their skeleton crews rigid in a final posture of convulsive movement.

To be a pilot is to feel what language does not say. A Tern that climbs, swoops, circles, and spirals in three dimensions is not the same as a Tern that taxis on a runway whose geometry is stricter than any found in nature. On takeoff and landing, the accomplished pilot slips between two and three dimensions with ease and grace. The student pilot, on the other hand, lurches along, in mortal fear of stalling too soon or too late, of crossing the unseen boundary between aereal and linear movement at the worst possible moment—too low to recover from a spin, too high to survive the fall.

As a student pilot in my mid-twenties, I went through three instructors, cracked one control tower trainee, and sorely tested the patience of a crusty FAA examiner. For weeks before my first solo, I lay in bed at night, wide awake, my hands compulsively configuring the Tern for landing: mixture rich, carb heat on, trim set, mags *check*; nose up and throttle back for slow flight; pull a notch of flaps, hold a steady sixty miles an hour. Turn left downwind to base, base to final. Now forget the instruments and look at the ground. See the VASI lights? What are they telling you? *White on white, too much height. Red on red, you're dead.*

The first time I soloed, I did everything by the book, and everything went wrong. On takeoff, the Tern threw itself into the air. Squaring the corners of my pattern, I felt fast and light. Turning final, I was fast and high. Using two hands, I pulled the flaps down all the way. That slowed me down some. I lined up with the runway and "flared"—the term for applying gentle backpressure to the stick until the plane stalls. The tail wheel ricocheted off the asphalt and the Tern bounced into the air. OK, I thought, *the runway is long, and I am determined.* I set down a second time. The Tern bounced and careered sideways toward the runway lights. I throttled up for the go-round.

There is a fairly simple explanation for what was happening. I couldn't stall because I was carrying too much speed, and I was carrying too much speed because I was carrying too little weight. For the first time in my experience, my 155-pound instructor wasn't sitting in the rear seat, the one closest to the tail wheel. Barring a stiff headwind or muddy field, the pilot of a tail wheel–equipped airplane usually lands the tail wheel first. Landing the tail wheel first is easiest when the plane's center of gravity is on the aft side of the normal range. With a 125-pound pilot in front and a 155-pound instructor in the back, the center of gravity lies farther aft than with a 125-pound pilot in front and no one in back. By the time I soloed, I knew how to fly. I just didn't know how to fly solo.

In flying, less weight leads to greater speed. Too much speed translates into a surplus of lift. Lift is a pilot's best friend, except on landing. To land is to execute a controlled stall: the gear touches down, and the air stops flowing smoothly over and under the wings. The airplane crosses an invisible line between power and potential. One second you're flying a plane, the next, you're driving an ugly car with wings.

Before I became a pilot, I had all sorts of romantic ideas about flying. I caught them like viruses from memoirs such as Beryl Markham's *West with the Night* and Isak Dinesen's *Out of Africa.*

"The death of a beautiful woman is unquestionably the most poetical topic in the world," writes Poe, which probably explains why images of Amelia Earhart and Marvel Crosson, an Alaskan aviatrix killed during a 1929 air race, went deep. That's what I wanted for myself: luminous skin, a level gaze, high cheekbones, khaki jodhpurs, and fitted flying helmet. The fringed silk scarf I could live without: it struck me as an affectation.

In those days, I thought of myself as soft. Learning to fly would be hard. I wanted it to be so. I didn't really grasp the principles involved. If anything, I thought of flying as an act that defied gravity. Of course, I didn't know much about gravity, what with majoring in English at Smith College, selected partly on the grounds that it had no distribution requirements: I could read as many novels as I wanted without enrolling in a single math or physics course. As for lift, I knew even less. The lifelong observation of cereal-box gliders had apparently taught me nothing, because I naively believed that a plane whose engine quit in midair would tumble end over end out of the sky, like a Slinky falling down stairs.

My first instructor, Scott, taught me that flying is, in fact, the act of harnessing lift. Our classroom was a few square feet of tarmac in front of the hangar. Scott used the air as a blackboard, sketching unseen currents in the air: prop wash flows off the propeller and tends to swipe the nose around to the left, especially on landing. Wingtip vortices and wake turbulence are powerful forces capable of slinging a small plane upside down into telephone wires (which is what happened to a pilot in Washington recently). I listened closely, scribbled down notes, then took the written exam to become a pilot. Having passed it with a score that roughly translated as a B+, I could no longer put off flying solo.

"The first solo is the point where you suddenly discover that flying is pretty wonderful," rhapsodized my flight manual. "You'll be so busy flying the plane that you won't even notice the back seat is empty."

I was busy, but not *that* busy. It was the strangest sensation, to be moving, to be *flying*, and to be stuck at the same time. You may not like the semantics of "stuck": Pistons were firing in the 165-horse Lycoming engine. Wings were functioning as air foils. I was up. I just couldn't get down. To be stuck is to be imprisoned in the present, with the future bearing down hard. When I was in third grade, my friends and I dared each other to lick the monkey bars in winter. When we stripped our tongues away, our mouths filled up with the taste of blood and steel. Now that metallic taste of fear was filling my mouth. *Calm down*, I told myself. *Slow down.* I didn't need to land on the next try, or even the next. I could shoot a series of approaches, shaving five miles an hour off each time. I could ignore the thunderheads elbowing in from the east. I could circle for another ninety minutes or so before running out of gas. Then, one way or another, I was coming down.

Part of me wishes to believe, against all logic, that each of us gets the death we deserve. In that case, mine would probably be a drawn-out ordeal. Breast cancer or MS. Perhaps a rare unpronounceable wasting disease contracted in some far-off jungle. If I were lucky, I'd have time to read the works of Borges and Chekhov and Cheever. A nurse with muscular cool hands would shoot me full of lovely morphine. Propped up against high-thread-count cotton pillowcases, wearing a pink satin bed jacket, I'd look frail, tragic, long-suffering. A few years ago, a friend died after a wing fell off in midair. Not for me that kind of death: one second whole; the next, a case for a forensic dentist.

Another friend, Dick Flaharty, is an outdoor clothing manufacturer and part-time mountaineer who leads search teams to remote crash sites. I wish it were possible to say he leads "search-and-rescue" teams, but such is the nature of flying in Alaska that rescue is rarely involved. Over beer one night, I asked him a burning question.

"Dick, how *do* people die in plane crashes?"

He looked at me. Hard.

"No, really. I want to know what happens to their bodies, what the actual thing is that kills them."

"Their hearts explode."

Just before the first solo takeoff, Scott stood beside me on the tarmac. He squeezed my shoulder and steadied me with his gaze.

"You're ready. You can do this. You've already done it a hundred times. If it'll help, just pretend I'm in the back seat."

Yeah, right.

We made a plan, Scott and I. Or rather, he made a plan, and I acceded to it. As long as everything was OK, he'd stay near the intersection of two taxiways, in the spot where I'd dropped him after shooting some dual takeoffs and landings.

"What if it's not OK?" I asked.

"Then I'll talk you down."

Every time I skittered onto the runway—too high, too fast, too light, then powered up for the go-round—the Tern leaping back into the air like a sparrow freed from a net—I saw Scott standing right where I'd left him, his right hand shielding his eyes like a visor. Inscrutable. Immovable. Utterly useless. God, how I hated him.

I'd known him forever, it seemed. His parents and mine went to the same parties, and he'd been my brother's best friend for as long as I could remember. Back in high school, he and I had both been on the cross-country ski team. He was handsome and whippet smart; quick with encouragement, slower with praise. He could laugh at himself but, like most pilots, he preferred not to. In some ways, he knew me better than I knew myself. If he went to the tower to talk me down, I'd never fly again.

Four times I radioed air-traffic control, requesting clearance to land. Four times, the controller's voice came back, saying evenly, "Cleared for the option."

"Cleared for the option" is tower-speak for, among other things, the option *not* to land.

I learned to fly not because I loved it (that came later) but because I was in love with the idea of it. I wanted to be able to say, "I'm a pilot." Looking back on my early twenties, I see peaks and troughs, the unbearable ecstasies and exquisite despairs available only to the truly indulged and self-absorbed. My parents had scrimped on red meat, fresh vegetables, whole milk, new shoes, and long-distance phone calls so they could afford to give me and my sisters riding lessons, French lessons, piano lessons, violin lessons, sewing lessons, ballet lessons, drama lessons. If we learned nothing else, we learned this very big lesson: A woman may be nothing more—or less—than the sum of her accomplishments.

Flight manual: "It is interesting to note that the perfect landing is always made on a day when the airport is deserted."

On my fourth try, I wrestled wings to earth, setting an unofficial and ignominious field record. The guy in the tower sounded as relieved as if he'd just caught a falling vase. "Interstate Five-Seven-Alpha-Tango, contact ground point-niner off the runway. And . . . congratulations."

In the decade after that day, I met a guy, married him, quit my job as a journalist, went to graduate school, gave birth to three daughters, left my husband, and took a teaching job on the other side of the country. I dealt with frozen pipes, surly contractors, private preschool, Clorox, Xanax, and pain. Also, I furnished my life with the things I love—furnished it so well that sometimes I can hardly breathe. Once upon a time, I thought soloing in the Tern was the hardest thing I had ever done, possibly the hardest thing I'd ever do. Now it seems like a piece of cake compared to getting out of bed most mornings.

In "Stillness," an essay from *Burning Down the House*, Charles Baxter points out a peculiarly American tendency in literature and film to frame violence or mayhem with motionlessness. The eye lingers on some aspect of setting or detail: heat shimmers, snow suffocates; then, after a slow-motion intake of breath, things go haywire. He argues that the mark of a good writer or filmmaker is the ability to pull off stillness. Here's a question: What if the truest measure of any talent, even the talent for living, is the ability to navigate stillness? Recently I ran this question by a friend. An English professor who collects as much art as he can afford on his academic salary, he saw right through my cheap philosophizing. "Charles Baxter is talking about stillness as an aesthetic," he said. "You're talking about life."

I believe the best thing anyone can (and does) say about me is that I am a competent woman. It is also the worst. I start each day with a list of things to do; most days, I get through it. I over-prepare for classes. I reply to e-mail and hand in my grades promptly. I show up on time for meetings and stay until the end. I feed the cats and water the plants. As a writer and mother, I traffic in unparallel universes: the realm of ideas and the realm of the produce aisle. Militant competence is the mask worn by panic. What if, one day, I realize that the hatches of my life have battened down so tightly I can never move again?

To return to that morning in March, my father took off from the ski strip and climbed to three thousand feet. After flying south for twenty miles or so, we spotted a snow-covered pond marked by the telltale tracks of another ski plane. Dad throttled back and descended. The tracks looked fresh. The fact that someone else had landed there recently meant the pond was probably safe for us.

We landed slowly, thirty-five or forty miles an hour. At first, the Tern settled lovingly in the snow's embrace. There was a loud crack, and we began to sink. Beneath a meringue-like surface, the snow was the texture of confectioner's sugar. It collapsed under our weight.

Sometimes you read a person's mind simply by studying his scalp, especially if that person is, like my father, bald. At this moment, the skin on the back of his neck was corrugated. Without saying a word, he throttled up and plowed through the fine powder.

Just shy of the shoreline, Dad punched the left rudder. I knew what he was thinking. If he could just swing the Tern around 180 degrees, so the skis were resting in their old tracks, he might cobble together enough speed for a take-off. He almost made it. Halfway through the turn, a wing tip snagged the snow. *Whoomph.* We sank to our belly.

To live in Alaska is to experience as ordinary what others elsewhere might experience as extraordinary. Like getting stuck. In the wilderness. In a plane. With ten years of flying under my belt, I could imagine worse scrapes. With thirty-five years of flying under *his* belt, my father had *been* in worse scrapes—plenty of them. My family has always subscribed to the actuarial notion that the more you use something, the more likely you are to ding it up. When the subject of one or more of his crashes comes up, Dad grins boyishly and says, "The only thing that matters is that you walk away afterward." He is not speaking metaphorically.

One spring day in 1973, a woman took off from Circle Hot Springs for the 125-mile southerly flight to Fairbanks. Halfway, clouds moved in, obscuring the terrain. The woman, who was not an experienced pilot, kept her wits about her. She climbed, stuck to her compass heading, and prayed for a crack in the concrete-colored clouds. Finding one, she slipped through. A while later, she saw below her a boundless body of blue water. The Fairbanks region contains no such body—only the sullen, slate-colored Tanana and Chena rivers. It turned out the woman was nearly two hundred miles off course, over Lake Minchumina in the dead center of the state.

Flying stories such as this one have taught me useful things: comedy is not always incompatible with tragedy. Humiliation often follows hard on hubris. On occasions when the instruments say one thing and the instincts say another, one ought always, *always*, to rely on the instruments. Look out the window once in a while to see what topography is telling you. What matters is not how well one stays the course but how gracefully one copes with the unforeseen. In their purest form, joy and terror feel strangely alike, monozygotic twins separated at birth.

My own flying stories will never feature me in a starring role, pulling off amazingly daring feats, or even slightly daring feats. For one thing, my snap decisions are almost always bad, awful in the same way my rough drafts are awful. For another, I have children to think of. Motherhood rewards sameness. A biologist would doubtless scoff at the notion of a female gene for stillness, but I believe in it. And is it not an American prerogative to transform the molecular into the moral? Remember the rush to judgment when a mother named Alison Hargreaves set out to summit K2 in winter? Remember the heartless censure when she died on the way down? Movement is about self-becoming, motherhood about self-erasure. Society punishes mothers who set their own pursuits above the demands of their children, who feel desire instead of fulfillment, who crave movement over stillness.

One of my closest friends is a woman who has always wanted to have children but, for reasons too complicated to go into here, cannot. She tells me I want it both ways, as if the occasional public rant against motherhood, this one included, somehow nullifies deeply felt private emotion. The truth is, I love my daughters—love them as a sow bear loves her cubs, protectively, unambiguously, and with a force and breadth beyond the reach of language. Is it OK to confess that sometimes I love them best when they are sleeping?

Motherhood's dirty little secret is boredom. When the girls were little, every morning was a study in perpetual motion: changing diapers, finding socks, cleaning up spilled juice, emptying the dishwasher, loading the dryer, turning on *Pocahontas*, bandaging the spot on one twin's arm where the other twin bit, bribing the big girl to dress herself, putting the biter on time out, trying not to forget when time out was time up.

The inside of my station wagon was a midden of crushed Froot Loops, goldfish crackers, and stale french fries. I'd put the girls in their car seats, drive to Fred Meyer, hunt for a parking space, then slip into public persona of The Mother: long-suffering, tolerant, weary, and indulgent without being a push-over. Too young for masks, the girls intuited they could get away with a certain amount of bad behavior in public. They begged for Barbies while I shopped, whined for M&Ms in the check-out gauntlet. Well-meaning strangers clucked sympathetically: "You have your hands full, don't you?"

Yes, I've got my hands full, goddammit. Tell me, what is it about the way I look right now that makes you think I want to be your friend, to ooh and aah over snapshots of your four-year-old twin nephews back in Kissimmee or Scarsdale or wherever the hell they live. Get out of my way. Motherhood is not performance art. I am busy, busy, busy. Too busy to think. Too busy to be still. Too busy to stop and pick up the parts of myself that are falling away like dead things. Round and round and round she goes. Where she stops, nobody knows.

I feel different when I fly. Whole somehow. The static that is the background noise of life with children fades. Flying engages senses and intellect in one exhilarating conversation.

Eyes sweep from the instrument panel to the windows and back again, absorbing data about airspeed, height, oil temperature, and the location of targets. Ears separate skeins of sound in the engine noise. One strand says both magnetos are firing in sequence; another, pitched lower, says the fuel mixture is a shade too lean. (Rereading these sentences, I wonder at the way the first-person singular "I" becomes absorbed in flight.) If I hold myself still, the sounds of the engine and the wind fill my thoracic cavity like a second heartbeat.

Outside lies a landscape vastly altered from the everyday. Things that seem monumental from the ground become foreshortened, flattened somehow. Mountains tread knee-deep in clear water. Patterns emerge where chaos dwelt. The word "ice" becomes absurdly inadequate to describe its many natures. On a river, ice looks like stalagmites poking up from the bottom of a cave. On the ocean, ice looks like onionskin viewed under a microscope. Ice on a glacier tumbles in pleats and ruffles, like the underskirts of a wedding gown. When I fly, I feel as if I am reading a text, really reading it, without ever learning the language. Alone in the Tern, I've whispered death to myself, just to feel the shudder that reminds me I'm alive. Less subject to my will than fear, joy sometimes catches me unawares; it, too, makes me shudder.

In *Out of Africa*, Isak Dinesen writes that to fly is to discover afresh what you've known all along: "I see . . . This was the idea. And now I understand everything."

Is stillness, then, the fleeting equilibrium between conflicting forces? The paleontologist Stephen Jay Gould says we ought to pay more attention to equilibrium, less to punctuation. Perhaps the stillness *is* the story.

When I was a kid, my family lived in the country outside of Fairbanks. On summer afternoons, we sometimes heard a thrumming sound. We kids would look up to see the plane lofting low, like a fat dragonfly, over the horizon. Once, then twice, it circled a field near our house. Then a hatch opened and red streamers, twenty-five or thirty feet long, slithered out. The streamers lolled and writhed on the air currents. Their purpose was to test the wind's strength and direction. Sam and

Hannah and I didn't know that then. We were too young. We just hopped on our banana seat bikes and pedaled as hard as we could, standing up, the mile or so to the field. As we pedaled, men dropped from the plane, each one trailing a parachute like a sac of spider's eggs. If the men saw us pedaling below, they probably thought we were watching them, awestruck at their bravery and prowess. In truth, we just wanted the streamers. Foxtails tickled our legs as we scoured the field. Later, we wrapped the streamers around our handlebars and hauled them home, booty from a far-off world. We hung them from our tree house. I don't think I've ever felt that happy since.

What about the gap between being still and being stuck? Is it purely a matter of perception, even of semantics? Is the glass half empty or half full? To say that you're stuck is to blame forces beyond your control, because, of course, they *are* beyond your control. When you're stuck, that's it: story over. "Stuck" could never be anything other than monosyllabic; not for it the "-ness" ending that transforms an adjective into a state. This "uck" ending has comical overtones: "muck," "buck," and "yuck." ("Fuck," a friend reminds me: the first word that comes to mind when you realize you're stuck.)

In contrast, the word "stillness" is exquisite, both the way it looks on the page and the way it sounds: the powerful doubling of consonants, the way the soft *s* at the beginning slides up to the implacable *t*, the fading to sibilance at the end. The act of being still has an element of will, even of responsibility. To be still is deliberately to foil the forces—internal or external—that would keep you moving if they could. And stillness is rich in erotic possibilities. In the bodice-rippers I read as a teenager, the arrogant, dark-haired, long-fingered hero always ordered the high-strung, hyperventilating heroine to "be still" while he stroked her quivering flanks. When she complied, a strange lassitude overcame her, the prelude to being ravished.

The language of flying is erotic, too, with its play of power and surrender, freedom and restraint. One glides, rolls, spins, and flares. "[I]n the air," writes Dinesen "you are taken into the full freedom of the three dimensions; after long ages of exile and dreams the homesick heart throws itself into the arms of space." Flying is a paradox, then: You throw yourself—body and heart—into the air, and then you are taken.

To be stuck is to be derailed from your will, also from the possibility of pleasure—though not, perhaps, from death. Stuck is when the car quits in the middle of nowhere and it's fifty below. Stuck is spending an hour at the grocery store before realizing you left your purse at home. Stuck is a book that my sister-in-law once pressed on me titled *Surrendering to Motherhood.* It's a pamphlet I once saw in the grocery store checkout line: *The Joy of Jell-O Molds.* Stuck is flying round and round in a pattern with no way to get down. Stuck is *not* a glorious spring afternoon when the Tern ends up belly-deep in snow.

"Look in back," Dad said. "I think there's a shovel. Snowshoes, too. I'll dig. You pack down a runway."

Hatless and gloveless, wearing only his workaday lace-up shoes, Dad shoveled snow away from the propeller and skis. I wallowed to my waist, cursing and struggling with the stiff rawhide laces on the snowshoes. Then with the peculiar, bow-legged gait of a bronc rider, swinging my arms to force the blood back into my frozen fingers, I tromped toward the shoreline.

"OK," Dad shouted. "I'm going to rock it out. When I yell, you push on the wing."

"Now!"

The Tern lurched out of the snow. Leaving me behind, Dad swept around the pond once with the door propped open, packing down my provisional runway. On the second pass, I grabbed a strut and ran alongside for a few paces. Dad snagged my left arm and hauled me in while the plane was still moving. I tossed the snowshoes behind the seat, bolted the door, and negotiated, with wooden fingers, the intricacies of my shoulder harness. The skin on the back of Dad's neck looked as smooth as a baby's butt. It occurred to me that he might be enjoying himself.

"Hang on," he yelled. "We might not make it on the first try, but I'm going to give it the cob."

When my father says things like "give it the cob," he is definitely enjoying himself.

A line of spruce trees bore down on us, then snow sprayed from our skis as we lofted skyward. We barely cleared the treetops. When we did, they bent in our wind, as if in homage.

Over the engine, I heard a sound like boulders tumbling over a river bottom. It was my father singing: *'Twas grace that brought me safe thus far, and grace will lead me home.*

Instead of turning for home, Dad set a course for the Tanana River. There, on the snowmachine-packed surface, I could and would grease a few landings, boost my confidence enough to fly solo the next time. The two of us would pull into my parents' driveway by 5:00 p.m., in plenty of time for the family dinner my mother cooks every Sunday. Between forkfuls, Dad might interject, "By the way, Jen and I had a little excitement this afternoon . . ." Then again, he might say nothing at all.

EIGHT ~ Angle of Attack

On account of books, I went AWOL from my own adolescence. Summer afternoons, I'd slather my legs with baby oil then lie outside on the sagging nylon chaise lounge with a can of TAB in one hand and a fat paperback in the other. In winter, I'd tent my yellow ruffled bedspread and read inside by flashlight. I read with an intensity that frightened my family, or so they tell me now. Mostly, I read dreadful books—Harlequin and Silhouette romances, two or three a day, still warm from the hands of the friend who'd loaned them to me. By the time I was fifteen, I had, like Eric Carle's very hungry caterpillar, methodically munched my way through everything on my parents' bookshelves: *Gone with the Wind, From Here to Eternity, Marjorie Morningstar, Mila XVIII, Trinity,* and an anthology of war stories. (My father was the reader.) When I found Henry Miller on a topmost shelf, then *The Joy of Sex* under my parents' bed, I read them, too.

Meanwhile, I grew a head taller than most of my classmates, including the boys. I gained scaffolding in the form of braces, glasses, and a training bra. I barely noticed; I was too busy reading. Years later, friends would ask what it was like to grow up in Alaska, which seemed as foreign to them as Outer Mongolia. I'd gaze back, speechless and stupid as a cow. No, we didn't live in igloos. No, we didn't mush our huskies to the 7-11. Yes, we had summer in Fairbanks. Hadn't I grown up just like they had? I didn't know. Somehow, I'd used bad literature the way other people use drugs and alcohol, to escape the dullness of daily life. In novels, people fell in love or fell off cliffs. They joined the circus, leapt onto runaway horses, blew up bridges and, when caught, gave away nothing under torture. In Alaska, nothing exciting happened to anyone I knew. Or so it seemed.

One day when I was thirteen or fourteen, I was reading on the brown tweed sofa in our living room. I must have been babysitting Ben and Rebecca. Nothing short of $2.50 an hour would otherwise have induced me to enter that region where the savages roamed freely. I was lying down, of course. My white cat, Friday, curled like a fat incubus on my chest. Mom was running errands. Dad had left that morning for the Bush, flying one of the company planes to a village whose name began and ended with a *K* sound: Kobuk, Koyukuk, Kwingillingok, Kongiganek, Quinhagak, or perhaps (an exception) Eek.

Within a year or two, my father's company would be flush enough to hire a full-time pilot. In the early days, though, when he needed to fly somewhere, he or one of his business partners (aka Uncle Sam or Uncle Andy) flew themselves. He rarely returned inside of a week; sometimes he was gone for months.

In the landscape of my childhood, my father's frequent and prolonged absences were the salient feature: he missed birthday parties, recitals, concerts, confirmations, and graduations. He wasn't the one to console us after bee stings or tonsillectomies or Mom's speeding tickets. He nearly missed the birth of one of my sisters. He was gone for the August 1967 Chena River flood, which forced us to flee our ground-floor apartment by canoe; and he was gone in 1975, when our mother, blinded by spring sunlight, drove our TravelAll into the side of a slow-moving train. Just a couple of days earlier, we'd moved our belongings into a new house. After the accident, Mom lay immobile for weeks, casts binding her arms and legs. At the end of every day, she rolled from the recliner in the living room onto a mattress beside it. There she slept fitfully among a field of unpacked boxes. It was a long time before my father got the news. He was running a Cat train across the Arctic in the days before satellite communications. Nope, nothing exciting ever happened to us.

With the help of Mrs. Fowler, a housekeeper-cum-babysitter, my mother ran a tight ship. When Dad came home, things loosened up. Dad built us helicopters out of Tinker Toys; elaborate forts that colonized the house, a tree house with a working trolley; a complex system of snow tunnels on the back porch. We had grilled steak for dinner and ice cream sundaes for dessert. Loose change from his pockets spilled into cracks between sofa cushions; we dug it out like grizzly cubs wild with the scent of a marmot colony. During dinner, someone—often my mother, gone giggly as a schoolgirl—slipped an ice cube down someone else's back. Once (but only once), we had a whipped cream fight. Indoors. "Roughhouse us! Roughhouse us!" we'd beg, and Dad would fall onto all fours, head-butting us into walls, bucking us off his back, growling so fiercely we were afraid: maybe he wasn't really our father after all; maybe Dad had gone away for good this time. "Stop! Stop!" we'd cry, but he kept coming, thundering after us as we bolted for the bathroom. He picked the lock; we blocked the door with drawers. He ran into the utility room and threw the breaker; we ran squealing from the dark bathroom into the dark hallway where he crouched, ready to pounce then tickle us to death. With my mother, play was as formal as a Shakespeare sonnet. It was something you did sitting at a card table sipping cocoa from a demitasse made from china so thin it was translucent. We played Monopoly, Clue, Parcheesi, Battleship, Chinese Checkers, Yahtzee, Gin Rummy. With Mom, you followed the rules, and both of you tried your darnedest to win. With Dad, play was more like a Jackson Pollock painting, something on the edge of unbearable ecstasy and visceral terror. You cheated whenever you could. Winning was beside the point; mostly, you just wanted to survive.

Before taking off from Fairbanks International Airport (I always thrill to that juxtaposition of "Fairbanks" with "International"), Dad would have filed a flight plan with the FAA. The verb "file" is misleading. Below the tower, in a dingy room smelling of grease and tobacco, he would have dictated the details of his flight to the FAA guy on duty. That's the "filing" part. After takeoff, pilots "open" or "activate" their flight plans via two-way radio. On landing, they "close" them. As long as a flight plan is open, the FAA is supposed to keep track of it and, by extension, of you. Fail to close a flight plan when you say you will, and someone will start looking for you.

I was deep in a book when the phone rang that afternoon, so I ignored it. A few seconds later, a shadow fell across the page.

"Jen," my brother began.

"What? *What?*"

Sam's mouth worked wordlessly. His skin was white beneath the freckles. His hands flopped like helpless, dying things at the ends of his arms. I dropped my book.

Where does the story of a death begin when death is, by definition, the end? How do you draw the narrative arc of a life that lacks any kind of denouement, that gradual falling off of action followed by the wrapping up of loose ends? "There is a kind of dying for which very little or no preparation is possible, and perhaps not advisable," writes Dr. Sherwin Nuland in *How We Die.* His subject, like mine, is violent death: severe blunt-force trauma and rapid exsanguination—the medical term for the rapid outpouring of most of the body's blood. Despite the dreadful language, it is probably a merciful death, quick and painless compared, say, to being gut shot by a stray bullet or roasted alive in a space shuttle, suffocated in an avalanche or eaten by a black bear.

The myth of the merciful death: *He never knew what hit him. At least she didn't suffer. There was no pain.* Milling around the outside of the church or the dog musher's hall or the airplane hangar pressed into sad service, mourners murmur these pat phrases. Like all platitudes, they serve a purpose: to salve our wounds, console our spirits, assuage our guilt for the unreturned calls, short-circuited conversations, rushed good-byes. Like all platitudes, they're as useless as pebbles when it comes to filling the yawning chasm between what is felt and what is said.

The next story, too, begins with a phone call. A Monday morning in July. I was in my thirties, rinsing cereal bowls and stuffing them into a crowded dishwasher. Before answering, I took the time to dry my hands on a dishtowel.

"Hey," said my father, without preamble, "doesn't your friend the lady doctor—I forget her name—fly a Maule?"

"I'm not sure who you mean, Dad."

"Yes, you do. The one whose husband was killed a few years back. Didn't they fly Maules?"

"Oh, you mean Nancy Lewis. She used to fly a Maule, uh-huh. Not anymore, though."

I was, in the graceless idiom of my husband's kayaking buddies, talking out of my butt. I hadn't seen or spoken with Nancy in years, not since the memorial service for her husband, Joe Finkel. Joe died in a crash that was blamed, in part, on the structural failure of a Maule: a wing fell off in midair. After that, what widow in her right mind would keep flying a Maule? The more I thought about it, the more sure I was. Yes, Nancy was still a pilot. No, she didn't fly a Maule.

"Why do you ask?"

That morning's paper carried a front-page story about a crash in the Brooks Range. This being Alaska, and the *Fairbanks Daily News-Miner* being the farthest north daily newspaper in the United States, such stories, while not common, are not exactly rare. This particular crash stood out because it involved multiple fatalities, including someone—as yet unnamed—who lived in Fairbanks. I registered these facts as sad but not unusual.

"No names?" I asked.

"Nothing yet."

"Well," I said firmly, "it's not Nancy."

On that long-ago afternoon when the FAA had mistakenly reported that my father's plane was overdue, I learned a couple of things. It's best to keep grief at bay for as long as possible, to hold off until the actual moment, not just the rumor of it, when a familiar name attaches to a beloved body that has stopped breathing. For one thing, the vomiting isn't as bad. For another, anything can happen in the gap between the idea of a thing and the thing itself.

Miraculously, she . . .

Against all odds, she . . .

I hung up the phone. As if my body already knew what my mind would not, I climbed the stairs on leaden feet, the dishes forgotten. I yanked sundresses from hangers and tugged them over the twins' heads as they watched a Scooby-Doo video. They protested when I switched off the TV. *Go outside,* I said. *It's a beautiful day.* As they toddled past me, I grabbed the loose fabric at the back of their dresses and reeled them in for hugs. By now, I was on my knees. Inside the circle of my arms, their bodies squirmed like grayling. As long as we stayed just like this, I thought, Nancy could not be dead. Then I let them go.

Downstairs, sunlight streamed through the south-facing windows, forming parallelograms on the honey-colored wood floor. The dishwasher hummed. Etta James was on the stereo, singing "Only Women Bleed."

Please god please please please don't let it be Nance.

"How sad," I'd say on Tuesday, skimming the unfamiliar names in the newspaper. But I wouldn't be sad, not really. I'd be relieved. Not my father. Not my brother. Not my husband. Not my friend. Not me.

Not this time.

In a poem titled "Dream of Safety," Dana Goodyear writes, "What it is hard to know we misconstrue." Of course Nancy kept flying a Maule after Joe's death, and of course she was flying her Maule the day before in the Brooks Range, showing off Alaska to a friend from medical school, the friend's husband, and their young son. The family was from a big city in the Southwest, where they'd left an older, teenaged son. His world was about to fall apart. Probably already had.

Verb tense matters. The teenage boy *was* the son of doctors; now he *is* an orphan. I *am,* luckily, the daughter of a civil engineer. As such, I think first of the literal meaning of "misconstrue"—to misconstruct, to undermine by flawed workmanship. Next, I see its figurative meaning, a misconstruction as a fixed idea whose center will not hold. Flimsy, yes, but not evil or malign. Before toppling or caving in on itself, a misconstruction buys us time to think the heretofore unthinkable, to reimagine the world with one less friend or lover or child or mother. To the living, time matters. Seconds matter. It's not as if we're stealing them from the dead. And Nancy, of course, is dead—had been dead nearly eighteen hours when I began bargaining with the powers-that-be to save her.

The teenage reader of novels grew up to be a writer of true stories. It was almost as if books let me escape from the world at a time when it seemed painful or boring then, gradually, to engage with it when I felt ready. For me, fiction and nonfiction are roughly equal to theorem and proof. For years, I studied theorems. Now I'm gathering proofs. Though I still admire and read it, fiction seems as alien to me as sculpture to a painter. (And yes, I know that some artists—Michelangelo and DaVinci, for example—worked in more than one form; so do some writers, just not me.) That said, I sometimes wonder what or who gives me the right to analyze not just myself and my own life but the lives of my acquaintances, friends, and family. Being a nonfiction writer feels like being in the business of stealing souls, of being a tourist in other people's lives. To speculate in print on the thoughts and motives of another, ultimately unknowable, human being strikes me as morally bankrupt and breathtakingly presumptuous. It's enough to make a smarter person turn to nature writing. As Annie Dillard writes in "To Fashion a Text"—an essay about her memoir, *An American Childhood*—"Things were simpler when I wrote about muskrats." Yet the genre chose me, not the other way around. If I were superstitious, I'd say it might be a cosmic revenge plot for the years I spent living in books. Now I can't get enough of gritty reality. (Not, however, made-for-TV gritty reality.) Sometimes my subjects come unbidden and must be reckoned with, else they'll never go away. Nancy is one of them.

In an essay titled "Other People's Secrets," Patricia Hampl replays a conversation with a friend who's struggling to translate her life into fiction. "Why not write it as nonfiction?" Hampl suggests, horrifying her friend. "Because I want to tell the truth," she replies, as if that's only possible behind the veil of fiction.

Is it crazy to want to tell the truth, or at least to be as honest as possible, in nonfiction? Defending my better self against my worse, I wish to say my motives are pure, untainted by *schadenfreude.* My questions are equally real and compelling. They concern a woman I knew briefly; our friendship kindled then flickered out over a period of five years or so. In truth, I'd be surprised if Nancy thought of me once in the months before she died. She'd moved on purposefully to new friends, new pursuits, a new love, while I'd remained behind somehow—snagged, mired, stalled in the past.

Nancy always struck me as the quintessential Alaskan of the late twentieth century—even more so than someone like me, who was born here. Does that sound strange? If so, measure the zeal of the convert against that of a believer born into the faith. Reared in the East, Nancy moved to Fairbanks after her residency. I don't think she was trying to "find" herself in the North; she pretty much invented herself against the backdrop of Alaska's extravagantly harsh, lavishly sublime landscape. After the crash, her second husband, a photographer, set up a link on his Web site to a slide show: Nancy mountain biking, Nancy skiing, Nancy fly-fishing, Nancy rafting, and Nancy rock climbing. In one photograph, Nancy—swaddled in red nylon Cordura—pedals past a bank thermometer, which reads minus forty-four degrees. Whatever the activity, Nancy always had the requisite gear: padded bike shorts, Patagonia or North Face fleece pullovers, nylon wind pants, climbing boots, hip waders, Ray-Bans, custom-made Apocalypse Design anorak and matching bibs; the skis, poles, kayaks, canoes, paddles, fishing rods, crampons, carabiners, ropes, helmets, sleeping bags, fold-up chairs, pop-up tents, and mountain bikes. Like her Subaru station wagon and her float-mounted, single-engine Maule, Nancy's gear was high caliber but not flashy. She might not have owned the newest product on the market, but she usually owned the best.

It's true, as you've probably guessed, that I envied her—envied her looks, envied her career, envied her top-of-the-line-in-everything gear, envied the way she seemed self-sufficient but not lonely. I made a study of her intensity, somehow missing that corollary to intensity, which is humorlessness. Her every gesture—the casual way she slung her kayak over one shoulder—seemed to say she needed no thing, no *one* to complete her. Now that I'm older, I think she needed something after all, though not in a craven way. She could be restless and fractious, exacting and impatient, perhaps because she was never fully at home in her own skin. She had to *do* in order to *be.* She courted the admiration of friends and acquaintances, and she won it. Easily. There, in our refracted gaze, she saw the self she had so carefully constructed. How do I know? Because I am, in this respect, just like her.

Nancy was forty-nine when she died, a decade older than I. She wasn't conventionally pretty but she was sometimes beautiful. Her face was long and narrow, framed by a cascade of dark-chocolate hair. Freckles played across the bridge of her nose. She was a shade shorter than me, maybe five-foot-four or five-foot-five, and wiry. My own face is, to put it mildly, forgettable; I'm the woman with her hand half-frozen in a wave at an acquaintance who fails to recognize her. Once, at a party, Nancy complimented me on my outfit, a shirt and skirt in woven black and green stripes, saying she'd nearly bought it herself. Wasn't it from Beaver Sports? Yes, it was. I felt a surge of warmth toward her.

I saw Nancy's parents for the first time in the late '80s, when she married Joe Finkel. The wedding invitation was a still life of kayaks, canoes, bikes, skis, even a motorcycle; the kicker was something like, "Nancy and Joe are putting away their toys for a day in order to get married, and they'd like for you to join them." Theirs was a summer wedding in the back yard of Nancy and Joe's house in the hills overlooking town. It was easy to pick Nancy's parents out of the crowd as the lone Easterners. Her father was tall and elegant. Her mother wore big sunglasses and a helmet of strawberry-blonde hair. Her slenderness brought to mind the Tom Wolfe phrase, "social X-ray." They had the indescribable whiff of New York about them. We Alaskans kept a respectful distance, not sure how to approach people who obviously came from a world of comfort and privilege, manicures and maitre d's who welcomed them by name.

For the wedding, Nancy wore a feminine gown of pintucked white voile. Someone told me it wasn't actually a wedding gown but a Jessica McClintock robe, a bit of gossip I found believable and endearing. Joe wore a charcoal suit and lavender tie. He and Nancy recited vows they'd written themselves; surprisingly, hers was the voice that broke under the weight of too-powerful emotion. Joe's baritone carried to the edges of the crowd. The manager of a trucking firm, he was the kind of man who made you feel, when he spoke to you, as if you were the only person on earth. With his white teeth, black hair, and beard, he was as sexy as a pirate.

The second time I saw Nancy's parents was at Joe's memorial service, in the fall of 1996. It was indoors, in a private hangar near the small-plane field in Fairbanks. Friends and family spoke briefly, sharing off-the-cuff anecdotes and memories. Nancy's father stood up, too, but I can't remember what he said—something about Joe's contagious love of Alaska and flying, I think. The grief in his face and his wife's said that they, like the rest of us, never imagined something so terrible could happen to someone they loved.

In the years before Nancy died, she'd begun traveling several months a year, sometimes for work (Doctors without Borders), sometimes for pleasure. She went trekking in Nepal and skiing in Switzerland. She played the cello. A year or two after I became a pilot, she took up flying herself, quickly surpassing me in hours and ratings. She earned her commercial license as well as instrument, multi-engine, and single-engine seaplane ratings. A friend told me she was considering a career change, from doctor to pilot.

In several pictures posted on the Web site, Nancy is sleeping: in an airport, legs sprawled over the metal seat dividers; in a sleeping bag propped against the side of a grounded canoe; on a sofa, snuggled up to her golden retriever, Jackson. I'm not sure how to read these images. Perhaps they mean that Nancy had only two speeds, "Full" and "Off." Or maybe they mean that, wherever she is, Nancy is at peace—that death is like a catnap stolen in the lounge of an airport where flights arrive every few minutes but none ever depart.

Among the images of Nancy skiing, Nancy boating, Nancy biking, Nancy hiking, and Nancy sleeping, there is one of Nancy delivering a baby. It seemed that no skill was beyond her. She worked hard and played harder, often against the backdrop of Alaska's profligate beauty. What is most striking about the images—and I may be over-interpreting—is that Nancy is almost always alone. It's almost as if her life were a one-woman play.

In Nancy's presence, one felt that her passion for the outdoors and its accoutrements did not necessarily extend to other human beings. She was smart and tenacious, physically daring; she was not warm. I don't recall ever touching or being touched by her, even on her wedding day. She did not want to have children, and, except for two nearly grown stepsons by Joe, she never did. Are these faults? I don't know. I, too, feel a kind of electricity in the presence of men that makes me bristle at competition. I, too, have been accused of standoffishness, and it's true that I rarely touch my friends. A casual arm around a shoulder or even a kiss on the cheek feels like an overloaded gesture. As for children—I don't know what to say. My brothers and sisters and I competed viciously for our parents' attention. One morning at breakfast, my mother asked each of us in turn, "What do you want to be when you grow up?" Hannah said she wanted to be a nurse, just like our mother. For a few seconds, the sun shone more brightly on Hannah's brown curly head than on anyone else's. Then I said, peevishly, "Well, *I* wouldn't want to be a nurse if I could be a doctor." That got me sent to my room. Within a few years, it would seem as if every conversation with my mother ended badly, with loud voices and slamming doors. Our worst fights took place in the car, where there was no backing down nor any escape. Frustrated, she'd fire off one of her favorite salvos: "Someday you'll have children of your own, and you'll understand how I feel right now," or "God help you when you become a mother." I'd reply in the way best calculated to cause her pain, saying, "I'm never having children."

Selfishness, not despair, was the unforgivable sin in our household. Our father's income was tied to the size and number of contracts that Brice Incorporated was able to win. This meant the family fortunes often rose and fell with government funding for capital projects. Even so, our parents'—mostly our mother's—admonitions not to wolf our food or drain the hot water supply, to share our toys and books and clothes and records, were not just about money. They reminded us that the group—the family unit, the community—always came first. I was always pushing against that principle, and not just when it came to things (although I'm ashamed to say that when my mother forced me to loan Hannah a favorite navy blue blazer, I stormed out of the room shouting, "She's too fat for it! She's going to ruin it!"), but when it came to my developing self. I was and am solitary by nature. I liked nothing more as a child than to curl up in the quiet corner of an empty room with a book. Early on, I sensed that I had to withhold my self from my family in order to find it. So did my mother. She was always hunting me down, rousting me out, urging me to finish my chores, set the table, join the family. On family vacations, I held myself aloof, pretending to be a foreign exchange student from a non-English-speaking country, oblivious to the noisy, demonstrative, quarrelsome, lumpen crew sharing the same car or restaurant as me. That was my dearest fantasy as a child—Bruno Bettelheim claims it's every little girl's fantasy—that I was a princess who'd accidentally been born into a middle-class, middlebrow family that suffered from terminal weirdness. Compared to *that,* Alaska always seemed, well, irrelevant. But Nancy had grown up in more privileged, urban surroundings; perhaps she needed something bigger than a noisome family to push against. In Alaska, she found it.

In the North, flying is the most quotidian form of travel. I was a few months old the first time I flew in a light plane; I was seven before I rode in a taxi. From the beginning, Brice Incorporated's work depended on someone's being able to land at remote airstrips or on beaches or gravel bars. Flying is so deeply embedded in the company and family culture that if someone says he or she is going out of town, the question is not, "What time is your flight?" but "Are you going private or commercial?"

To fly as much as we do is to incur a certain amount of risk. When an Alaskan dies in a plane crash, I'm rarely more than two degrees of separation from knowing him or her. Nick Begich was a family friend and Democratic candidate for the U.S. Congress in October 1972 when the Cessna in which he and House Majority Leader Hale Boggs of Louisiana were passengers disappeared. (Two weeks after his plane disappeared, Begich won the election. The sitting governor of Alaska, a Republican, appointed Begich's opponent, Republican Don Young, who remains Alaska's sole representative to the U.S. Congress.) Earlier, pilot Don E. Jonz of Fairbanks had elected to take off from the Anchorage airport in marginal weather. Jonz was a well-regarded pilot who'd once written (in an article titled "Ice without Fear"), "If you are sneaky, smart and careful, you can fly 350 days a year and disregard ninety-nine percent of the b.s. you read about icing." Another family friend, John Chalupnik, suffered a cerebral hemorrhage at the controls of his single-engine PA-12. His non-pilot wife and soon-to-be widow, Joan, landed the plane from the back seat and, years later, married one of my uncles. There was the twenty-something park ranger who kindly offered me and my hiking companions a lift from the Wonder Lake campground to the Eielson Visitor Center at Denali Park a few years ago. He died when the plane in which he was a passenger went down in bad weather after trying to rescue stranded climbers on Mount McKinley. And then there was Joe Finkel, Nancy's first husband. Then Nancy herself.

The sequence of events after any fatal plane crash is nearly always the same. The media report the *who, what, when,* and *where*; readers, friends, and family speculate on the *how* and *why*, which seem forever under investigation. Hungry for narrative, we fall ravenously on any crumbs that fall our way. Speculation is better than nothing. The first rumor emerged the day after Nancy's crash: the Maule's ignition key had been snapped in two. For a few hours, I believed it because I wanted—no, needed—to believe that, in the end, Nancy mustered superhuman strength, acting heroically but futilely to restart the engine in the face of faulty technology. In fact, everything I know about physics and matter belies that rumor. What we cannot bear, we misconstrue.

Something about the day-in, day-out pursuit of a death-defying hobby or profession nurtures a moralizing streak in many pilots. Every crash yields an instructive lesson. In *The Right Stuff,* Tom Wolfe calls this lesson or moral a "theorem": "There are no accidents and no fatal flaws in the machines; there are only pilots with the wrong stuff. (I.e. blind Fate can't kill me.)" After Nancy's death, a pilot friend sent me a long e-mail advancing this moral/theorem: "When mountain flying, you should always put maximum distance between your plane and the ground. Nancy did not, and it killed her." The National Transportation Safety Board seems to concur, albeit in more disinterested terms. It issued a report on the crash of Maule 9237 Echo one year afterward. The report's language is bone clean, rigorously non-narrative, stripped of any emotion, ornament, judgment. Nancy had logged nearly 650 hours as a pilot—the equivalent of sixteen forty-hour workweeks. She'd passed the required physical with nothing more than the stipulation that she wear—as I too must—contact lenses or glasses. She'd passed a biennial flight review a few days before the crash.

The NTSB report is heavier on description than analysis, and mostly what it describes is machinery. Investigators found the cables that connect the rudder and ailerons to the cockpit intact, meaning the airplane didn't break apart in the air. A thorough examination of the engine turned up no "pre-impact" anomalies. The report states: "The primary crush zones extended from the firewall area back to about the forward doorpost, and encompassed the pilot and front seat passenger area. The fuselage was buckled and folded, and the empennage was positioned downhill." (I had to look up "empennage": an elegant term for the rudder-, elevator-, and trim-assembly.) The likely cause of the crash, according to the NTSB, was "[t]he pilot's inadvertent stall of the airplane during an unknown phase of flight."

Therein lies the crux. In one sentence, the NTSB advances a theory of causality. Nancy's husband disagreed. In a lawsuit, he alleged that a fuel company employee failed to replace the cap on Nancy's private tank, thereby allowing water to seep into the fuel supply. Fuel contaminated by water might cause an airplane to stall, likely on takeoff, when it sucks the most fuel. Lending credence to such a theory might be evidence—not mentioned in the NTSB report—that the ignition key was broken in half. If so, Nancy might have died trying to restart her engine.

Put simply, Nancy's husband's theory is that mechanical failure caused by a fuel deliveryman's error led to the crash. Finding no evidence of mechanical failure, the NTSB, on the other hand, advances a theory of pilot error. Those two words, "pilot error," may not appear anywhere in the report. They don't have to. The phrase "pilot's inadvertent stall of the airplane" adds up to only one thing, which is pilot error. To understand why, you must understand that, in an airplane, a stall is what happens to the wing or wings, not the engine. Mechanical failure can and often does contribute to a stall. Even then, the agent of a stall is almost always the pilot. In the simplest possible terms, engines quit; pilots stall.

Once airborne, the pilot's single biggest task is to prevent the airplane from stalling before it's time to land. At the risk of getting too technical, a propeller-driven plane climbs out due to a complex combination of forces, one of which is lift. The equation for lift is

$$L = C_L S \frac{\rho}{2} V^2 \text{ or } L = C_L \times S \times \frac{\rho}{2} \times V^2$$

Bear with me. You don't have to get the math in order to get what's next. (In fact, you don't have to get the math in order to fly: I'm living proof.) In addition to lift, there's the rate of climb, which is controlled by the throttle. Then there's the angle of attack, which is controlled by the elevators. Technically, the angle of attack is the angle between the relative wind and the chord line of the airfoil (airfoil being a fancy term for the wing). A nose-high profile or attitude creates a steep angle of attack; a nose-low attitude creates a shallow one. Airplanes fly in part because, like birds, they've got the anatomy for it; in part because they've got engines to propel them through the air; and in part because the pilot arbitrates between wind (strength as well as direction), power, and angle of attack. To get angle of attack, think of the paper airplanes you launched in your second-grade classroom. If you threw yours straight up to get it higher than everyone else's, it probably went into a spiral and crashed. Smarter the second time, you flattened out the angle of attack to maximize glide. Angle of attack is what you get when you temper ambition (the desire to ascend as swiftly as possible) with efficiency (the necessity of ascending safely).

I wish to god it were that simple. Look once more at the formula for lift. It takes into account air density (ρ) or barometric pressure. Barometric pressure explains why a fifteen-degree angle of attack combined with a seventy-knot airspeed suffices for takeoff on one day but not the next. On a cool morning, a light aircraft with half a tank of fuel and one person on board catapults into the sky with a steep angle of attack and low airspeed. On a hot afternoon, that same aircraft with four people on board and a full load of fuel pulls substantially more power to clamber off the runway. That's what's known as flying "heavy" as opposed to flying "light." When the weather is warm, air molecules cluster together, making the air denser and more difficult for an airplane to penetrate. Therefore, climbing out heavy on a ninety-degree day requires a (seemingly paradoxical) low or nose-down attitude and lots of power.

On the day of the crash, Nancy was flying heavy (three passengers, plenty of fuel, floats) in unseasonable (seventy-five-degree) heat. She took off from the float pond at Fairbanks International Airport in the morning and landed a couple of hours later above the Arctic Circle, at Lake Sithylemenkat, which is ringed by 3,000- and 4,000-foot peaks.

In my imagination, Nancy and her friends picnicked on ham sandwiches, hiked around for a bit, and even scavenged for blueberries, although mid-July is pretty early for them. Perhaps they posed for goofy group pictures, Nancy in the middle with her arms looped around the shoulders of her med school colleague and the colleague's husband. Was she happy at that moment? I like to think so.

Around 3:30 p.m., a satellite picked up Nancy's emergency locator transmitter signal. A pilot in distress can set off an ELT deliberately, or it can be set off by turbulence. Most often, though, it goes off in response to a sudden impact. Given the state of communications technology, 3:30 p.m. is probably, give or take a moment or two, when the crash occurred. In lieu of "crash," the NTSB prefers "collision"—as in, an airplane and a mountain were involved in a collision: *On July 15, 2001, at an estimated time of 1530 Alaska daylight time, a float-equipped Maule M-5-235C airplane . . . sustained substantial damage during a collision with mountainous terrain, about fifty miles south of Bettles, Alaska.*

The news that the "certificated" pilot and three passengers died—"received fatal injuries"—doesn't come until the report's fourth sentence. Instead of the straightforward "died" or even the passive but sufficient "were killed," we get three multi-syllabics: "received fatal injuries." This bureaucratese might be meant to elide some kind of knowledge gap, perhaps the time of death. No one can say for sure that Nancy and her friends died on impact, only that they were dead by the time the first rescuer arrived.

A state Fish and Wildlife Protection officer spotted the wreckage around 6:00 p.m. It was strewn along the side of a mountain three miles from the lake. The officer landed his wheel-equipped plane along a ridgeline roughly a thousand feet above the wreckage. According to the report, he encountered southeasterly winds from seventeen to twenty knots, significant gusts for a light plane. I'm fascinated by the report's relish for numbers—dates, times, aircraft IDs, wind strength, temperature. Facts always trump emotion. We find out that the wind was blowing between seventeen and twenty knots, but not what it felt like for the pilot to pull off a fairly technical tundra landing then walk toward that mangled airplane. Did he hope against hope that someone had survived, becoming more certain with every step that no one had?

In pilot lingo, crash victims "bought the farm" or "bunched it," as in, "Harold ran out of fuel in Windy Pass and bunched it." The FAA tends toward acronyms such as "C-FIT," meaning "Controlled Flight into Terrain." The NTSB report describes Nancy's crash this way: "Post-accident investigation revealed that the nose of the airplane impacted in a near vertical attitude, on the soft, tundra-covered terrain." The vernacular for that kind of crash is "augered in."

By focusing on the cause of the *crash*—"the pilot's inadvertent stall . . . during an unknown phase of flight"—the NTSB sidesteps speculation on the cause of the *stall.* The agency is acting more like a coroner testifying at an inquest ("the bullet tore through the abdominal wall and nicked the heart before exiting the body") than a witness at trial ("I saw him shoot Bobby! I swear it!"). Why? Perhaps as a hedge against the inevitable lawsuits. It's not easy for survivors to file a wrongful death suit based on a report that says an inadvertently stalled airplane collided with mountainous terrain, resulting in "fatal injuries" to those on board. More likely, the report ducks the question of who's at fault largely because that question is largely unanswerable. Of course, its open-endedness doesn't stop Nancy's and my friends, especially the pilots, from blaming Nancy's death on a combination of hubris and heat. "I believe," says one, "that the combination of a full load, warm weather, and a nice breeze are what caused Nancy's demise . . . What makes it tragic to me is that no matter what you say about cause, she failed to fly a route that would maximize separation between the ground and the plane."

Before takeoff from Lake Sithylemenkat, Nancy would have pumped excess water from the floats. She would have checked the engine, fuel supply, and control surfaces. She would have done a simple test designed to detect water in the fuel supply. Detecting any, she would not, presumably, have taken off. Yet shortly after takeoff, something went terribly wrong. Perhaps the takeoff was sluggish. Perhaps Nancy felt (rightly or wrongly) that she needed more height to clear the high peaks ringing the lake. Perhaps she behaved instinctually, pulling back on the stick and steepening her angle of attack. I say "instinctually" because it makes sense to point the nose of the plane where you want it to go. But a pilot as accomplished and mature as Nancy would have tempered gut-level instinct with a practical grounding in physics, especially Newton's Law: "For every action there is an equal and opposite reaction." Raising the nose inhibits the flow of air over the wing, which in turn slows the airplane. To a point, such slowing can be counteracted by the addition of power. Raise the nose too high, though, and the airplane will stop flying even if its throttle is wide open. This event—the engine is running, but the plane is not flying—is called a stall. Pilots call this particular stall a "power-on" or "takeoff" stall. It is nearly always deadly.

Nancy may have poured on the power at the same time she steepened her angle of attack. That would have been a reasonable response to a reasoned perception that she needed altitude. Perhaps a downdraft slid over one of the peaks, palming the plane like a giant's hand and introducing a fresh variable. The textbook response would have been to dip a wing into the wind, ease up on the throttle, lower the nose, and ride out the draft. In short, to reduce the angle of attack and climb out more gradually. But Nancy couldn't climb out gradually: those peaks were *close*. My guess is that she shouldered into the wind, poured on the power and maintained a relatively steep angle of attack. That strategy might have worked if the wind hadn't quit abruptly, as mountain winds are wont to do, catching the plane in an untenable attitude: nose high and wing low. The plane stalled then rolled over on its back, the first loop of a death spiral. With 3,000 feet between her and the ground, a pilot as experienced as Nancy could have recovered. But Nancy didn't have anywhere near 3,000 feet.

Post-accident investigation revealed no anomalies with the Maule's airframe or engine. The NTSB exposed Nancy's fuel to a water-detecting paste that turned out negative. The preponderance of evidence suggests that unlike her first husband, Nancy wasn't the victim of mechanical failure. Blind Fate didn't kill *her*; pilot error probably did.

In the mid-1980s, Nancy and I both hung out with a tight-knit group of kayakers, "The Crack of Noon Club," on the Nenana River near Denali Park, roughly 140 miles south of Fairbanks. Nancy and I were at roughly the same level in terms of risk-taking and skill, so we often paddled together, trading off the lead through the fiercer rapids. Once, at the end of a downriver race, I slipped into a nasty recirculating hole. My boat floated free, then my paddle, but not me. In the idiom of boating, I was getting "maytagged" by water pouring over the rock, striking the river bottom then furling upward. After thirty seconds of this, I surfaced to see Nancy's red Dancer cresting the pillow of water above me. It bonked me on the head then flipped over. Like me, Nancy got sucked out of her boat; like me, she went through the high-speed wash cycle. The dynamics of that particular hole were such that it couldn't handle two of us. For the sake of the metaphor, I wish I could say that I was the one who got lucky and floated free while Nancy stayed in the hole for what felt like an eternity, until a couple of guys got their act together to stage a rescue. Instead, the one who nearly drowned that day was me.

I married one of my rescuers. Nancy and I had both been drawn to him, the most daring kayaker in the group. She never told me so, but I saw the way her eyes followed him on the river. He was strong and silent and kind, an accomplished climber as well as kayaker. For reasons I still don't get, he picked me over Nancy. The morning after I stayed overnight for the first time, the phone rang. It was Nancy, inviting him to a movie that afternoon. He turned her down, saying that "we"—meaning he and I—had plans. We went as a couple to Nancy and Joe's wedding, and to Joe's funeral. By the time Nancy died, my husband and I were leading two separate lives in one house, too caught up in the pain of our unraveling marriage to pretend for the sake of old friends that everything was all right. I'd changed as a result of graduate school then motherhood. Risking my neck every weekend was no longer my favorite pastime. Housebound, my husband and I found we had less to say to each other than on a river or a glacier. Our silence filled rooms. I began reading again. Essentially, I fell back in love with books. In Nabokov and Neruda, Didion and Mailer, Bishop and Agee I found beauty, wit, and wisdom. Their voices filled my head. They shed light on the world, and I saw that it was bigger than I'd ever imagined.

A few weeks before Christmas '94 or '95, I bumped into Joe Finkel at the grocery store. He pulled his cart up alongside mine and told me all about Nancy's gift: fluorescent lights and shelving for a basement greenhouse. "I hope she likes it," he said.

"She's going to *love* it," I told him. What else could I say? Marriage might have domesticated Nancy more than I thought.

On Christmas afternoon, he and Nancy showed up at our house for a gathering of kayakers. Nancy's lips were tight, Joe's expression hangdog. I grabbed his arm.

"What's going on?" I whispered.

"Wrong present."

When I was in junior high, my parents bought a house in a new development outside of Fairbanks. Our neighbors were mostly professionals with children. On one side lived a veterinarian, his glamorously named wife, Belle, and their pampered only daughter, Billie Jo. On the other side lived an air cargo pilot and his wife, Dee. I don't remember ever setting eyes on him; he did most of his flying at night. Dee seemed exotic in comparison to my mother, the buttoned-up New England surgeon's daughter. Dee had bleached blonde hair, cotton-candy fingernails, sun-bronzed skin (those were the early days of tanning booths), and a smoker's husky voice. My mother might have described her as "brassy," a word she frequently paired with "divorcee." Dee and my mother were friendly without being friends. They spoke whenever they saw each other, and my father surely exchanged flying credentials with Dee's husband. We children barely knew the two of them existed. Certainly, we never set foot inside their house.

For an airplane to fly, two things are required: lift and momentum. The airfoil, or wing, creates lift, and the engine provides momentum. An airplane can fly without an engine, though not forever; it cannot ever fly without wings. What makes the wings work is the flow of air above and below them. This air flows at two different speeds: slower on top, faster on the bottom. Air flowing over the top races to catch up to air flowing under the bottom. It never succeeds. In physical terms, what makes a plane fly is disequilibrium. In metaphoric terms, it's the tension of wanting what can never be had. To grasp the principle of lift is to see why a pilot's worst nightmare is not losing an engine but losing a wing.

One day, Dee's husband was flying a cargo jet at altitude when a wing fell off. The house next door to ours went dark, insulated shades drawn against puny sunlight. My mother rang the doorbell, casserole in hand, but no one answered. I may have seen Dee once more before she sold the house and moved away. She may have been thin and haggard, shriveled like a raisin inside her suntan. To be honest, I don't remember. What I do remember is the way her house went overnight from being a home to being an empty shell.

It's possible to lose a wing without really losing a wing. To stall is temporarily to lose both wings—a slightly better scenario, by the way, than losing just one. Student pilots practice stalls the way that beginning musicians practice scales. Over and over again, until they become second nature. Some student pilots think they're boring. Not me. To this day, every stall is as scary as a dress rehearsal for my own death.

A mile or two southeast of the Fairbanks airport lies a three-dimensional practice area for student pilots. The terrain is nearly flat, the tundra crisscrossed only by four-wheeler trails, dotted by decaying cabins. No houses or people. Here and there the wreckage of an airplane being reclaimed by earth. The drill here is to ascend to 3,000 feet then perform what's known as a clearing turn, a 360-degree scan for traffic. One or more clearing turns are *de rigeur* whenever you practice slow flight. Entering slow flight, you raise the nose, reduce the throttle, add carb heat, and pull a notch of flaps. Slow flight in the Arctic Tern falls between thirty and seventy miles an hour, roughly the range of rush-hour traffic on the New Jersey Turnpike. In slow flight, the airplane's controls feel spongy, its responses sluggish.

An airplane configured for slow flight is also configured for landing, the trickiest leg of any flight. Of the myriad things that can go wrong, a premature landing stall is one of the deadliest. That's why you practice slow flight and power-off (or landing) stalls at altitude before the first solo. To perform a power-off stall, you enter slow flight then simultaneously cut the power and lift the nose until you feel as if you're flying through plasma. The stall, when it comes, feels like a gentle tug on the tail feathers. Then falling. To recover, you push the nose forward and lay on the power.

Compared to a takeoff stall, a landing stall is a piece of cake. You practice the takeoff stall with the throttle wide open. Then you pull back on the stick until the airplane is practically standing on its tail. At the same time, you dance on the pedals to prevent one wing or the other—though usually the left one—from dropping. You hold the plane, protesting, in this position for uncountable seconds. Then it shudders, jerks, and drops. You recover by releasing backpressure on the stick and permitting the nose to fall, meanwhile using the rudder pedals to straighten out the wings.

The likeliest scenario for a landing stall is that the pilot, realizing he might touch down prematurely, pulls back on the stick to keep the plane in the air longer. The likeliest scenario for a takeoff stall is that the pilot, realizing she might crash into a copse of trees or a mountain pulls back on the stick to gain altitude faster. To recover from either kind of stall, two things are necessary: presence of mind and altitude. Presence of mind is a learnable skill. Dozens of practice stalls teach you to feel the limits of the aircraft and to override that instinctual stick-back response. Altitude, on the other hand, is neither state of mind nor skill. As a standard part of every private pilot check ride, the examiner pulls the throttle to simulate engine failure and asks the student to set up for an emergency landing. To ask an ordinary pilot (as opposed to a stunt pilot) to execute a low-altitude stall, however, would be madness. Only someone with a death wish would do it. With stalls, it's possible to replicate the event and the recovery, but not the context in which they commonly occur.

One of the awful corollaries to growing older is crafting condolence letters. I went to more funerals in the year 2000 than weddings and baby showers combined. Every time a colleague's father drops dead of a heart attack, a friend's husband kills himself, or a cousin is diagnosed with inoperable cancer, I stare helplessly at the blank insides of a card. Grief is a country whose boundaries cannot be breached by language or even gesture. Words won't suffice, but they're all we've got. Once or twice, I've actually written the line, "Words fail me when I try to say something meaningful about your loss," but it seems not only self-conscious but selfish, as if to suggest that my struggle to find the right words even registers alongside the struggle of the bereaved—as if *she* ought to feel sorry for *me*.

So language not only fails but, paradoxically and frustratingly, it fails worst when we need it most. In this essay, I'm trying to work my way back to the language of accident reports. In the effort to be objective and just, such reports often sacrifice an even higher objective, which is humanity. Accidents happen not to people but to airplanes or cars or ships, all seemingly acting without human agency or consequence. Even natural disasters get described principally in terms of the havoc they wreak on objects.

A historical marker along Route 29, in Nelson County, Virginia, recalls the events of August 19, 1969: Torrential rains, following remnants of Hurricane Camille, devastated this area. A rainfall in excess of 25 inches largely within a five-hour period, swept away or buried many miles of roads, over 100 bridges, and over 900 buildings. 114 people died and 87 remain missing. The damage totaled more than $1,000,000 and Virginia was declared a disaster area.

This is history as a spreadsheet: Camille = >25 inches of rain. Destruction = X miles of road, >100 bridges, >900 buildings, ≅201 people. Cost = >$1 million.

It must've felt like an apocalypse by water. Rain melted hillsides and swelled mountain brooks to ravening rivers that devoured houses, barns, churches, bridges, and tractor-trailers. Most of the victims did not drown but were beaten to death by debris such as trees, boulders, steel beams, truck tires, antiques, and livestock. Identifying them was not easy. Newspaper accounts describe doctors doing autopsies in a tent behind a funeral home. On the strength of stomach contents, they were able to sort the dead into families: *The Smiths had spaghetti for supper, so this must be little Billy . . .*

We are a nation in love with statistics. The narrowing of the gap between prose reports and numerical spreadsheets ought not to surprise me, but it does. I'm not talking about language pressed into political service, to finesse a lie into truth or to shame silence out of dissent. At forty-three, I'm not so naïve as to register outrage or even surprise at the means of propagandists. My question is, what or whose interests are served by a version of history so bland that the body count ranks behind damage to property and just ahead of the money problem?

Sam Dragga of Texas Tech University and Dan Voss of Lockheed Martin write about accident reports. They conclude that, by and large, such reports force writers as well as readers to "divorce themselves from their humanistic impulses and perceive accident victims as simple archaeological artifacts."

The NTSB report on Nancy's crash focuses in a fetishistic way on the aircraft, thereby turning her into a kind of artifact or irrelevancy. One is given to understand, in the first few sentences, that "the accident aircraft" and mountainous terrain have been involved in a collision, causing "substantial" damage to the airplane. Even after the fourth sentence, with its "received fatal injuries" circumlocution, neither Nancy nor her passengers are identified by name. Nancy is merely the "accident pilot" or "the certificated commercial pilot." The plane, in contrast, is known by its make and tail number: Maule 9237 Echo. The Maule logged 1,207 hours of flight, Nancy only 643. Tests revealed there were no contaminants to the Maule's fuel supply, just as an autopsy revealed there were no contaminants—drugs or alcohol—in Nancy's body.

According to Professor Dragga, the language of marine accident reports tends to be more humanizing than that of airplane, automobile, or industrial accidents. When I asked him why, he said he wasn't sure. He pointed out that machines are relatively recent inventions compared to boats, whose history dates to the first observation that wood floats. Our collective modern unconscious (if there is such a thing) may cleave to the notion that drowning is a more natural, and therefore more *human*, form of death than a mangling in a machine. Professor Dragga also observed that the corpses of shipwrecked sailors or fishermen are rarely found unless they wash ashore separately from the wreckage of their ship. It makes sense, in a sick kind of way, that a corpse entangled in wreckage becomes, in the language of the accident report, conflated with that wreckage.

Even the most factual, objective, and neutral reports offer up a moral. The very act of depersonalizing—of *depersoning*—a report is the act of casting judgment. It's the ultimate revenge of the guy with the notebook or the girl with her nose in a novel. Like Icarus, the pilot seeks to transcend our too-human condition and fly like a bird or a god. For a while, the trick works; giddy with pleasure or fear, she steepens her angle of attack and flies into the sun. Who can say when or why transcendence becomes transgression? Then she falls. Like Icarus she falls, a ball of melted wax and feathers. Is it any wonder that our scribes sometimes treat as less than human those whose failed enterprises seek to make us more?

In *Wind, Sand and Stars*, Antoine de Saint-Exupery writes, "When a pilot dies in the harness his death seems something that inheres in the craft itself, and in the beginning the hurt it brings is perhaps less than the pain sprung of a different death." It's a lofty way of saying, "At least he died doing what he loved." In Saint-Exupery's phrasing, I like the ambiguity of the word "craft." If I were to check it against the original French, I'd probably find that the conflation of "craft" as in "art" with "craft" as in "machine" was purely accidental. So I won't check. Furthermore, the poetry of Saint-Exupery's phrasing (again, in translation)—"inhere" and "in harness"—lends the pilot's death a kind of dignity that less beautiful language ("received fatal injuries") cannot.

According to the autopsy report, Nancy died of "multiple blunt force impact," another indigestible hunk of verbiage: what, precisely, does "multiple" modify, "blunt force" or "impact"? And what, precisely, is "blunt" force—presumably, the opposite of "sharp" force, but what is *that*? Finally, what does it *feel* like to die from "multiple blunt force impact"? (It may not be as bad as it sounds, according to the physician Sherwin Muland. In *How We Die*, he writes, "Endorphin elevation appears to be an innate physiological mechanism to protect mammals and perhaps other animals against the emotional and physical dangers of terror and pain.") Parsing the prose of accident investigators must look like a cheap shot. On the contrary, I feel nothing but respect for those who conduct serious and detailed investigations of baroque complexity then write up their findings as carefully as they can. The work matters. I just want more: the outtakes or behind-the-scenes footage, if you will. What's it like, the back-and-forth between investigators at an accident scene? Or do they even talk as they measure impact craters, trace cable lines, apply water-detecting paste? Do they rail against the pointless waste of human life? Crack off-color jokes? Sometimes I wonder if the language of NTSB reports is antiseptic not because the authors feel nothing at all but because they feel so much.

You may well ask, if it upsets you, why bother to read the NTSB report? If it depresses you, why bother with any story that ends badly? The answer, in part, is that stories about other people's dying remind me, the reader, I'm alive. I don't think I'm alone. After hearing that someone has died, and how, those of us blessed—or burdened—with reflection tend to feel our own lives more acutely. Also, we read because we want to slip inside the skin of someone who's crossed over, if only for a moment. In life, Nancy was a kind of doppelganger for me; in dying, she stole the death that I, the reader and homebody, had imagined for myself time and again. Of course I read the report.

My estranged husband brought back a program from Nancy's memorial service. In one photograph, she reclines like a tundra odalisque. Her legs are crossed, and she leans on one elbow. Yellow poppies spring up around her, picking up the yellow in her Patagonia fleece pullover. Instead of an elastic band, clips hold her hair back off her face. Behind her, barely visible, rise shale cliffs dusted with snow, softened by fog. Nancy smiles knowingly for the photographer, her new husband Hugh. It is 1999, and they're on the Charlie River together. Joy lights Nancy from the inside. She's incandescent with it. Seeing that, I cried for a long time.

The summer before she died, I was flying home from my family's cabin on the Salcha River when I heard Nancy's voice. She was flying away from Fairbanks, north to the Brooks Range.

For thirty seconds or so, we shared a radio frequency. The controller asked each of us for our position, and we gave it. We didn't speak to each other. That's one of the rules: no kibbutzing on the radio. Even so, I flatter myself that Nancy recognized my voice, too. Hearing her, I felt the old envy well up: she was bound for somewhere interesting while I was headed home with a kid in the back seat. I might as well have been at the helm of a minivan. If there'd ever been a contest, it was over. Nancy had surpassed me as a pilot, outdoorswoman, and Alaskan. She'd found happiness—or so I heard—in her second marriage. Who was I to begrudge her any of it? After a moment or so, the envy subsided. What rose up next caught me by surprise. It was the warmest kind of kinship, as if I'd just passed my own self in midair.

NINE ~ Blue Storm

In my second week of graduate school, a slip of paper appeared in my campus mailbox. It listed the books I was to read in preparation for the comprehensive exam, eighteen months hence. There were forty-odd titles on the list, including Saint Augustine's *Confessions,* Rousseau's *Confessions,* Thomas de Quincey's *Confessions of an English Opium-Eater,* James Agee's Let *Us Now Praise Famous Men,* and John Haines's *The Stars, the Snow, the Fire.* Being the sort of person who often gets things almost right ("'Almost' only counts in horseshoes," my mother's father used to say), I picked up a copy of Antoine de Saint-Exupery's *Wind, Sand and Stars.* It was pure serendipity. In paperback, Saint-Exupery's memoir is a little book, maybe four by six inches, roughly the size of *The Book of Common Prayer* or my open palm: 243 pages of densely packed, no-frills serif typeface and such laconic chapter titles as "The Craft," "The Men," "The Tool," and "The Elements." The writing is as fresh as if Saint-Ex were seeing the world—"the naked rind of the planet"—for the first time, which is how flying must have felt to him and his compatriots, the men who put the "Avion" in "Par Avion." In the early years of the twentieth century, the first international mail pilots took off from tiny fields in "tenebrous" darkness and "tacked in the direction of Mercury." They landed on runways lit by flickering gas flares. Or they didn't.

My copy of *Wind, Sand and Stars* has suffered in the decade or so since graduate school. The word "Wind" has blown off the spine, the corners have curled into ringlets, and the innards have been worn to the texture of cotton sacking. When shuffled, the pages fall open to certain passages the way that conversations with certain friends slide into certain grooves. It's not exactly friendship I feel toward the book, though. Over the years, the contours of Saint-Exupery's prose have become as familiar as a lover's body; like a lover's body, I can count on them to surprise and—marvelous archaism—to pleasure me.

Is it naïve to believe that one or two books or even a poem can change your life? Isak Dinesen's *Out of Africa* and Beryl Markham's *West with the Night* made me want to become a pilot. *Wind, Sand and Stars* made me want to become a writer. It also made me despair—as the best books tend to do—that I ever would.

A book is what made my father want to become a pilot, too. He read it in the mid-1950s, shortly after he'd won an ROTC scholarship to Yale then flunked the Navy physical on account of his overbite. (In the days of close combat at sea, sailors had to be able to grip musket balls in their teeth.) Yale then offered my father an academic scholarship on the strength of his math score, but he turned it down. He'd just read *Battle Cry* by Leon Uris, a novel about the Marines in World War II, and he was going to become a Marine pilot. On a recruiter's handshake, he enlisted. He flunked the Marines' flight physical on account of a rare visual defect: under extreme duress, he might be prone to seeing double. The doctor prescribed an exercise with a pencil, which my father performed every day for three hours before re-taking the physical. This time, he flunked it decisively. Nearly seventy years old now, he has never in his life suffered a bout of double vision.

The Marines wouldn't make him a pilot, but they wouldn't let him out, either. My father went to boot camp. Afterward, everyone else in his platoon received orders for Korea. He was sent to electronics school. The military electronics shop in Albany, Georgia, ran along civilian lines. My father likes to say it was the first and only time in his life that he punched a time clock. A quick study at electronics, he soon found himself, a mere corporal, supervising sergeants and warrant officers. Just before his stint ended, his commanding officer called him in to say he was Annapolis-bound.

"Thank you very much, but no, Sir," my father recalls saying. "He got pretty unhappy with me then, but my feeling was, if I couldn't fly, I just wanted to get my time in and get it over with."

Antoine de Saint-Exupery was born in 1900 in Lyon, France, to a family of provincial nobles whose fortunes, like those of provincial nobles everywhere at the turn of the twentieth century, were declining. His paternal grandfather was a count, his maternal grandfather a baron. When Saint-Exupery was four, his father died of a stroke, leaving his mother a widow with five children and very little money. If not for the kindness—freely and cheerfully given, it seems—of family and friends, Madame Saint-Exupery and her brood would have been homeless. Instead, they and their retinue of tutors, governesses, and servants shifted every few months from one chateau to another. A mischievous but charming boy who was always tearing the knees out of his pants, young Antoine tried to design and build a flying bicycle. According to his biographer, Stacy Schiff, the wings were made of bed sheets mounted on wicker supports. As a fledgling pilot in the early 1920s—in *his* early twenties—Saint-Ex found his passion and his meaning in flight. The more I think about it, the more I believe he became a writer *because* he could fly.

In 1926, the general manager of Compagnie Latecoere, the French mail line, interviewed him for a position. On being offered a desk job, Saint-Exupery reportedly (again, according to Schiff) rose to his considerable height and spluttered, "Monsieur, I especially want to fly . . . only to fly!" The manager allowed as how that might eventually happen. First, however, Saint-Exupery had to serve an apprenticeship as a mechanic. Later that same year, he got his first assignment, to fly "the mails," as they were known, over the Pyrenees from Toulouse, France, to Alicante, Spain, then back. His craft was an open cockpit Breguet 14. The elements were wind, fog, rain, and snow. On his return, bad weather forced him down in a field miles from his base—an ignominious start to a career in which even the low points were to become the stuff of legend.

My father was born in Dade City, Florida, between world wars, in 1934, to Luther and Helen Brice, a pair of self-starters who reared four natural-born sons (my father was the eldest) as well as two adopted sons and an adopted daughter. My father's birth was a difficult one. My grandmother liked to tell the story of how, on seeing little Alba Luther for the first time, my grandfather drawled, "Well, now, Helen. If that's the best we can do, we'd better quit now."

Nearly twenty years later, the Marines would run a background check on my father for a security clearance and find no record of his existing before age fourteen. They would see this as somewhat suspicious. My father would then have to explain. At age fourteen, he had had to produce a birth certificate to play high school football. Neither he nor his parents had ever bothered with the birth certificate before then. If they had, they might have discovered even sooner that my father's name was not, in fact, Alba Luther but Luther Alba. The source of the mix-up is murky. My grandmother blamed her mother-in-law, Ada Brice Loudon, who stepped in while my grandmother was still weak from childbirth. It was, after all, Ada's son, my grandfather, who was named Luther. The less favored name of Alba belonged to the other side of the family, descending from my grandmother's father.

In pictures from when they were courting, Luther looks movie star handsome in the mold of Clark Gable or Robert Duvall: tawny complected with a high forehead, golden eyes, and sensual lips. In contrast to the dashing looks, he possessed a mild disposition. My grandmother brought vivacity and charisma to the relationship. As a young woman, she had the round face and broadly drawn features of an Eastern European peasant. (Her ancestors, the McNutts, were in fact Scotch.) Her short blonde hair blew away from her face like dandelion fluff. She was not beautiful, but she had enough personality to fill a room. When she met my grandfather, she was, in her words, "just out of the conservatory," having finished a degree in piano performance at Macon Wesleyan. My guess is, from the moment she set her cap for him, he never had a chance.

When my father was growing up, Luther worked as a logger and sometime sawmill operator. The family moved around between northern Florida and southern Georgia, following the work. They were in Augusta, Georgia, when the Japanese bombed Pearl Harbor. My grandfather enlisted in the Navy Construction Battalion. The Seabees, as they were known, filled up with men young enough to serve but too old for the infantry; my grandfather was thirty-two. When he went to war, my grandmother went to work. She hired a woman to look after the boys and took a job at a radio station. Every afternoon at the appointed hour, eight-year-old Alba and his three brothers—Sam, Andy, and Thom—tuned in to find out when their mother would be home. If she signed on saying, "This is WGAC Augusta," it meant she'd be in the kitchen fixing their dinner within the hour. If she said, "This is WGAC Augusta, Georgia," it meant she was working late and might not be home before their bedtime.

In 1943, the Associated Press offered my grandmother a job in California. She moved herself and the boys across the country, to the town of Richmond. She covered local and state politics. (In 1978, Richard Nixon would stride through the lobby of Claridge's Hotel in London, where she and I were guests. To my chagrin, she would step into his path, put out her hand, and say, "Mr. Nixon, I haven't seen you since I covered your House campaign in '46." To my surprise, he'd shake her proffered hand and say, feelingly, "It's good to see you again.") She enrolled the older boys in military school in Oregon for a few months then pulled them out when money got tight. The war ended, and Luther came home. He and Helen tried to pick up where they'd left off, but the war had changed them both. Helen had always been the kind of cook who could transform a breast of chicken, a cup of cream, and a handful of beans into a gourmet dinner for six. With a gallon of paint and a few artfully arranged pieces of fabric, she could turn a house into a home. Having unleashed all of that creative energy on the outside world, she wasn't about to go back to the kitchen.

My grandparents' marriage, stormy from the start, became even stormier. More than once, they split up for a few weeks or months then got back together. During the years when I knew them, they led separate lives, sometimes on opposite ends of the country, sometimes under the same roof.

My grandmother was brilliant, eccentric, thin-skinned, generous, flamboyant, and narcissistic. She was meant to be an actress or a stage director, a career that could have fed her ambition and cordoned off her real life from her imagined one. *A real dynamo,* people used to say, admiringly. *A great lady.*

A piece of work, I used to think, disloyally. Studying abnormal psychology in college, I found an ailment to explain everyone in my family. Delusions of grandeur was hers.

Granddad was unflappable. Also hard working, gentlemanly, dignified. Faint praise, perhaps, but I adored him. He was easier to love than my grandmother. Sweeter, for one thing. Funny, too. She'd harangue ("Now *Daddy,*" she'd begin, exasperated, "you *know* . . . "), and he'd retreat.

In her dotage, my grandmother spent several months out of every year traveling, either by herself or with one of her grandchildren. She took me to Europe and to South America. My grandfather stayed home. Home was sometimes a 2,400-acre cattle ranch called Kanapaha, outside of Gainesville, Florida, sometimes a first-floor bedroom at the farm, my grandparents' home north of Fairbanks. My grandparents renovated the farm in the '70s, rebuilding it from the ground up. They turned its rabbit warren of tiny rooms into half a dozen large, light-filled spaces. My grandmother created a kind of great room for herself on the second floor. It had a walk-in closet, library, fireplace, balcony, and an atrium. It was elegant but a little weird. My grandmother staged elaborate theme parties with the farm as her set. (For Christmas one year, she had my uncles and cousins staple spruce boughs to the wood-paneled walls. Then she interspersed them with lit candelabra. It's a miracle we didn't all burn up.) She invited dozens of people: artists and politicians, restaurateurs and doctors, professors and priests. Also hitchhikers and hangers-on; her hairdresser, her travel agent, and her secretary; the owner of her favorite boutique; even the policeman who'd issued her a speeding ticket the week before.

My grandmother's party-giving talent was wasted on Fairbanks, Alaska, but it was wasted lavishly. She never let reality get in the way of her idea of how it should be. Like all hostesses who, given the great good fortune to be born half a century later, might have captained ships or companies, she was a bit of a bully. In the hours before one of her spectacles was set to begin, the phone at our house rang incessantly. It rang until my father surrendered, silently gathering his pipe, jacket, and car keys, and driving to the farm. For Christmas, my grandmother had horse-drawn sleigh rides that would have been fun if she hadn't forced us to sing "Jingle Bells" the whole time. For the Fourth of July, she had Lady Liberty (a legislator's wife) riding a white horse around the grounds. One year, she turned the field nearest the house into a range for golfers and skeet shooters. My job—if you can fathom it—was to fetch the golf balls. For indoor parties, she often shooed us grandchildren upstairs. The staircase began at the end of the buffet line, so strangers, not knowing any better, sometimes followed us up. They'd emerge at the top of the stairs into a room that was part stage set, part bedchamber. And there we'd sit, balancing plates of food on our laps, chatting politely in full view of my grandmother's bed.

If my grandmother's room was meant to inspire awe, my grandfather's was a refuge. It was on the first floor, at the back of the house, in the same place as the original master bedroom. After the renovations, it seemed smaller, though it may not have been. It was furnished cozily with a daybed, a camel-colored couch and chairs, built-in bookshelves, and a bulky TV that seemed forever tuned to football. A sideboard held a brass tray with a bottle of Old Granddad and three or four crystal tumblers. Cigarette smoke hazed the air. At family gatherings, the men gathered in this room. They sprawled on the couches and chairs. They propped their feet on the low, newspaper-strewn table. And they talked in construction code, what my mother calls "job talk." In my family, job talk is the male vernacular. To an outsider or a girl, it's profoundly impenetrable.

From the age of three on, I often spent Friday or Saturday night with my grandparents. "Can I spend the night at the farm?" I'd ask my mother, and she'd place the call. Or else my mother would say, "Grandma's on the phone. She wants to know if you'd like to spend the night at the farm." This spending-the-night-with-the-grandparents stuff was new to my mother, whose own grandparents had been wizened ancients not just from the time of her birth but, seemingly, from the time of their own. She said yes anyway, sensing that nights at the farm supplied something not on offer at home.

She was right. For one thing, spending the night with my grandparents let me indulge my dearest fantasy, which was to be an only child and the center of adult attention. For another, I liked the irregularity of my grandparents' household. They ate when they were hungry and went to sleep when they were tired. My grandmother fixed my favorite dish, lima beans in cream sauce. My grandfather let me watch whatever he was watching on the TV, snuggled between the two of them in the big bed (in the days before separate bedrooms). They woke in the middle of the night, switched off the crackling TV, then puttered around for a while. Low whimpers from the springer spaniels, Bubba and Sissy, were met by low murmurs from my grandparents. Drowsing in a bed still warm from their bodies, I felt strangely secure. What every child wants, perhaps: to be sure that while she's sleeping, the ones who love her are awake.

I was drawn to the undercurrents in that household, to the drama of my grandparents' marriage—more than to my own parents' staid and steady love. At the farm, anything could happen; few things surprised me. They surprise me now, in the telling: teeth grinning in tumblers beside the bathroom sink. Dog turds fossilizing in unused rooms. Wicker trunks sighing with filmy flesh-toned nightgowns and peignoirs with satin-trimmed mules to match. My grandmother let me parade around in the peignoirs and mules as well as her makeup and perfume. At bedtime, she ran me a bath just like hers, with water so hot it pinked up my skin. She had a profligate hand with the Vitabath, too. At the farm, the line between childhood and adulthood, so clearly drawn in my mother's Yankee household, all but disappeared.

Until her death in 1992, my grandmother was the weather in all of our lives. Even now, her secretary (who still works for the company) sends a fat manila envelope of my grandmother's letters and papers every few months. Whenever I see one of these envelopes addressed in Beverly's hand, I feel as if my grandmother is trying to boss me from beyond the grave. It's unfair of me, I know. But the truth is that if she could, she probably would. My grief for this woman who may have glimpsed in me something I failed to see—*fail* to see, even now—in myself is so great that I still weep, fourteen years on, at her salutation: "My Darling Jennifer." The intimate, intricate pattern of her thought is everywhere present in her letters. In the scrawled amplifications and emendations that spoke out from their mother sentences like so many speciation charts. In her lavish overuse of dashes, exclamation marks, and underlining. At their best, my grandmother's letters were ebullient songs of herself. At their worst, they were vehement exertions of her will to crush the imagined reader. My grandmother's letters were an education. They taught me that writing *matters.*

I said earlier that my grandmother was meant to be an actress or stage director. She was meant to be an artist of some kind, anyway, and epistolary drama was her form. She often spent several days on a single letter, picking up unfinished sentences or incomplete thoughts in a new color of ink. Or letting them lie on the page like dropped stitches. As a young, unformed woman, I hated her letters. They arrived sporadically, every few weeks or so, regardless of how much time had passed since one, or even since our last meeting. In fact, I was *more* likely to hear from her a day or two after dining *a deux* at the Bear and Seal, Fairbanks's best restaurant, than after several months of silence. She wrote to elaborate on a point from dinner or to comment on my eyebrows. (She was ever a fan of my eyebrows. In fact, she may be the only person who ever noticed them.) She wrote to continue the conversation. Or rather, to continue *controlling* the conversation. I, as the hapless recipient, was forced into silence, as helpless to get a word in edgewise as I'd been at dinner, when she'd imperiously ordered Caesar salad and scallops for us both. (I despised anchovies and scallops, craved the Bear and Seal's beef Wellington.)

Prude that I was, my grandmother's letters smacked to me of excessiveness bordering on promiscuity. I felt obligated to reply, which I did in the pinched and formal prose that has served since time immemorial as a fortress for otherwise weak or undefended psyches. She rightly saw these replies as provocations. As often as not, the next salvo came via the telephone, when she tartly observed that "resume" requires accents over both *e*s, as anyone who'd studied French for as many years as I had, and who'd been to France in the company of her grandmother, ought to know. I smarted at that. I'd been careless and gotten caught. She telephoned to say she didn't approve of the way I addressed my envelopes to her.

"I am *not* Mrs. Luther Liston Brice," she said. "*My* name is helenka Brice." In her mouth, "helenka" was a roller-coaster ride that climbed up at the beginning, lolled through the middle, then leapt off the end. It was an open secret that she'd invented the name herself—a bit of arty pretentiousness, I was tempted to say, but I didn't. I had to concede, grudgingly, that she was right. Petty, but right.

Some years after my grandmother's death, a carefully worded letter addressed to my father and his brothers showed up in the company mailbag. The four of them conferred over its contents in the front office with its horseshoe desk that had belonged to Grandma. Afterward, they crafted a warm reply. A few months later, a woman named Scott stepped off an Alaska Airlines jet. I wasn't there; the thinking was that we shouldn't overwhelm her with too many Brices at one go. Even so, she must've felt overwhelmed, walking toward that clutch of men a few years older than she, strangers who were unmistakably—that breadth of forehead, that hint of overbite—her brothers. My father, the oldest, had known about the dalliance between his father and Scott's mother in the vague way of a child who sees something happening but who doesn't bother to make sense of it. His parents were separated at the time. When Scott's letter came, a half-century later, he knew it for what it was: the genuine article. She'd waited until both of my grandparents were dead. Neither of them had known about her, and she hadn't wanted to cause them any pain. She wasn't after money or revenge. She just wanted to meet her brothers.

My grandparents' marriage stuck for more than fifty years. In a poem titled "Notes for a Sixtieth Wedding Anniversary," Jane Mayhall writes, "Because we didn't believe in obligations, / we never thought about divorce." Maybe that was it. My grandfather wasn't a storyteller, and he rarely spoke of what happened during the war. In the twenty-odd years that I knew him, he told me only one story. At Iwo Jima, Rabaul, New Georgia, Guadalcanal, and Bouganville, his unit of Seabees went ashore shortly after the infantry assault and started felling trees for roads and airstrips. My grandfather supervised the logging and sawmill crews that created lumber for hangars and barracks and hospitals.

My father's five hundred–page *Time-Life Books History of the Second World War* has this to say about the Seabees:

> [They] magically reshaped the coral-pocked face of the Pacific; their wand was the 20-ton bulldozer . . . [T]hey blasted away reefs to make channels for the fleet, leveled hills, and laid down landing strips in their place, lashed pontoons together to create artificial docks and brought to many a remote Pacific isle its first roads and hospitals. On more than one occasion they used their bulldozers to entomb nests of enemy snipers who were menacing Marine or Army mop-up squads. The [Seabees] had as their core many master craftsmen too old for the infantry, men with a zeal that matched their skill. Their advanced age led the Marines (average age: 20) to crack, "Never hit a Seabee—he may be your grandfather."

One day, my grandfather told me, he and two of his buddies were scouting in the jungle. He was in the middle. Suddenly, he heard my grandmother's voice. "*Luther,*" it was saying. Then, more insistently, "*Luther?*" He ignored it. This was crazy. Helen (*he* never called her helenka) was back in Georgia with the kids. "*Luther!*" He stopped. He meant to ask his buddies if they heard anything. He never got a chance. A moment later, one of them stepped on a mine. There was an explosion, and the two of them vaporized. He would have vaporized, too, if he hadn't stopped. The story has always struck me as odd for a couple of reasons, not least because my grandfather was the one who told it to me. Grandma had always been the repository of family stories, the true as well as the apocryphal. If a story that powerful—and that flattering—was floating around in the ether, how come she never wrested it away from him? Decades later, I told the story to my father and asked if he'd ever heard it. He had not. I asked him if he believed it. After a moment's hesitation he said, yes, he did.

At the age of seven, my father developed a limp. X-rays led to a diagnosis of Perthes disease, in which the ball of the hip softens abnormally. The cause of the disease is still unknown, although it is more prevalent in boys—especially first-born sons—than girls, and in children who are on the short side. The course of treatment in the 1940s was draconian. My father spent two years in bed followed by another two and a half years in a wheelchair or on crutches. Zane Gray was his constant companion through the bedridden years. Every day, when school let out, his brother Sam sat on the end of the bed and regurgitated everything he'd learned. My father was nearly twelve before he walked again without the benefit of braces or crutches. He'd missed two years of school but, thanks to Sam's tutoring, re-entered only one year behind, in Sam's grade.

The war split my father's childhood in two. Before: carefree years spent living in the lowlands of Georgia and Florida, where the boys ran as wild as bobcats while their father logged pulpwood with one or two hired men. After: years of moving from place to place while my grandfather tried—and failed—to make a go of the sawmill business. After his discharge in 1945, Luther took Alba along on a trip to Fortune Branch, Oregon, to see a man about a sawmill. They rode a bus. In the middle of the night, the driver drifted off to sleep and ran through a guardrail. The bus rolled over a couple of times then came to rest on one side. Shaken but unhurt, Alba cried out for his father. Luther moaned. A fat woman had landed on top of him. The same bad luck pursued him into the sawmill business. Postwar, the demand for wood products soared. So did the number of willing workers. Before long, the market was glutted. The sawmills that survived were the ones with enough financial capital to invest in modern machinery. Muscle was the Brice boys' only source of capital. Eventually, they gave up on sawmills and went back to stump logging.

At thirteen, my father was setting chokers for his father. At fourteen, he was felling trees himself. The summer before their junior year, Al and Sam bought two flatbed trucks, a Ford and a Chevrolet. They subcontracted for their father, loading wood by hand in the days before logging trucks came equipped with winches or cranes. At prom time, the Ford was the cleaner of the two trucks, so they drove it, along with their dates, to the dance.

Well into their thirties, my father and his brothers behaved like teenagers whenever they got together. A couple of times a year, our four families would caravan to a hot springs resort fifty miles north of town. My father led the way with us kids bouncing up and down in the back seat like a bunch of charged electrons. He sped up gradually until "Al-BA," my mother would say, emphasizing the second syllable. It was a warning. A few minutes later, Uncle Andy or Uncle Thom would zoom by us with my cousins Helen and Luther or Steven and Tommy thumbing their noses at us out the back windows. "*Al-ba,*" my mother said again, more ominously. He floored it.

"*Alba*! Slow down! You'll get us killed!" my mother shouted. This was the only drama of their marriage, repeated endlessly, with very little variation.

When our father zipped around Uncle Andy as if he were standing still, the back seat went wild. Pale-faced, my mother gripped the dashboard.

We hit a hairpin curve at eighty miles an hour. At least one wheel—maybe two—of our station wagon left the ground. My father kept the wheel wrenched around so we overshot Chena Hot Springs Road, careening onto a nearly hidden lane that ran perpendicular to it. He hit the brakes, spun around in a whirlwind of dust, and hid behind a clump of bushes. The finned tail of the wagon stuck out a ways, but it didn't matter.

Three seconds later, Andy blazed past, then Thom, then

Sam. None of them spotted us. My father gave them a head start then pulled onto the highway as sedately as if we were on our way to a church social. In the resort parking lot, we pulled alongside my uncles' cars. They knew they'd been had, but they didn't know how. My father cranked down the car window, grinning.

"Wow," he said, mock incredulous. "What were you boys chasing? You were sure flying when you passed us. Bet you didn't even see us."

In *Wind, Sand and Stars*, Antoine de Saint-Exupery grasps something that often eludes adventurers who take up the pen. The story of a human being waging battle against Great Nature is not really a story at all. Nature is too impersonal and impervious for the role of antagonist; it is incapable of deception, betrayal, malice, or evil. We humans might engage with it, but it does not engage with us. Similarly, a battle waged within the heart or mind of one angst-ridden individual signifies nothing because the stakes are too low. "There is nothing dramatic in the world, nothing pathetic, except in human relations," Saint-Exupery writes. He repeats it several times: no drama except in human relations.

A Civil War buff, my father can hold forth for hours on the merits of this or that general, the tactical miscues and flawed assumptions that tipped certain battles in favor of the North or the South. He makes a study of human drama in far off times and places. Of the upheavals in his own life, he says little. A jagged half-inch scar runs down one leg from knee to ankle, a relic of the time when he and his father were clearing land in Petersburg; a chained-up log snagged on a stump then snapped free, tearing open my father's leg. He's grilled a steak on the radiator of a bulldozer, shooed a black bear out of the cab of his truck, and fallen asleep at the controls of a log skidder just before it rolled down a sixty-foot embankment. He's gone without food and sleep for days on end (which is why he snoozed at the controls of the log skidder).

Here's a story he will tell, but only when coaxed. Sometime

 in the late '60s, he was hauling gear to someone else's job at Bettles, just north of the Arctic Circle. It was March, unseasonably warm. When my father tried to cross the Yukon River in a brand-new D-8 dozer, the ice gave way beneath him, and he dropped fifteen or twenty feet, to the bottom of the river. As the dozer settled into the silt, jagged panes of ice fell all around the canopy, imprisoning my father. He shoved frantically, but they were too heavy to move, especially with the current of the river pressing against them.

Well, you've really done it this time, he recalls thinking. *This is a stupid way to go.* Then he thought, *No, it's not going to be like this.*

He tried again to dislodge one of the sheets pinning him in the cab, and this time it moved. He was able to climb on top of the canopy and, from there, to swim up through the hole in the ice. An Alyeska Pipeline Service Company helicopter was on the scene within minutes later. "You're in shock," a medic told my father, who disagreed weakly. He let himself be bundled into the helicopter and flown back to Fairbanks, where he spent a night in the hospital. The next day, he hauled the D-8 out of the river, built a tent around it, and warmed it up. When it was completely dry, he flushed the engine with a special mixture of antifreeze and diesel. In the end, the D-8 revived, its only ruined parts the electrical ones.

"How did you know what to do?" I asked. "Is this part of mechanic's training: 'How to Rehabilitate an Engine After It's Been Under Water for Twenty-Four Hours'?"

He laughed. "No, it was because I'd been in the river a few times before that."

Between the letters on the left and the numbers on the right, Alaska's license plate shows a raggedy line of miners, picks slung over their shoulders, climbing the Chilkoot Trail. The Chilkoot was the legendary poor man's route to the Klondike during the 1896 gold rush. Now a popular hiking trail, it begins in Skagway, just over the Alaska-Canada border. As trails go, it is not to be underestimated: "[It] can be rough with deep mud, standing water, unstable boulders, slick rocks and roots making footing difficult," writes the Canadian park service. Vertigo is a typical problem. "[S]evere rain or snow storms are possible even in the middle of summer," continues the park service. "Avalanche hazard persists until mid-July." In 2004, my parents hiked the trail with a group of friends that included my oldest daughter. Kinzea was eleven; my mother and father were sixty-eight and sixty-nine. My parents went for several reasons: to see the sights they'd admired in photographs, to prove to themselves (and to all doubters) they were fit for a young person's adventure, and, in my father's case, to walk in the miners' footsteps.

They spent a week on the trail. At the end of the hike, in the ghost town of Dyea, they had to wait for several hours for the train to carry them back to Skagway. Most of the group spread their sodden gear in the sun then sprawled, weary and footsore, alongside it. My father lit his pipe and strolled along the railroad tracks. From their vantage point on a small rise, my mother and friends watched idly as my father puffed away, staring at his feet. Moments later, a grizzly sow surfed down a hillside to the tracks. My father was too far away to hear the shouts of his companions. Because it was one of them—not my father—who told me the story, I play the scene from the point of view of someone standing helpless on that rise. For the next minute or two, bear and man, each unaware of the other, shambled toward each other. The bear sensed my father first. Twenty feet away, she rose up on hind legs and sniffed the air. My father looked up then, too. He paused for just a heartbeat then resumed walking. The sow dropped to all fours and bolted into a copse of trees.

"In those days," writes Saint-Exupery, speaking of the early mail planes, "the motor was not what it is today." He was writing in 1939. "It would drop out, for example, without warning and with a great rattle like the crash of crockery. And one would simply throw in one's hand: there was no hope of refuge on the rocky crust of Spain."

A great rattle like the crash of crockery. Then *no hope of refuge*.

After leaving the Marines in 1956, my father studied engineering at Columbia University. He couldn't afford to stay, so he transferred after a semester to the University of Florida. After one semester there—restless and broke—he hitched a ride with a friend driving a minibus to Alaska. The two of them hired on with the military for a land-clearing project on the Kenai Peninsula. When the job ended, the friend went back to Florida alone. My father lucked into a job at Clear Air Force Station, sixty miles south of Fairbanks. The superintendent, a Floridian, owed the Brices a favor. A few years earlier, he'd run into a cash-flow problem. One step ahead of the repo men, he sold his home to my grandfather for a price that was more than fair. As soon as his cash-flow problem was solved, the man bought his house back. Then he went to Alaska. For the Clear job, he hired my grandfather (who'd driven up from Florida, too, by then) as foreman and my father as a laborer. When the job shut down for the winter, the pair of them stayed on as caretakers.

At that time, my father and his father were intent on breaking into the Alaska timber industry. They had their sights set on southeast Alaska, where the mild climate and prodigious rainfall nurture sky-scraping Sitka spruce. The cold, arid climate of the Interior, on the other hand, yields a scrawnier product known as black spruce. The more time they spent there, though, the more they saw the advantage of staying in the Interior, where the competition was nonexistent. Luther and Al applied to the federal government for a small business loan to build a sawmill near Fairbanks. They rented a cabin outside of Fairbanks, on Chena Ridge, and my father went to work for Pan Am as a mechanic.

After months of hemming and hawing, the SBA approved the loan application but imposed so many conditions—a consultant to design and oversee the sawmill, for example—it wasn't feasible. Meanwhile, the cabin on Chena Ridge was becoming more crowded. The moment to cut their losses came and went. My father's people have always been gamblers. They staked everything on Alaska, which had, only a couple of years earlier, traded up from a territory to a state. At 378 million square acres, it was by far the biggest state in the Union. It had by far the smallest population and the fewest roads. In those days, it took twelve hours to drive from the state's second-largest city (Fairbanks) to its largest (Anchorage), a distance of just over 300 miles as the crow flies. The capital city of Juneau was (and still is) accessible only by air or sea. Only a smattering of Native villages had runways back then. Villagers traveled by dog team or snowmachine in winter, riverboat in summer. As recently as 1925, dog mushers bearing precious serum had rescued Nome from a diphtheria outbreak. By 1960, it didn't take much foresight to see that Congress would appropriate funds to bring its shiny new acquisitions—Alaska and Hawaii—into the twentieth century. There was money to be made in the timber industry, but not in the way that my father and his father had envisioned.

In 1963, Brice Incorporated won its first contract, to clear timber and brush for a new road north of Fairbanks. Within months, they won another similar contract and purchased their first bulldozer. Their big break came a year later: good fortune on the heels of bad. The Good Friday earthquake of 1964 (9.2 on the Richter scale) and ensuing tsunamis had washed away the Kodiak Island village of Afognak. Lions Clubs from all over the United States sent funds to rebuild. The company—as it is always known in my family's shorthand—won a contract to construct an airstrip at the place that would henceforth be called Port Lions. By then, my father had quit his job at Pan Am, and his brothers Sam, Andy, and Thom had joined him and Luther in Alaska.

The rare eye defect that had dashed my father's dream of becoming a military pilot wasn't even detected during the private pilot medical exam. My father began his flying lessons in the late 1950s but quit because of his work schedule: seven days a week plus evenings moonlighting as an aircraft fueler. In February 1962, he married my mother, and in February 1963, I was born. My parents couldn't afford the $19,000 asking price of the house they were renting. How could he justify flying lessons? He couldn't. A few months after I was born, he flew East with my mother and me for two weeks. While my mother looked after her newly widowed father, my father took just enough lessons to pass the private pilot check ride. Back in

 Alaska, he and his brothers pooled their savings to buy a used Aeronca Champ, the aeronautical equivalent of a one-speed Schwinn bicycle. They sold it within months, when money got tight. With the $5,000 my mother inherited from her mother's estate—and, more important, with my mother's blessing—my father bought a Stinson 108 Station Wagon. He hadn't owned it for more than month or two when he flew some supplies out to the Chena Hot Springs Road job. My mother held me in the back seat. My father set the Stinson down on a gravel bar that turned out to be rockier than it looked. The gear made an unholy racket as it scudded along the rocks. Hearing what sounded like a crash, my grandfather and uncle tore through the underbrush between their camp and the gravel bar. They forded the Chena River in their work clothes. Expecting the worst, they came upon this tableau: the Stinson, intact, with my father and mother and me beside it. Seeing his wild-eyed father and brother, my father grinned his *Aw, shucks* grin. It faded. He says he never saw his father angrier than at that moment. A vein throbbed in his forehead, and his face turned bright red.

"Son, what were you *thinking*?" he shouted. "What if something happened to you and you got stuck out here in the wilderness with no baby food or diapers? What if something happened to *her*? Did you even think about that?"

A few years later, my father sold the Stinson for a low-winged Bellanca. It held a family of five, which we numbered by then, and flew faster than the Stinson. As a rule, airplanes that are fast in the air are fast on the ground as well. Where they existed at all, bush runways in the 1960s tended to be narrow and short—well suited to such craft as the Piper Super Cub or Arctic Tern but not the Bellanca. Sam was a toddler and Hannah an infant when it overshot the runway at Noorvik, just north of the Seward Peninsula, plowing into a thick stand of willows. They scratched like fingernails on the windows. No one—not even the Bellanca—got hurt that time.

The company won a contract to build an airstrip near the village of Wainwright on the North Slope. One day, a scraper broke down in the middle of the unfinished strip. Without a new hydraulic pump, it wasn't moving. The only way to get such a pump—short of waiting months for it to arrive via barge—was to fly it in. With less than five hundred feet of useable runway, my father took off in the Bellanca and flew into Fairbanks to purchase the pump. Conditions were dicey when he returned. Wind off the Arctic Ocean buffeted the Bellanca from every direction. To avoid a collision with the scraper, my father tried to set down on the extreme end of the runway, just beyond an embankment. Only the nose gear cleared the embankment. Clipped of its main gear, the Bellanca tobogganed down the runway, coming to rest safely short of the scraper. My father was unhurt. A few days later, shorn of its gear and—for convenience's sake—its wings, the Bellanca left Wainwright on the back of a barge. It never flew again.

Since then, Brice Incorporated has bought and sold several models of Cessnas, a Helio Courier, a Beechcraft Bonanza, and two twin-engine planes, an Aztec and a Navajo. At the age when many successful businessmen either get a divorce or a Porsche, my uncle Sam bought a flame-orange stunt plane called a Navion. (He has since sold it.) The company employs a pilot who's ready to fly at a moment's notice. When he's not in the air, Gordon maintains the fleet. His office is a cubby in the company's hangar on the East Ramp of the Fairbanks airport. Its tiny overheated bathroom is papered from floor to ceiling with pilot pornography: soft-focus watercolor prints of airplanes in scenes that vaguely suggest a narrative—parked on a glacier, say, or pulled up in front of a wilderness cabin. The fleet has shrunk as Alaska's runways have grown in number and size. Runways capacious enough for a DC-6 are common now. Brice Incorporated built a fair number of them. Because it's cheaper to charter a DC-6 than to buy, maintain, and insure a small plane, the company fleet now numbers only two: a six-seater Cessna 206 and a two-seater Arctic Tern.

I took flying lessons under Gordon's watchful eye. He kept the Tern fueled and ready, the engine oil and brake fluid topped off. He helped me roll it onto the tarmac or back into the hangar. He didn't offer me flying tips. With the deceptive casualness of a father checking out his daughter's boyfriends, he made idle conversation with each of my instructors in turn. They must have passed muster. If they hadn't, my father would have heard about it. Because of the nature of his work, Gordon kept (and keeps) irregular hours, but he was always at the hangar when I left on a solo flight, always there when I returned. His attention wasn't warm but steady and impersonal. I used to think that if I were to wreck the Tern, it would be harder to face him than my father.

At eight o'clock on a Sunday morning years ago, Gordon's red pickup truck was parked outside the hangar when I drove up to pre-flight the Tern for my first solo cross-country flight. Winds en route to Circle Hot Springs resort were forecast to be light and variable, meaning negligible, not a factor. I took off. Somewhere over the White Mountains, two-thirds of the way there, the wind picked up. It rocked the Tern roughly from side to side, like a resentful big brother toying with the baby's cradle. It was the kind of wind that gets your attention when you're a forty-hour pilot flying solo outside the pattern for the first time. The sky was cloudless, shellacked in blue. I throttled back, which is what the manual says to do in moderate turbulence. My airspeed dropped from ninety-five miles per hour to seventy-five; the controls felt sluggish. Probably, I should have turned around. My instructor's parting words that morning had been: "Don't forget, there's no shame in aborting." It's true that I learned to fly to prove something to myself, not my father. It's also true that he would never shame me on purpose. Even so, I could imagine our conversation that evening:

> Dad: "So how'd your flight go, Jen?"
>
> Me: "Um, I had to turn back. Too much turbulence."
>
> Dad, incredulous: "You mean, you turned around because of a little *wind*?"

I kept flying. When the runway slid up under me, I executed what's known as a mid-field crosswind. When landing at a field with no controller (an uncontrolled field, of course), you're supposed to transect the runway. This way, you can check for traffic and study the windsock. You want the windsock to be doing one of two things: hanging as limp as a deflated party balloon or pointing straight down the runway. The windsock at Chena Hot Springs that morning stiffly saluted a spot in the trees directly across from the runway. Great. That meant a direct crosswind of fifteen or twenty knots. The Tern is tough: it can handle a crosswind of twenty-five or thirty knots without sustaining structural damage. The pilot was less tough. Whether or not she could, at that precariously early moment in her career, successfully land the Tern in such a stiff crosswind was an open question.

The trick to crosswind landings is to dip one wing into the wind. In an especially stiff crosswind, you try to land on two wheels: the tailwheel and the windward wheel. Confident, even aggressive, use of the rudder is required. "Confident" and "aggressive" are two words that no one, not even I, would have applied to my piloting skills—not then, and probably not now. Flying is a pursuit that runs contrary to my nature. I've long sensed that other pilots are guided by a calm and supportive inner voice that says things like, "Hey, this looks like a great opportunity to test those crosswind landing skills you've been practicing for months." My inner voice is always shouting, "*WHAT THE HELL DO YOU THINK YOU'RE DOING? ARE YOU OUT OF YOUR GODDAMN MIND? TURN AROUND RIGHT THIS MINUTE BEFORE YOU KILL YOURSELF!*" In any sticky situation, it is too much to hope that my inner voice will offer up a sane and plausible course of action.

For that reason, I've come to rely on a mental technique that I call powering through. The phrase comes from whitewater kayaking, where it means paddling so hard and so fast that the hydraulics can't snag you. It's equivalent to brazening out an awkward social situation—accidentally squeezing the butt of a stranger wearing the same costume as your boyfriend at a Halloween party, say. Powering through or brazening out is almost always what I end up doing, but only after stifling my initial impulse to surrender or sink through the floor. On final for the runway at Circle Hot Springs, I ducked my right wing, pressed firmly on the left rudder, and crabbed my way, curled around the wind, to the runway. If you live near an airport or are in the habit of watching small planes land, you've seen them in this windy-day configuration: the nose is pointed thirty degrees or more away from where the plane is headed—a bit like a person whose body is walking north but whose head is turned to the east. A moment before touchdown, I switched over to the right rudder. I was now leaning into the wind. If I'd been less tentative, more sure of myself, I might have succeeded. Instead, when the wheels touched, the wind seized the Tern, sweeping it sideways toward the orange cones marking the edge of the runway. Beyond them, the woods' dark mouth gaped. I powered up and took off, skittering over the treetops. *So close. So close.*

Even though I'd logged forty hours before my first solo cross-country, I was still a scared pilot. Statistically speaking, I didn't pose nearly as much of a danger to myself and others as a 200-hour pilot. The moniker "200-hour pilot" is an insult, as in, "The guy who bought the farm in Atigun Pass the other day was a 200-hour pilot." A 200-hour pilot combines a surfeit of cockiness with a paucity of experience. In short, he's not afraid enough.

In his terrifyingly titled book, *The Killing Zone: How and Why Pilots Die*, Paul A. Craig postulates that people become pilots because they like to take risks. He charts the fatal accidents recorded in the United States between 1983 and 2000 and correlates them to pilot hours. The result looks like a snake that's swallowed a rabbit. Contrary to the myth, it's pilots in the 100- to 150-hour range who rack up the most fatalities. Somewhere in that range—short of 300 hours, anyway—is what Craig ominously describes as "the killing zone." His theory is that caution almost always overrides the risk-taking impulse in the most inexperienced pilots. The safest pilots—those with more than 300 hours—haven't lost their taste for risk, writes Craig; rather, they're risk takers who've scared themselves silly once or twice, gotten lucky a passel of times, and learned a lot about flying that can't be taught on the tarmac.

My father, as precocious in flying as everything else, nearly bought the farm at the ninety-hour mark. It was during the Port

Lions job, when I was just a toddler. Dad was a newly minted single-engine pilot flying regularly over the North Pacific. Without sophisticated instruments or the rating to use them, even if he'd had them, he was at the mercy of the wind, waves, and fog that often blew in without any warning. A guy could run up against the limits of his capabilities pretty quickly. He was flying from Kodiak Island back to the mainland and, from there, back to Fairbanks when heavy clouds muscled in. He had a passenger, a state Department of Transportation inspector, on board. As a Visual Flight Rules or VFR pilot, my father had two choices: fly above the clouds, or fly below them. To fly into them is verboten. In such situations, flying above the clouds is scarier but smarter; the worst that can happen is that you lose your bearings then run out of fuel. Below the clouds, you might augur into a mountain or the ocean. My father tried to do the smarter thing. He flew the Bellanca as high as it would fly, but it topped out still swaddled in gray cotton. Then he descended until the plane's belly was practically perched on white caps. He was still in the clouds. Then he went back up, topping the clouds on his second try.

Despair followed on the heels of elation. In the effort to get clear of the clouds, he'd lost his bearings. The "visual" part of being a Visual Flight Rules pilot means you're supposed to see the terrain at all times. If not, you're in an IFR (Instrument Flight Rules) situation with VFR skills. Navigation becomes dicey at best. This was even more true in the early '60s, before satellite-assisted navigation aids such as transponders, Lorans, or Global Positioning System devices became common. Navigation back then (and even when I began flying, in the '80s) was guided primarily by compass. In the Far North, a physical phenomenon known as magnetic variation exerts a strong and deceptive pull on the needle. When flying blind in heavy weather, as my father was on that day, it's nearly impossible to rely on the compass alone. It's marginally better to pick up a signal from a radio tower positioned near an airfield. A disoriented pilot might be able to hone in on such a signal, but he wouldn't know how far away the airfield was, or whether he had enough fuel to reach it. My father kept fiddling with the radio dial. Suddenly, he raised a scratchy voice belonging to the controller in Homer, a tiny fishing town on Kachemak Bay. Based on a radar blip that might or might not have been the Bellanca, the controller was able to offer my father a compass bearing. It was a bit like throwing numbers into the wind. Even if the bearing brought him directly to Homer before he ran out of fuel, my father would have no way of knowing he was there. As far as the eye could see, the clouds formed a floor as dense as poured concrete. A blind descent to the jagged coastline would have been tantamount to suicide. Then the pilot of a Northern Consolidated cargo jet broke in. He'd overheard my father's exchange with the controller, and he had an idea. Where he was flying, he could see a pinprick of light in the clouds. It was big enough for a plane to slip through, and it was right above Homer. He was willing to mark the spot by circling there for a while. Within minutes, my father spotted the jet, fluttered his wings in thanks, and dropped through the hole. He landed safely and hung his head while the controller chewed him out. Meanwhile, his passenger, the state inspector, rented a car to drive the 600 remaining miles to Fairbanks.

In the forty-odd years that he's been a pilot, there have been two occasions when my father would have felt safer leaping from the plane with a parachute than continuing to fly. Neither was on the flight from Port Lions to Homer. The first was on a flight from Kotzebue, in northwest Alaska, to Fairbanks, in the Interior. A toothy grin of a mountain range known as the Brooks Range separates Arctic Alaska from the milder (relatively speaking, of course) climate zone to the south. In the '60s, pre-flight weather briefings in rural Alaska were sketchy to nonexistent. At best, pilots who were planning to fly consulted other pilots who'd flown recently. At worst, they held a spit-dampened finger up to the wind to see how quickly it dried. Shortly after my father—by then a 200-hour pilot—took off in the Bellanca, thunderstorms checker-boarded the sky. For a time, he slalomed between them, a time- and fuel-consuming tack. Then he thought, "What the hell, how bad can it be?" The answer: "Pretty bad." Inside the thunderhead, visibility dropped to nil. Heavy rain turned to hailstones the size of golf balls.

Somehow, my father was able to fly out the other side. After landing in Fairbanks, he dismounted on spaghetti legs. Grabbing a wing to steady himself, he saw something strange. It took him a minute to figure out what it was. The hailstones had blasted all of the yellow paint off both wings, cowling, and fuselage. The Bellanca was now the color of sky.

Antoine de Saint-Exupery saw death so many times it became a shadowy familiar that kept showing up without invitation or warning. The ordinary flight, the ordinary storm, even the ordinary person: these had no place in his life or his memoir. (With bemusement, he recounts how the lover of a particularly dashing pilot friend killed herself—*in her lover's bed*—on hearing that their affair was to end at sunrise.) Saint-Ex himself flew through hurricanes and cyclones, sandstorms and hailstorms—though not, one assumes, their metaphoric equivalent in human relations. At a time when flying fatalities were common, he survived more crashes than anyone. After a crash in the Libyan desert, he survived for four days with no food or water, a situation he later described, with typical sangfroid, as "hardly ideal."

Like the best memoirs, *Wind, Sand and Stars* is about the author only incidentally. Mostly, it's about Saint-Ex's efforts to make sense of a world that, with the invention of flight, had grown exponentially more knowable and more mysterious. What sets *Wind, Sand and Stars* apart from the reminiscences of equally intrepid explorers? The effortless elegance of the prose, for one thing. The elasticity of the metaphors, for another. And the offhand modesty of a voice that, if it were American (i.e., more colloquial and less elegant), would say, Buck Rogers–style, *Aw shucks, folks. These shenanigans of mine don't hardly add up to nothin'.*

Here is Saint-Ex describing a storm off the coast of Argentine Patagonia—a place where "the crust of the earth is as dented as an old boiler"; where the only vegetation, he archly notes, is a "plantation of oil derricks"; where "rises a chain of prow-shaped, saw-toothed, razor-edged mountains stripped by the elements down to the bare rock." On a typical day, flying this desolate, wind-swept route demands every bit of concentration and strength a pilot can bring to bear. On an atypical day, it asks more. Here is Saint-Ex's description of an atypical day:

> The sky was blue. Pure blue. Too pure. A hard blue sky that shone over the scraped and barren world while the fleshless vertebrae of the mountain chain flashed in the sunlight. Not a cloud. The blue sky glittered like a new-honed knife . . . The purity of the sky upset me. Give me a good black storm in which the enemy is plainly visible . . . I can get my hands on my adversary. But when you are flying very high in clear weather the shock of a blue storm is as disturbing as if something collapsed that had been holding up your ship in the air.

Despite feeling as if he's falling, he finds a way to fly upright. Something strange, something *unnatural*, is happening, though. Saint-Ex feels the "secret little quiverings" that presage a storm: the "warning drum on the wings . . . little intermittent rappings scarcely audible and infinitely brief, little cracklings from time to time, as if there were traces of gunpowder in the air."

"Then," writes Saint-Ex, "everything round me blew up."

During the explosion, he struggles mightily with the aircraft; after it's over, he wrestles with words. Had such a storm ever been described? Had one ever been experienced—and survived—before? Perhaps not. At a loss, he turns to the alchemy of metaphor: "I was wrestling with chaos," he writes. Below him, the earth was rearing, buckling, spinning. "The plane," he writes, "was skidding as if on a toothless cogwheel." He likens himself to a waiter juggling an enormous pile of plates, a porter bowed underneath a heavy load, a man clinging to the end of a monstrous, cracking whip. The sky is a "slippery dome" on which he can't find footing. Fighting a force that would hurl him into those toothy, slavering mountains or, failing that, to rip him to shreds in midair, Saint-Ex loses feeling in his hands. He fears they might let go of the wheel without his consent or knowledge. "Any minute now," he writes, reliving the moment in the present tense, "I should be overcome by the indifference born of utter weariness and by the mortal yearning to take my rest."

That moment, of course, never came.

The second time my father wished for a parachute was on a flight from Northway to Cordova. The company had contracts in both places, and my father was splitting himself in two trying to supervise both jobs. The forecast said a storm was brewing over the Wrangell Mountains, but my father was in a hurry; he told himself he could beat it. At the helm of the Bellanca, he swung around the flank of Mount Sanford and tucked into the Copper River Valley. Within minutes, he was caught in the gears of a low-pressure system rolling in from the coast and a high-pressure system swooping down from the Wrangells. The first sign of trouble was a bump or two in a blue sky. Then the real turbulence began. The Bellanca slid across the sky and back again, a toy mouse being batted across the kitchen linoleum by a playful cat. It lay up on one side then the other. Still the sky was blue.

"Later on, a guy asked me, 'Why didn't you turn around and go back?' The answer was that I was doing everything I could to keep the plane upright and flying down the valley," my father says.

Clouds stampeded through the valley. They swept up the Bellanca then carried it down toward the canyon floor, now obscured by wind-sifted silt from a dry riverbed. My father could barely see. He felt as if he were flying through a dust storm in the Sahara Desert. At such moments, one's choices funnel down to one or two at most: surrender or fight.

After thirty minutes or an hour—one loses one's sense of time—the storm spat the Bellanca out onto the coast. My father set down on the strip at Cordova, taxied to his parking spot, then sat for a long time. He tried to remember whatever bit of business had seemed so damned pressing just a couple of hours earlier. He thought about his wife and his children and everything he'd risked. He thought about luck and skill and how the fact that he was sitting there, alive and able to think at all, was due entirely to the former and not at all to the latter. Years later, after I'd wrung the story out of him, I asked if he'd

 been afraid. Not when it happening, he said. Not until it was all over. Then he was too afraid to move for a long, long time.

Antoine de Saint-Exupery can hardly bring himself to tell a story—even one as exciting as the blue storm—without interrupting himself to muse on the shortcomings of narrative. "The reason why writers fail when they attempt to evoke horror is that horror is something invented after the fact, when one is recreating the experience over again in the memory," he writes. Facing death, a pilot is less likely to feel fear than a panoply of other emotions, among them fury at himself for getting into the situation in the first place. Later, it's not only narrative but words that fail. Reading the story of the cyclone in the Andes, I sensed that Saint-Ex was throwing up his hands, saying, "Why keep trying, futilely, to evoke the horror of that moment when I can do these nifty loop-de-loops with language?" The loop-de-loops get in the way. They're supposed to.

Perhaps sensing that he hasn't gotten it right yet, Saint-Ex tries to describe how he felt. The second time, his mind veers away from metaphor, toward something more raw and inarticulate: "Had I been afraid? I couldn't say. I had witnessed a strange sight. What strange sight? I couldn't say. The sky was blue and the sea was white. I felt I ought to tell someone about it since I was back from so far away! . . . You cannot convey things to people by piling up adjectives, by stammering." Yet he doesn't pile up adjectives, doesn't stammer—at least, not in his written account. His is the candor of a man who spends a great deal of time in solo conversation, and who holds himself to the highest standards of precision and lyricism. Watching him struggle to get it right—to hoist words and frame sentences—we see something of the difficulty of flying, too.

My father is always working. If he's not working at the office, putting in twelve-hour days, he's working in the Bush, putting in even longer hours while supervising a road or runway job. He's in his seventies now. In Puerto Rico this winter, on one of the rare vacations he could be cajoled into taking, the captain of a sailboat said, in the slightly patronizing tone that middle-

aged people often adopt when addressing those who are old enough to be their parents, "So, what kind of business were you in, Al?" *Wrong verb tense,* I thought.

When he visits me in New York, where I live now, I barely have time to heave his suitcase in from the car before he's asking what needs to be done around the house. He's always up an hour or two before dawn. For the first day or two, he beats a path from the hardware store to the plant nursery to Wal-Mart and back around again, collecting tools and nails and paint and bulbs. Then he gets to work filing the front door so it will shut, shoring up fieldstone around the foundation, anchoring my wrought-iron railing, taping Visqueen over the bedroom windows, and rerouting the dryer vent. The whole time, he's whistling bits of whatever piece of music is stuck in his head: "Amazing Grace" or "Rock of Ages," most likely. In the evening, he and my mother and I play a savage game of Scrabble or, if we can rustle up a fourth, a rubber or two of bridge. On such days, I crawl into bed around eleven o'clock and fall asleep to the riverine sound of their settling in, just like when I was a child.

Around the time my father reached retirement age, fifteen years ago, he and my mother planned a trip to Europe. It was to be a reprise of their honeymoon in the Scandinavian countries. At the last minute, my father backed out. He was too busy at work, he said. For the first time, my mother saw with an awful clarity that he would never slow down, never retire. He would die in harness. The decades of five o'clock risings weren't a means to an end but ends in themselves. For my mother, it was as if something collapsed that had been holding her up in the air. She fell into a clinical depression. At odd moments, storms of weeping swept through her. She was unable to eat. She kept her bedroom dark and slept past seven in the morning.

After a few months of rattling around inside the ill-fitting shell of the sunny, selfless woman she'd been, my mother came back. Almost. Now, when she teases my father—she's a big tease—her teasing has an edge. On one of our road trips in Puerto Rico, my father, who doesn't speak a word of Spanish, innocently observed, "We must be close to the town of Salida. I keep seeing signs for it." Someone—maybe it was me—said,

 "Dad, *salida* means *exit* in Spanish." All of us laughed, including my father and my daughters, who had no clue what *salida* meant, either. But my mother laughed longer and harder than anyone. She laughed until tears rolled down her cheeks. She laughed until my father said, in a tight voice, "OK, Carol. That's enough."

My father's winter uniform consists of Pendleton wool shirts and wide-wale corduroy pants; in summer, he switches (or rather, my mother switches him) to cotton plaid shirts and permanent-press khakis. That's what he wears to the office. When he's out on a job, he wears blue mechanic's pants and shirts or insulated Carhartt coveralls over long underwear. The ubiquitous white crew-necked Hanes T-shirt. My father's shirts, especially the woolen ones, soak up the smell of his pipe tobacco, which lingers even after washing. Because my father sometimes sticks his pipe in his breast pocket before the ashes are cool, nearly all of his shirts have tiny holes at the base of the pocket. My mother used to patch them. Not anymore. Because the holes make her feel helpless and angry—especially when they appear in brand-new shirts—my father tries to hide them. For the rehearsal dinner just before my wedding, she set out his clothes along with a fifty-dollar silk tie she'd purchased for the occasion at Nordstrom. The tie, which had little airplanes printed on it, was a splurge; my mother had sworn me to secrecy about the price. A day or two after the wedding, she took the tie to the dry cleaners to have a stain removed. When she went to pick it up, the owner—he'd known her for years—said, "Mrs. Brice, I don't know how to tell you this." She knew exactly what he was going to say: my father had burned a hole in the silk tie then slathered it with gravy to buy himself some time. When she confronted him that evening, he said, "Well, it worked, didn't it?"

When my father is out of town and my mother has the evening free, she is likely to spend it ironing his shirts in front of an old movie on the TV. When he's home, she irons between turns at Scrabble or Parcheesi or Upwords. Russian mazurkas play on the stereo. The steam iron hisses and sighs. My father, choosing his words carefully, broaches a delicate matter.

"Carol, how come I never wear blue jeans?"

"Because you never *ask* to wear blue jeans."

"That's because you never buy me any."

So it came to pass that my father began wearing blue jeans at the age of seventy. He owns two pairs now, one or the other of which he puts on nearly every day, the deep hems turned up several inches, a sign of late-blooming sartorial rebellion against the L.L. Bean catalog and, of course, my mother with her pins and needles and patches.

Like his father before him, mine is not a storyteller. Social situations often turn him taciturn or, worse, loquacious at the worst possible moment. For a stretch in my early twenties, it seemed as though every one of my childhood friends was getting married, and I was buying a new bridesmaid's dress every other week. Some dresses were worse than others. The worst was a hideous confection of low-cut white taffeta with a huge black bow on the butt, as if to say, "X marks the spot." I was walking down the aisle wishing I were invisible when I heard my father whisper in a voice that carried at least as far as the choir, "Look, Carol, Jen doesn't have nearly as many pimples on her back as she used to." Then, "*Oof,* Carol, that hurt! Did I say something wrong? I just meant . . . *Oof!*"

When I was younger, he'd sometimes appear at the door of my bedroom at six o'clock in the morning. He'd ask if I wanted to skip school that day to ride with him to a job site. I always said yes. If we were flying, I knew he'd hand over the controls shortly after takeoff. "Maintain this altitude and heading," he'd say, pointing his pipe at the windshield and, beyond that, a bluish mountain. "You want to pass just to the right of that peak." Then he'd pack his pipe with tobacco and smoke it pensively for a while, occasionally checking the altimeter. Eventually, he'd drift off to sleep. I was twelve or thirteen years old. My brother Sam, also a pilot, once cracked that the only time our father *doesn't* sleep is when he's flying over water.

On our travels, he asked me what I thought of Jimmy Carter's policy of turning most of Alaska into national parks, or whether I believed in the death penalty. What about euthanasia? Legalized prostitution? Who was the best president of all time? The worst? And who wrote better, Faulkner or Hemingway? I can't remember a time when my father wasn't interested in what I was thinking. He was the first person to take me seriously; he taught me to take myself seriously as well. Giddy at the controls of the Helio Courier, I told him I wanted to be a pilot someday. Never mind that I was merely maintaining straight and level flight in a single-engine aircraft on a calm day, or that I was already struggling in algebra and earth science and was about to struggle a lot more in trigonometry and physics.

"You'll make a good one," he said.

Seconds later, he'd point wordlessly to the mountain that had somehow drifted into the left-hand corner of the windshield. The mysteries of the rudder as yet unplumbed by me, I'd correct by turning the wheel. He'd empty the cold ashes from his pipe onto the floor. Within minutes, his chin would drop to his chest again.

Near the end of *The Killing Zone* is a personality quiz like the ones that usually appear in *Glamour* or *Cosmopolitan.* ("Are you the kind of girl men love, or the kind men leave? Take this quiz to find out!") Among the forty questions are these:

Who would you rather be?
a. Astronaut Hoot Gibson
b. Talk show host Oprah Winfrey
c. Scientist Albert Einstein

It is 3 o'clock in the morning and you are stopped at a red light (that may be stuck). What would you do?
a. Look both ways and go
b. Wait for the light to turn green
c. Call the police to report a broken traffic light

When I see a hitchhiker I—
a. Drive past and never give it a second thought
b. Drive past but feel guilty that I didn't stop
c. Give him a ride

If you answer "a" to the majority of questions, you've got a "pilot personality": you are, to paraphrase Paul Craig, an independent achiever who enjoys mastering complex tasks. If you answer "c," you've got the anti-pilot personality (my phrase). In that case, Craig writes, you shouldn't despair: if you muster the courage to fly, you'll be safer than most pilots. Like all personality quizzes, this one fails to register much in the way of complexity or ambiguity. For instance, I nearly always answered "c" (I confess I'd rather be Einstein than Oprah) or "a" (Who *wouldn't* run a slow light on a deserted street at three o'clock in the morning?). I rarely answered "b," except in the case of the hitchhiker—a silly question, really, if the driver is female and the hitchhiker is male. But my average score, tallied then divided by the number of questions, hovered right around 2, or "b": 2.105, to be exact. I read the questions to my father over the phone. His answers averaged 2.05. We both belong to the category of people who are meticulous and cautious, unlikely to take unnecessary risks and—*drum roll, please*—unlikely ever to become pilots.

When my father isn't working, he's reading. (Or, as my mother tartly observes, snoring with an open book on his chest.) If passion for books is something you can catch, like a cold or a bouquet, then I caught it from him. The first books I loved were fairy tales. Then Nancy Drew and Cherry Ames mysteries. The Little House series by Laura Ingalls Wilder. Louisa May Alcott's *Little Women, Little Men, Eight Cousins,* and *Rose in Bloom.* Biographies of famous women: Mary Todd Lincoln, Dorothea Dix, Marie Curie, Amelia Earhart. For a shamefully long stretch (detailed elsewhere), I read nothing but Barbara Cartland, who taught me that romance happens in the ellipses, and Danielle Steele, who taught me that sex happens on the page (this in the days before she became squeamish about the details of anything but plastic surgery). Fat paperbacks got me through the years when my only brush with true love happened on a youth group hay ride, when I brushed away groping hands. One day, I woke up wanting more than stories of imperiled milky-throated heroines trading barbs with the blackguards they'd eventually tame then marry. I turned to my father's bookshelves. Mostly, they held volume after volume of dry history. I associated the dust on those shelves—dust that I probably should have been cleaning on Saturday mornings—with the distant past. My father's favorite topics were the Civil War and General Robert E. Lee. If pushed, he might read a book about Ulysses S. Grant or William Tecumseh Sherman. He read books about flying and books about the North. He read books about flying in the North. And he read fiction: Ernest Hemingway, Leon Uris, Herman Wouk, Irwin Shaw, John Le Carre, James Michener, Patrick O'Brian. When he found an author he liked, he read everything that author wrote. The first decent books I read were my father's: *War and Remembrance*, *From Here to Eternity*, *Lie Down with Lions*, and *Exodus* (Leon Uris, not the Old Testament). The characters in these books were looking for more than a clue in a clocktower, more than their missing half. Some of them met with sad endings, or sad-happy ones. I couldn't get enough.

My father taught me not to be afraid of difficult things. When I was fifteen years old and learning how to drive, he wouldn't let me use his company car, a Ford Granada with an automatic transmission. Instead, I had to learn in my mother's car, a Volvo with a stick shift. Driving lessons ratcheted up the tension between me and my mother. We hadn't been getting along because of my compulsiveness (her version) and her desire for control (my version). Now we weren't getting along because I couldn't master the fine art of pumping the brakes on ice.

One March or April morning, he shook me awake an hour earlier than I'd set my alarm to wake up for school. He had some bit of business in Valdez, 365 miles southeast of Fairbanks; he needed to drive there and back inside of a day. Would I like to come along and practice my driving? We took one of the mechanic's trucks, a temperamental beast whose stick shift tried to yank my arm out of its socket. On our way back, it began snowing. By the time we reached Isabel Pass, the weak sun had already set. The wind was blowing forty miles an hour, at least. Tentacles of snow reached halfway across the road. My eyes were bugging out of my head and my palms were sliding off the wheel.

"Dad," I said. "*Dad!* Wake up!"

"Whoa, Jen. Pull over carefully. Not too far. You don't want to get over on the shoulder in this powder. It'll suck you in . . .

" . . . just like that."

With my father, there were never any recriminations—not for ending up in a ditch, not for wrecking a truck, not (decades later) for ending my marriage. We stood for a while beside the snow-mired mechanic's truck. After half an hour or so, Dad waved down a guy in a Peterbilt that wasn't pulling a trailer. The guy was willing to help as long as he got to laugh at someone else's stupidity. It was, after all, the going price of samaritanship. My father didn't give me up. Just said, a little gruffly, "Yup, we got a little too far over on the shoulder, and the soft snow sucked us in. Got a chain?"

In July of 1944, the war that Saint-Ex had signed on for was about to end. One night he took off on an Allied spying mission. His assignment: to gather data on German troop movements in the Rhone River Valley. He never returned. For more than half a century afterward, he dwelt in that special purgatory of disappeared pilots—Amelia Earhart among them—whose death is an unverifiable truth. Then, in 2004, a team of divers off the coast of Provence brought up bits of wreckage from a Lockheed Lightning P-38. A piece of the tail bore the serial number 2734L—Saint-Ex's. There was no body, however, and no clue as to the cause of the crash. Perhaps he was shot down. Perhaps he fell asleep or lost consciousness. Perhaps he suffered a mechanical failure. *A great rattle like the crash of crockery. No hope of refuge on the rocky cliffs of Provence.*

One snowy afternoon in 1981, my father flew to Quinhagak to drop off a part for a job. Quinhagak (pronounced QUIN-hock) is a village on the Yukon-Kuskokwim River Delta. He had a cup of coffee there. At home, my father uses half-n-half or evaporated milk; on the job, he uses non-dairy creamer and likes it fine. In either place, he dumps in two or three tablespoons of sugar. The result is so thick and sweet it's closer to coffee ice cream than anything. After half an hour of job talk with the mechanic and foreman, he rose. It was snowing outside, and it was getting late.

Clumps of wet snow clung to the Bonanza's wings. They'd blow off while he was taxiing, he figured. With no passengers or parts, he'd be flying light. Good thing, too, because the Quinhagak strip was short, under two thousand feet. There was a hill at one end, something to get over. When you take off in a light plane, you tend to feel the moment when the plane is ready to fly. That sounds like a Zen koan but it's not. You're up on step, tail in the air, driving down the runway, then suddenly the stick feels weightless. Now the plane is begging to fly. Except it's not, really. It's in ground effect. Ground effect is like a cushion of air. Pilots use it to accelerate on takeoff, decelerate on landing. Physics has no answer for it; probably it's created when the plane's proximity to the ground prevents wingtip vortices from forming. Wingtip vortices are coil-shaped currents that trail from—you guessed—a plane's wing tips. They destroy lift, forcing the pilot to pull back on the stick or the wheel to increase the angle of attack. Depending on the circumstances, ground effect can be a pilot's best friend or worst enemy. On landing, an inexperienced pilot carrying too much speed can get caught in ground effect and drift hundreds of feet down the runway. An overly confident pilot carrying too much weight on takeoff can be lulled by ground effect into thinking that he's going to get away with it. If you think of takeoff as a transaction whose currency is lift, then the first stage—getting off the runway and into ground effect—is cheap; the second stage—getting out of ground effect and into the air—is expensive. Sometimes—forgive the cheesy metaphor—a pilot overdraws his account.

On takeoff from Quinhagak, the Bonanza gobbled up a thousand feet of runway. It wanted to stay in ground effect. More than once, my father pulled back on the stick to see if it would fly. It wouldn't. Meanwhile the hill was bearing down. He could try once more to coax the Bonanza into the air, or he could abort. If he tried again, one of two things would happen: he'd get away clean, or he'd smash into the side of the hill. If he aborted now, he'd walk away from the wreckage of an expensive aircraft, a loss he could ill afford. Since then, he's second-guessed himself a thousand times. So have his friends and family, many of them pilots. There's a contingent that thinks he would have gotten away clean. "If I'd tried to get over that hill, I would've been plastered against the top of it," he told me.

A few days after the crash, he spoke with an NTSB investigator.

"How did it happen?" the guy asked.

"Pilot error," my father replied.

The guy nearly dropped his pencil.

"In all the years I've been doing this job," he said, "I've never heard anyone blame an accident on pilot error."

My father told him how he'd cut the throttle and set down on some tussocks between the runway and the hill, mangling the propeller and landing gear. It could have been worse. My father walked away without so much as a bloody nose.

I was a freshman in college the year of the Quinhagak crash. Now I make a living teaching college students who weren't even born then. Last summer, when I was visiting in Alaska, my father went for his annual flight physical, the one that's required for every pilot over sixty. The doctor checked his pulse, blood pressure, and reflexes, his eyesight and hearing. My father's hearing is the family joke. It's so bad he can't hear the ding of the alarm when he fails to fasten his seatbelt, which is pretty much every time he rides in the car. When they're feeling punchy, my twins call him up on his cell phone and shout, in unison, "*Ding, ding, ding.*" They think it's a hoot. Because the hearing portion of the flight physical isn't terribly rigorous, my father passed it. The vision portion posed more of a problem. The doctor lingered over it for a long time. Finally, he said, *Tell you what, I'll pass you this time on condition you make an appointment tomorrow to see the eye doctor. Tell him I said you're overdue for a new scrip.*

Will do, my father said.

He didn't add that he'd been to the eye doctor a week or two earlier. The glasses he was wearing for his flight physical were brand new, the best correctives that technology could offer.

Next summer, my father will schedule another physical, and the scene will probably unfold like this: The doctor takes his time. When it's over, he rolls back a few inches on his steel stool with the black leatherette top. Puts a little distance between himself and my father. He lays his hands, palms up, on his creased trousers. The universal symbol of helplessness. *I'm sorry, Al, but they just won't let me pass you this time.* My father grimaces, but he doesn't make a fuss. It's not his nature. Meanwhile, the news will be sinking in. After nearly half a century as a pilot, he's grounded forever.

TEN ~ Unlearning to Fly

"Practice makes perfect," my mother would quip whenever I bungled a Chopin nocturne. "Practice makes perfect," she'd say, handing over the Sunday sports section, which published the results of high school ski races, as if I *wanted* to see my name in last place. "I'm proud of you, honey," she said, years later, after reading my first book. Then she gave me a yellow Post-It with a list of typos.

She springs from the mid-twentieth-century American Enlightenment, my mother. Hers is the gospel not so much of perfection but of perfectibility: if something is worth doing then it must be worth doing well. Julia Child said it about French cooking, Benjamin Spock about child rearing, and Alex Comfort about joyful sex. (And doing something well, a friend who is a fan of *Mastering the Art of French Cooking* points out, does not preclude doing it with joy.) As a worldview, perfectibility can be annoying (if not cloying), but it beats the hell out of the inverse, which is cynicism. For better or worse, perfectibility is the worldview that shaped me, and roughly eighty-five percent of the time I like myself OK.

"Practice makes perfect," my mother said, latticing a lighter-than-air piecrust over strawberry-rhubarb filling. My own leaden lump of Crisco, flour, and water (ice cold, as per the instructions) had just gone *thunk* in the garbage can. To this day, whenever I bake a pie, my brother Sam thoughtfully offers to fetch the electric carving knife.

Practice makes perfect. My mother must've said it five or six times a week. It was her pat response to every sigh of frustration. *Keep trying, honey. You can do it.* The only time she quit singing that Pollyanna tune was when I got my learner's permit. Not long after, her prized Volvo wagon got T-boned by a Ford pickup in an accident that was one hundred percent my fault.

I never say, "Practice makes perfect." This is partly because I now see that excess practice fed my particular (though probably not pathological) neurosis when I was young: if you want to avoid your real life, playing the same *Allegro* movement from a Beethoven sonata twenty-three times, at twenty-three metronome speeds, is a nifty way to do it. It's partly because, as much as I love and admire my mother (I do, I do), I've managed not to *become* her.

If at first you don't succeed then try, try again. It's not practice per se that sets us apart from the four-legged beasts but the systematic and serious way we embark on the enterprise. Once a week, we pay an expert thirty-five dollars an hour to give us lessons in viola or painting or yoga. Then we practice and practice and practice some more. Perhaps we practice for the day when the invitation to Carnegie Hall or the Whitney Biennial appears in the mailbox; perhaps we just want our money's worth from all those lessons; perhaps, having invited Perfection into our lives, we find that we must put up with its gloomy sidekick, Guilt.

Growing up in a Tudor-style house on Cherry Street in North Adams, Massachusetts, the daughter of a surgeon and a socialite, my mother never dreamed she'd be rearing her own brood someday in the Frozen North with a husband who was gone more than he was there. "Compensations," writes Lauren Slater in her essay, "Black Swans," "can be gritty gifts." My mother's compensation was the gritty gift of culture. In Fairbanks, Alaska, in the 1960s, culture wasn't in the air or in the water. It was a commodity and, like other commodities—canned peas and winter boots and the like—paid for by check or in cash.

The guardians of culture were genteel ladies of my mother's

generation or older who had also grown up on the East Coast and who had also never pictured themselves as parky-wearing frontierswomen. But here they were, having followed their husbands who'd followed their work to Alaska. These ladies tendered ballet in the basement, piano in the parlor, and French in the front room. They turned parish houses into preschools. My mother bought it all. In the days before Excel spreadsheets and electronic day planners, she shuttled me and my siblings to dance lessons, art lessons, riding lessons, hockey practice, violin lessons, piano lessons, singing lessons, sewing lessons, French lessons, and confirmation classes. My sister Hannah took to riding and singing and sewing. I took to everything but riding and singing and sewing. (Every Halloween, she asks my daughters, "What do you want to be?" And then she turns them into bumblebees, butterflies, gypsies, fairies, witches, geishas, or cowgirls. Magic.) I felt lukewarm toward ballet. I stayed in it mainly for the sake of my friends, Dana Button and Mimi Lee.

"*Miss* Button, young ladies do *not* kick other young ladies on the bottom during *grand battements*."

"Yes, *Madame*."

Madames came and went, but the *barre* and the wall-length mirror remained. To grow up studying ballet is to grow up looking at yourself. A lot. It is also, perhaps, to stop seeing yourself as you really are. For performances, I was often singled out for roles—a fairy godmother in *Sleeping Beauty*, for instance—that combined heavy costuming with light dancing. At fourteen, I danced in the *corps* for a low-end production of *The Nutcracker*; I was the only Snowflake wearing a strapless bra under her tutu. The following August, my mother telephoned the studio to sign me up for another year's worth of lessons.

"I don't know how to say this," Miss Walsh began. "But Jennifer's class will be dancing *en pointe* this year."

"Is there a problem?" my mother asked.

"Um . . . well . . . Jennifer isn't ready to dance *en pointe* yet."

"Are you thinking of holding her back?"

"No," said Miss Walsh. "I'm thinking that now might be a good time for Jennifer to pursue other interests."

Afterward, I had to write a thank-you note to Miss Walsh, a

 final curtsey for all those years of lessons. A final apology would have been more like it, I felt so ashamed. And anxious. I'd grown up inside the frame of that forty-foot-long mirror. When I was little, it had reflected back a skinny girl in a sagging black leotard, black tights, and black slippers. Before every class, my mother brushed my hair into a high ponytail, sectioned it off then bobby-pinned it into a fat coil. Twelve years later, the tights and slippers were pink, sometimes covered by hand-knitted leg warmers for the *barre*. The long-sleeved leotard was still black, though, and my hair was still in the same bun. The mirror reflected a girl who was taller and curvier than most of her classmates. A girl who, unlike them, couldn't scissor her legs into Chinese splits or a ninety-degree *arabesque*. But her *chaine* turns were a beauty to behold. (Or were they?) She could spin as straight and fast as if she were being unfurled from a rope. (Or could she?) She didn't know. She'd spend the rest of her life wondering if she could trust what she saw in the mirror.

That thank-you note, by the way, was my mother's exquisite revenge on my ballet teacher: in our household we knew what good manners were, even if some people did not.

I missed ballet less than I thought I would. I cut my hair short. I wore my Snowflake tutu as a Halloween costume. I joined the cross-country ski team. My mother saw the latter for what it was: my rebellion against her culture. For once, she didn't say, "Practice makes perfect." Instead, she said, "Don't forget that someone has to cross the finish line last."

Racing hurt. I felt for the whole five kilometers as if someone were taking an axe to my sternum. After crossing the finish line (last), I strung my weight between my poles and heaved helplessly. Strings of saliva swung from my nose and mouth. I got used to skiing on feet as frozen as blocks of wood. My eyelashes fell out. My earlobes reddened then peeled. I kept at it, though. I liked ski practice, especially LSD—long slow distance. I skied alone or with a friend on a moonlit trail. The snow turned to indigo silk, the trees to black velvet. The only sounds were the rhythmic *swish-swish* of our skis and the bellows of our breath.

I got faster in my second season, eking out a few middle-of-the-pack finishes. In three years, I never made Junior Nationals, though, or even the varsity team. But I got out more. I made friends with guys, a first for me. At the ski team Christmas party, one of them presented me with a tin of fruitcake. Because it was dark in the basement of somebody's parents' house, I missed the tiny holes poked in the lid, which opened on a wad of shredded Kleenex teeming with baby mice. I'd never been the type to scream on a roller coaster, but I knew what to do at that moment. While I was screaming, the tin flew like a Frisbee from my hand and hit the wall. Baby mice spilled everywhere. I felt as if a door had opened, ushering me into my real life.

On a bus trip to Anchorage, a brown-eyed teammate slid into the duct-taped vinyl seat beside me. I saw that his eyes drooped at the corners, like a puppy's. When he started playing with my fingers, I thought my heart would bust out of my rib cage. That was another beginning. I didn't know how to like a boy, so I teased this one, which is how my mother has always shown affection. He took it pretty well. We snuggled in private and passed notes in public. In this manner—notes in the hall—we argued, broke up, and got back together. *"Amy says you're mad at me. Are you?" "No, I thought you were mad at me." "Why?"* Because I was older, I got my license first. I'd drive us to the Pizza Pub or the movies then to his house. We'd leave the engine running and steam up the windows of my mother's Volvo. I was, to borrow a phrase from Annie Dillard, learning with him "that unplumbed intimacy that is life's chief joy." *Practice makes perfect.*

It was always a given in my family that I—of all my brothers and sisters—would go East for college. The fact that my boyfriend's older brother was serving a life sentence for slitting a taxi driver's throat made my parents even keener to send me far away. Ruling out the big Ivies, my mother used the phrase "lost in the crowd." I was still retreating behind the closed door of the practice room for as many as four hours a day. My mother—no dummy she—had been alluding to the fine line between self-discipline and self-abnegation, between driving oneself hard and driving oneself crazy. She arranged for me to apply to Smith, and I arranged to like it. I did not, however. I was nobody in Northampton: not smart enough for the nerds, fast enough for the jocks, butch enough for the dykes, or rich enough for the preps. The only other girl from Alaska was Susan Lindauer. After one look, we gave each other a wide berth. She came from a well-known Republican family that owned newspapers; her father ran for governor once, a campaign undone by allegations of financial sleight-of-hand. I came from a well-known Democratic family in construction; a cousin had served in the state legislature, and my mother chaired the Alaska Children's Trust under a Democratic governor.

In college, I made myself invisible by wearing rugby shirts and jeans, penny loafers and a navy-blue pea coat. My girlfriends wore similar clothes, but only to classes. They had different clothes for parties: lycra bodysuits, Jordache jeans, metallic belts. I did not. I hated fraternity parties, anyway—the heat of closely packed bodies, the smell of sweat and beer overlain by too much Lauren perfume or Polo cologne. Boys' eyes slid over me then snagged on my roommate Christina, a former Ivory Soap baby. She was tall and curvy and gorgeous, a Spanish major whose ambition was to work as a simultaneous translator for the United Nations. I wasn't gorgeous (I was, then as now, the kind of woman who looks good to men who've been at sea a long time); I didn't dance; I didn't remember my SAT scores; I didn't sail; and I was from Alaska—a conversation stopper if there ever was one.

On Friday nights, I walked up Bedford Terrace from Baldwin House, cut through the center of campus, and went right on Green Street, a street of elegant shops that led to the music building, the gym, and Paradise Pond. I entered the music building. The practice room was the only place where I didn't feel boring and lumpen and stupid, like one of the woebegone and misbegotten left behind when the weekend shuttle left for Amherst or UMass. There, I could switch on the metronome and reassert control over the music, if nothing else.

The illusion didn't last. *Forget everything you've learned*, said Mr. Fern at my third or fourth piano lesson. (He'd strung me along for a while.) Gently (for he was a gentle if undiplomatic man), he closed Prokofiev's Piano Concerto in D-Flat—*Too difficult for you*—and opened Bach's French Suites. What Mr. Fern saw when he watched me play was a bundle of bad habits in need of breaking. I was too stiff, for one thing. I overused the pedal. And I played from my hands rather than my shoulders. For weeks, I clung irrationally to my old ways. Mr. Fern's voice and gestures grew sharper. He felt that what he was asking was fairly simple. Was it too much to ask that I try a bit harder? Apparently, it was. That semester, I was in danger of failing biology and Soviet history, my clothes were all wrong, and I didn't fit in with the girls on my hall, one of whom was dating Prince Albert of Monaco. I needed to play the Prokofiev for reasons I couldn't have articulated, even to myself. I needed to lose myself in its crashing dissonances and minor-chord despair. Bach's tidy consolations would not serve. The petty humiliations of leaving home for college in the East had scraped away my soul. At every lesson, Mr. Fern and I fought bitterly over the flimsy bit that was left. I know what was at stake for me; what was at stake for him was a mystery. On Friday nights, I snuck into the music building after the teachers had left for the day. There, I played music forbidden to me by day: Chopin's "Fantaisie Impromptu" and Rachmaninoff's Preludes, even Gershwin's "Rhapsody in Blue." At a November lesson, Mr. Fern suggested I check out *Zen and the Art of Motorcycle Maintenance* from the library. I did, and I thought it was a terrible book. At the end of the semester, to Mr. Fern's relief and mine, I quit the piano.

Somehow, I eked out passing grades in biology and Soviet history—grades that were nevertheless low enough to merit a stern talking-to by the dean, who deployed such words as "expectations," "standards," and "effort." The only course in which I was handing in above-average work was a year-long Great Books seminar led by a serious scholar named Ronald MacDonald. We read *The Iliad*, *The Oddyssey*, and *The Aeneid* there. Later, I encountered Chaucer, Milton, Shakespeare, Donne, Herbert, and Spenser. Keats and Dickinson. Eliot, Pound, and Stein. I liked the Moderns best. "These fragments shored against my ruins" and all that. Then Robert Lowell, Elizabeth Bishop, Anne Sexton, James Merrill, and Sylvia Plath. Class would end but we'd carry the conversation down the stairs of Seeley Hall, through the art gallery breezeway, across Elm Street, and up the front steps of Mary Ellen Chase House, where seniors lived. We spoke of the Ariel poems during high tea in the drawing room. We wondered whether Ted Hughes would ever permit the publication of the unexpurgated diaries. We fervently hoped so. After dinner, we sprawled on the floor of my friend Julia's room (she'd won the room lottery and drew palatial quarters with a fireplace), slugging twist-top wine and talking loosely of boys and clothes, professors and poems. One or two of us may have confessed to a crush on the twentieth-century Americanist. We felt we'd been born twenty-five years too late, but some of our professors had taught Plath as an undergraduate—then watched her unravel during the months when she and Ted Hughes were on the faculty. She caught him dallying with a student. He denied it, but we took her side. The more we drank, the more we spoke of her familiarly, as if she were in the room drinking with us. She killed herself in the year—1963—when most of us were born, on the day—February 11—that *I* was born.

In college, I dropped the piano for poetry; after college, I dropped poetry for kayaking. The boat and dry suit were expensive, the lessons cheap: a couple of six-packs of Corona or Foster's around the campfire after a day on the river. Like poetry, kayaking was beautiful and dangerous. On Willow Creek near Talkeetna, the jumping-off point for climbers of Mount McKinley, I got pinned upside down, smashed my right hand, and nearly succumbed to hypothermia before being hauled to shore. On the Nenana River, I got stuck in a whirlpool and spun around like a swizzle stick. That time, I rode out slung ignominiously over a friend's bow.

"How was it?" Someone wanted a play-by-play at the takeout.

"I saw God."

It was what you were supposed to say. It meant you'd come into contact with the Sublime. It meant you'd nearly peed yourself in fear. It meant you'd be telling the story around the campfire.

There were a lot of stories around the campfire, but they were really only one story. It went like this: (1) I came to the river; (2) I saw the face of God/Great Nature; and (3) I conquered God/Great Nature. It was a silly story mostly, an exercise in self-aggrandizement on the part of people who spent their weekdays as the shabbily paid minions of corporate giants. In one respect, though, it was not a silly story. When we told it, we were really unraveling a paradox. We were telling *ourselves.* Writes Thomas Weiskel in *The Romantic Sublime,* "There is simultaneously a wish to be inundated or engulfed by pleasurable stimuli and a fear of being incorporated, overwhelmed, annihilated . . . Fascination and dread coincide." Where fascination and dread coincide, there is nearly always a story.

I'd never been a storyteller before. Up until that summer, I'd been engaged in two essentially non-narrative pursuits: reading and practicing. To read is to consume stories, not generate them. To practice is to demystify a process, to excise the dread as well as the fascination. Also, the risk. Without the element of risk—*risk that something will go wrong*—there is no story. On the river, I saw that risk exhilarates in the truest sense of the word: it makes you notice your exhalations. It also creates the conditions for story.

I spent my first season on the river practicing the Eskimo roll. You snap your hips and sweep your paddle in a coordinated, committed way. In a swimming pool, it's a cinch. In a silty, frigid, and fast-flowing river, it's not. In one of my favorite stories, a perky young woman (not me) pivoted into an eddy already occupied by a less perky young woman (also not me). The perky one said, "Hey, let's do a practice roll!" The other one said, "Hey, fuck you!"

The roll has three levels: baby, combat, and bombproof. A baby roll is an extended paddle roll that's not pretty but gets the job done. Sometimes. A combat roll is the roll you need when you get incorporated, overwhelmed, or annihilated by the river god. It can be counted on. Usually. A bombproof roll is just what it sounds like: ironclad.

By the end of my second season, I had a combat roll. It served its purpose. Suddenly, I wasn't scared anymore. Suddenly, I had less to say around the campfire.

Now seemed like a good time to take up flying. My father and uncles were pilots, and so was my brother. Flying ran in my family. "You'll make a good pilot," my father said when I told him. He'd never seen me on the river. He had no way of knowing, as my kayaking buddies did, that I was a slow study with a yen for risk-taking. My mother was less sanguine. She said little but rose early from the table to bang dishes in the sink. I think she was more afraid for me than I was for myself.

To learn to fly is to companion yourself to death. It becomes your new best friend, talking in your ear at odd moments—when you're stuck in traffic or in bed, on the cusp of sleep. I wasn't suicidal. I didn't want to die. What *did* I want? I couldn't explain, even to myself. Especially to myself. Years later, I read Montaigne's essay, "Of Practice," and thought, *That's it.* He writes: "We can have an experience of [death] that is, if not entire and perfect, at least not useless, and that makes us more fortified and assured. If we cannot reach it, we can approach it, we can reconnoiter it; and if we do not penetrate as far as its fort, at least we shall see and become acquainted with the approaches to it." By learning to fly, I thought I might acquaint myself with death's approaches—take a little tour of the ruins, so to speak. I hoped it would be painless. Afterward, I'd redeem my nonstop ticket to the realm of the living.

I should have paid more attention to Montaigne. He was on horseback when a servant on a bigger, faster horse overtook him. He nearly died from the fall, nearly succumbing to "that sweet feeling that people have who let themselves slide into sleep." He awoke a few hours later, feeling "battered and bruised." Montaigne used the episode as an occasion to *essayer,* to sally forth on the topic of practice, which leads him to death, which leads him—of all places—to a defense of autobiography. "It is not my deeds that I write down," he says, "it is myself, it is my essence." If I'd paid more attention, I might have seen that the purchase-price of such wisdom was pain.

Like Montaigne, I was overtaken—in my case, by a pilot in a faster, bigger plane. That's where the similarity—already a stretch, I admit—ends. I was flying with my second instructor, a baby-faced boy named Don Conniff whose ambition, like my father's at his age, was to fly for the Navy. (Like my father, Don would fail the flight physical. A diabetic, he would become a submariner instead.) Like my first and third instructors, Don was more than competent when it came to the nuts and bolts: how to read a sectional chart, plot a course, check the oil, prevent a ground loop, talk on the radio, rest one hand on the throttle at all times, as if it were a child or a lover. Don was no shrink, though, and a shrink was probably what I needed. By the time he took me on, I was in my second year of flying lessons. I'd logged fifty hours in the front seat and passed the FAA written exam. I could solo. I could demonstrate short-field takeoffs and soft-field landings, power-on and power-off stalls, slow flight, steep spirals, S-turns, and maneuvers under the "hood" (a visor improvised from an empty Clorox bottle). With my heart in my throat, I'd gone up on the first and last days of hunting season. I hadn't done too badly up there with the camo crowd, jacked up on C-Rats and testosterone, straddling their 200-hp engines. I hadn't panicked. Long ago I'd passed the point at which a student pilot ought to plot her short then her long cross-country solo, the final hurdle before the FAA check ride. Instead I regressed back to logging dual time with an instructor. I was getting a reputation as a problem. There is a type of student pilot who likes learning to fly better than flying. Perhaps I was that type. Don thought not.

"You could pass if you wanted to," he said. "You just lack confidence."

"I don't feel confident enough to pass," I said.

For a long time, we stayed stuck in my tautology.

A weekday in late summer. Too early for hunters, not too late for tourists. Don put me through my paces in the practice zone, then we headed back to the airport. I remember a lot of chatter on the radio.

"Now," Don said. He had a headset, but I had the mic.

"Fairbanks Tower, Interstate Five-Seven-Alpha-Tango is three miles southeast with Juliet, inbound for landing on the ski strip."

On the east ramp of the Fairbanks airport, where small planes take off and land, the default runway is surfaced in asphalt. If you want to use the ski strip, which is gravel, you have to ask for it. Because gravel is more forgiving than asphalt, I always ask for the ski strip.

The controller told me to enter the pattern on crosswind, third in line behind a Cessna 172.

"Roger," I said. "I've got the traffic."

Next, the controller told the pilot of a Beechcraft Bonanza he was fourth in line behind an Arctic Tern.

"Roger," he said. "I'm looking for the traffic. Uh, what does an Arctic Tern look like?"

No answer.

Orange, I thought. *Tell him it's orange.*

At that moment, things went slightly awry. When the tower tells you to get in line, you're supposed to say, "I've got the traffic." If you haven't got the traffic—meaning you don't see it—you say, "I'm looking for the traffic." It's not rocket science.

Instead of calling back to say he had the traffic, the Bonanza pilot said, "Understand I'm third for Runway One-Right, behind an Arctic Tern."

At that moment, things went seriously awry. In his mind, if not in fact, the Bonanza pilot had jumped ahead of me. He should have had three airplanes in his sights; instead, he had only two.

I turned from crosswind to base. I was now about 800 feet above the ground, perpendicular to Ski Strip One, where I intended to land. Just beyond it was Runway One-Right, where the Bonanza was going to land.

"I don't know what to do," I said to Don. Panic tightened my voice.

"Confirm your position." He sounded calm. The grip on my throat eased.

"Fairbanks Tower, Seven-Alpha-Tango. Understand I'm second in line for Ski Strip One, behind a 172 on short final for One-Right."

"Confirmed."

In many ways, flying in traffic is like driving in traffic. Your only job is to watch out for the guy in front of you. As long as you're flying straight and level, the guy behind you is not your concern; he's also none of your business. It's considered bad form to correct or even point out someone else's error. By definition, controlled airspace is where pilots submit to the tower's authority, surrendering autonomy in exchange for safety. The tower's role is to space incoming and outgoing aircraft in such a way there's no danger of collision.

Confused or not, the pilot of the Bonanza was not, technically, my concern. I was, technically, his. *Forget him,* I told myself. As soon as the Cessna touched down, I turned final. The business with the tower had distracted me. I was higher than I should have been.

"Full flaps," Don said.

As a rule, I took off and landed with one notch of flaps. With two, the Tern fell out of the sky like a stone. That was our usual joke: *You want to fall out of the sky like a stone, eh?* Today, it didn't seem funny.

I needed two hands to wrestle with the flaps. When they were down, I set my left hand on the throttle, where it belonged. That was when shadow passed between me and the ground. It seemed to move in slow motion, a gigantic fish. A gigantic blue fish. It passed so close I saw the sandy-blond strands of the pilot's comb-over. I saw him working the controls. I saw him not see me.

In "Labor Day Dinner," Alice Munro describes a near miss at a country crossroads. An unmarried couple sit in the front seat of a pickup. They're on the way home from dinner with friends, and they've been quarreling in the oblique way that Munro's characters tend to quarrel: he started it by saying something mean about her clothes. The woman's teenage daughters sit in lawn chairs in the truck's bed. An unlighted car full of drunken kids speeds through the darkness and runs a stop sign, nearly ramming the pickup. Afterward, Munro writes, what the couple feels "is not terror or thanksgiving—not yet. What they feel is strangeness. They feel as strange, as flattened out and borne aloft, as unconnected with previous and future events as the ghost car was, the black fish."

Precisely. The Bonanza slid under me so fast that before and after, terror and reprieve, blended together. Afterward, I felt not only strange but a stranger to myself. I'd been overtaken on short final: the nearest kind of miss, a hair's breadth from a midair collision. It scared the bejesus out of me. Don, too.

"Hit the mic," he said to me.

Then, to the tower: "Did you see what just happened?"

"Seven-Alpha Tango, Fairbanks Tower. Yes, sir. Cleared for the option. Contact Gound-Point-Niner off the runway."

"Is that all you've got to say? Are you gonna let the guy in the Bonanza get away with that?

The Bonanza pilot cut in: "Is there a problem?"

"Yes, there's a problem," Don said. "You asshole, you're lucky to be alive right now. You just overtook us on short final."

Tower: "Watch your language, sir."

My brush with death was nothing like Montaigne's painful one, somewhat like Munro's fictive one. Yet the essay and the story—both of which I read years later—showed me ways to make sense of the moment. To bring it under control. To *civilize* it, if that makes sense. Describing other lives, the best writers—the wisest ones—help us enter our own more deeply. They see, as Montaigne puts it, that "Every man has within himself the entire human condition."

Afterward, I drove to my father's office. Fairbanks is a small town, and I didn't want him to hear the story from someone else.

"Jesus," Dad said, rubbing his head with both hands the way he does whenever he's flummoxed or angry.

"Jesus," he repeated.

Then, "I can't think of any reason why your mother has to hear about this."

Years went by. I passed the private pilot check ride. I went to graduate school. There, I read the Russian poet Osip Mandelstam. A co-founder of Acmeism, Mandelstam rejected the mysticism and abstraction of Symbolist poetry in favor of clarity and concision. More than a century later, even in translation, his poetry is eminently readable. Mandelstam rose to prominence before the Bolshevik Revolution, his reputation secured by two collections, *The Stone* and *Tristia.* In 1933, he wrote a poem known as the Stalin epigram. It begins, in W. S. Merwin's translation, with the line, "Our lives no longer feel ground under them." The poem, with its harsh criticism of the "fat-fingered" Kremlin dictator, was equivalent to a suicide note. It was as if Mandelstam authored, signed, and delivered his own death warrant. I know poets whose dearest wish is to live in a world where poetry matters. In Stalin's Russia, it was a matter of life and death. Before long, Mandelstam was arrested for counter-revolutionary activities and exiled. There was such a hue and cry from the public that he was released. Later, he was arrested again and sentenced to hard labor. He tried to kill himself and was reprieved. In 1938, Stalin's goons arrested him one last time. They sent him to the Gulag Archipelago, where he died that December. He was forty-seven.

A few years earlier, Mandelstam had written "Lines about the Unknown Soldier." It's not one of his better-known poems. It may not even be one of his better poems; I'm not one to say. Since the long-ago morning in June when I stumbled on it, a particular stanza has been speaking to me. Here it is, in a translation by Nina Murray:

> Teach me, unwell swallow,
> Who has unlearned to fly,
> How I could with no rudder or wing
> Elude this tomb in the sky.

Mandelstam liked swallows. Being at a loss for words was like being a wingless swallow, he wrote, more than once. In this particular poem as well as in the Stalin epigram, the speaker has lost touch with the earth, progenitor and protector of life. Here, the speaker lurches wingless and rudderless, a helpless supplicant: "Teach me." Neither nature ("unwell swallow") nor technology ("no rudder or wing") can liberate him from the oxymoron of "tomb in the sky." I'm riveted by what this speaker wants: not a lesson in how to fly but a lesson in how to die.

Practice makes perfect.

"There is, it seems to us / At best, only a limited value / In the knowledge derived from experience," writes Mandelstam's contemporary T. S. Eliot in "East Coker." Experience leads us beyond the approaches and up to the very door of death. But what then? I thought I was practicing when I was kayaking and flying. And I guess I was. But the lessons of reading, and, later, of writing, went deeper. Stories and essays and poems have taught me more about life than life has taught me about itself.

Every odd-numbered summer, I schedule a biannual check ride followed by a third-class medical. I pass these easily enough, even though I don't fly much anymore. In the foreseeable future, an odd-numbered summer—2007? 2009?—will go by without new entries in my logbook: the updated medical certificate taped to the inside cover, a fresh CFI signature in the back. That's when I'll quit flying forever. I won't miss it the way Proust misses his madeleines but rather the way an amputee misses his leg. The loss will ache, its compensations gritty as poetry—or life itself.

University of Nebraska Press

Also of Interest

Falling Room
By Eli Hastings

Eli Hastings recounts how a privileged, white, fiercely leftist American male tries to make sense of himself in relation to the contrary people and situations he finds in books and his travels to Cuba and Central America.

ISBN: 978-0-8032-7364-1 (paper)

Hannah and the Mountain
Notes toward a Wilderness Fatherhood
By Jonathan Johnson

Longing for a home in big, wild country that would keep them passionate and young, Jonathan Johnson and his wife, Amy, set out to build a log cabin on his family's land in a remote corner of Idaho. But what begins as a doable dream suddenly looks quite different when, on their first morning in the cabin—without electricity, a telephone, or running water—the couple learn that Amy is pregnant.

ISBN: 978-0-8032-2601-2 (cloth)

Just Breathe Normally
By Peggy Shumaker

Drawing from the geology of life's upheavals, *Just Breathe Normally* greets the shaping power of experience and the regenerative power of love. As if her life were passing before her eyes, in the wake of a near-fatal cycling accident, Peggy Shumaker faces not only a long convalescence but also a re-evaluation of her family's past.

ISBN: 978-0-8032-1095-0 (cloth)

Order online at www.nebraskapress.unl.edu or call 1-800-755-1105. When ordering mention the code BOFOX to receive a 20% discount.